The Literature of the Great War Reconsidered

The Literature of the Great War Reconsidered

Beyond Modern Memory

Edited by

Patrick J. Quinn

and

Steven Trout

palgrave

First published 2001 by
PALGRAVE
Houndmills, Basingstoke, Hampshire RG21 6XS and
175 Fifth Avenue, New York, N. Y. 10010
Companies and representatives throughout the world

PALGRAVE is the new global academic imprint of
St. Martin's Press LLC Scholarly and Reference Division and
Palgrave Publishers Ltd (formerly Macmillan Press Ltd).

ISBN 0–333–76459–5

This book is printed on paper suitable for recycling and
made from fully managed and sustained forest sources.

A catalogue record for this book is available
from the British Library.

Library of Congress Cataloging-in-Publication Data
The literature of the Great War reconsidered : beyond modern
memory / edited by Patrick J. Quinn and Steven Trout.
    p. cm.
    Includes bibliographical references and index.
    Contents: Beyond fiction? : the example of Winged warfare / Chris Hopkins — Literary images
of vicarious warfare : British newspapers and the origin of the First World War, 1899–1914 /
Glenn R. Wilkinson — Encoded enclosures : the wartime novels of Stella Benson / Debra Rae
Cohen — The self in conflict : May Sinclair and the Great War / Terry Phillips — "Lives mocked at
by chance" : contradictory impulses in women's poetry of the Great War / Deborah Tyler-
Bennett — "The huge gun and its one blind eye" : scale and the war poetry and writings of
Harriet Monroe / Allessandria Polizzi — French women poets' response to the Great War / Nancy
Sloan Goldberg — Myrmidons to insubordinates : Australian, New Zealand, and Canadian
women's fictional responses to the Great War / Donna Coates — "Dear, tender-hearted,
uncomprehending America" : Dorothy Canfield Fisher's and Edith Wharton's fictional responses
to World War I / Mary R. Ryder — Fatal symbiosis : modernism and World War I / Milton A.
Cohen — Artistry and primitivism in The enormous room / William Blazek — Mother's boy and
stationmaster's son : the problem of class in the letters and poems of Wilfred Owen / John
Gibson — The war poetry of Wilfred Owen / Malcolm Pittock — "Thought that you've gagged all
day" : Siegfried Sassoon, W.H.R. Rivers and [The] repression of war experience / Patrick Campbell–
– Siegfried Sassoon / Patrick J. Quinn.
    ISBN 0–333–76459–5 (cloth)
    1. Literature—20th century—History and criticism. 2. World War,
1914-1918—Literature and the war. I. Quinn, Patrick J., 1946– II. Trout,
Steven, 1963–

PN771 .L583 2001
809'.93358—dc21

                                                    00–054529

10   9   8   7   6   5   4   3   2   1
10   09 08 07 06 05 04 03 02 01

Printed in Great Britain by Antony Rowe Ltd, Chippenham, Wiltshire

For our wives

Contents

Acknowledgements

A very special thanks to R. Nathan Wilson, without whose computer expertise and keen editorial eye this project would never have been completed; even the 1999 flu epidemic at Fort Hays State University could not keep Nathan from heroically poring over chapters and providing invaluable assistance. The editors also wish to thank Dr James Forsythe, Dean of Graduate Studies and Research and Vice Provost at Fort Hays State University, for helping to defray the costs involved in preparing the manuscript.

List of Contributors

William Blazek is a Senior Lecturer at Liverpool Hope University College, where he teaches courses on American Modernism, literature and culture, technology and photography, and serves as MA Award Director for the American Studies Department. He previously taught at the University of New Orleans, Clarion University of Pennsylvania and the University of Glasgow. His current publication research includes a co-edited volume of essays on American mythology and contemporary literature for Liverpool University Press as well as a monograph on American writers in the First World War.

Patrick Campbell runs the MA in Performing Arts at Middlesex University. He has a Doctorate from the University of London and has been Visiting Professor at the Universities of British Columbia and Northern Colorado. His books include *Wordsworth and Coleridge: Lyrical Ballads* (Macmillan – now Palgrave, 1991), *Analyzing Performance* (Manchester University Press, 1996) and *Trent Park: A History* (Middlesex University Press, 1997). Both *Psychoanalysis and Performance* (Routledge), an edited collection of commissioned essays (with Adrian Kear), and a thematic issue of *Contemporary Theatre Review* on the performing body appeared in 1999. He was formerly editor of *MTD* (*Music/Theatre/Dance*). Patrick has written numerous literary articles in academic journals, many devoted to the work of Siegfried Sassoon. His full-length critical study of the poet (which includes a discussion of every poem written by Sassoon during the Great War) was published in the USA by McFarland in 1999.

Donna Coates teaches in the English Department at the University of Calgary. She has published a number of articles on Canadian and Australian women's fictional responses to the Great War. She is now conducting research on Canadian and Australian women's fictional and dramatic responses to the Second World War as well as examining the literature of Canadian and Australian women who are re-visioning these historical periods.

Debra Rae Cohen is an Assistant Professor at the University of Arkansas. Previously she taught at the University of Mississippi, where she is writing a dissertation on enclosure, space and citizenship in British women's fiction of the Great War. She completed her undergraduate work at Yale and returned to academia after over a decade spent as a cultural journalist in New York City. She has taught at the University of Helsinki and has guest-lectured on women's war literature at the Universities of Jyvaskyla, Joensuu and Tampere (Finland) and the University of Vienna.

Milton A. Cohen is Associate Professor of Literary Studies and Humanities at the University of Texas at Dallas. He has written on various aspects of Modernism and American literature, including Imagism, Futurism, Schoenberg, Stein, Hemingway, Fitzgerald and cummings. Recently, he has finished a book-manuscript entitled 'Movement, Manifesto, Melee: The Modernist Group 1910–1914'. Presently, he is writing a study of Hemingway's style in the first *In Our Time.*

John Gibson holds degrees from the University of London and the University of Hull in England and an MA in literature from the University of Massachusetts. He is currently teaching at the University of Southern Indiana where he has just developed and taught a synthesis course on the First World War. He lives in Evansville, Indiana, and Belchamp Walter, England. He has two books of poetry published in England, *Starting From Here* (1995) and *Folk Dancing* (1996), and a book of poems on Mexico accompanying the colour prints of artist Michael Aakhus (Evansville, IN, 1997).

Nancy Sloan Goldberg is Professor of French and Women's Studies at Middle Tennessee State University. She earned her undergraduate degree at the University of Wisconsin-Madison and her MA and PhD at Vanderbilt University. She is the author of *En l'honneur de la juste parole*, a study of French pacifist poetry of the First World War, and has published articles on French political and social literature in *Journal of European Studies, The French Review* and *The Minnesota Review*. Her forthcoming work, *Women, Your Hour is Sounding: Challenge and Choice in French Women's Novels of the Great War 1915–1919* (St. Martin's Press – now Palgrave), is the first comprehensive study of the literary response of established writers to the conflict.

Chris Hopkins is a Senior Lecturer at Sheffield Hallam University, where he is Course Leader for the BA (Hons) in English Studies. His research is mainly on the British novel in the 1930s, on Anglo-Welsh writing, and on representations of modernity in the twentieth century.

He has published on these topics in journals including *Critical Survey*, *Literature and History*, *Focus on Robert Graves and His Contemporaries*, *Notes and Queries*, *The Journal of Gender Studies*, *The Review of Irish Studies*, *English Language Notes* and *Style*. He has contributed chapters to books on the 1930s and on the writings of the Great War, and is currently working on a book for Palgrave: *Thinking About Texts – An Introduction to English Studies*.

Terry Phillips is Senior Lecturer in English at Liverpool Hope University College where she teaches courses on women's writing and nineteenth- and twentieth-century literature. Her main research interests are in the nineteenth- and twentieth-century novel, Modernism, and the literature of the Great War. She has published articles on May Sinclair in *Image and Power* (1996), edited by Sarah Sceats and Gail Cunningham, and *Women of Faith in Victorian Culture* (1998), edited by Anne Hogan and Andrew Bradstock.

Malcolm Pittock has taught at the University of Aberdeen and Bolton Institute. Although retired, he is actively engaged in research which is issue-based. Publications are forthcoming on Dickens, Orwell, Marvell and Owen's relation to Tailhade and Tolstoy. He is at present working on Mrs Gaskell's debt to Scott in *North and South*, after recently completing an article on the relation between *Redgauntlet* and *Bleak House*. Other publications include a volume on the German Expressionist dramatist, Ernst Toller, in the Twayne German Authors series and articles on, *inter alia*, Chaucer, Henryson, Marlowe, Ibsen, Lawrence, T. S. Eliot, David Storey and the Victorian poet, Sidney Dobell.

Allesandria Polizzi is a doctoral student at the University of North Texas, where she is currently writing a dissertation on work as a performance of cultural identity in American working-class literature. Her publications include an essay on H.D. in the *Journal of Imagism* and a chapter on Margaret Fuller in a collection of essays due in 2000. Her teaching inter- ests include American literature, film, popular culture and disability issues. Based on this latter interest, she is currently serving a three-year appointment on the MLA Disability Issues in the Profession committee.

Patrick J. Quinn is Professor of English Literature at University College Northampton and sits on the Management Committee of the St John's College Robert Graves Trust at Oxford. He is general editor of the 24 volume Carcenet Press Robert Graves Programme and has written a study of the early poetry of Robert Graves and Siegfried Sassoon entitled *The Great War and the Missing Muse*. He has edited several books of essays including one on Robert Graves and writers of the 1930s and edited two volumes for the *Dictionary of Literary Biography Documentary Series* on English poets of the Great War. He is currently preparing a study of American fiction written during the First World War and an edition of Robert Graves's essays, *Some Speculations on Literature, History and Religion* (2000).

Mary R. Ryder is Professor and Director of Graduate Studies in English at South Dakota State University. She holds a PhD in American Literature from the University of Illinois, with a speciality in Realism and Naturalism. Her book *Willa Cather and Classical Myth* earned the *Classical and Modern Literature* Incentive Award and the Mildred Bennett Award for distinguished Cather scholarship. Her work has appeared in journals such as *Style*, *Western American Literature* and *American Literary Realism* and ranges from studies of Cather's connection to writers like Frank Norris and Sinclair Lewis to a study of feminism and style. Her current research involves the recovery of Midwest farm fiction written by women between 1900 and 1930 and its portrayal of violence against women.

Deborah Tyler-Bennett is a poet and lives in Loughborough. She performs her work and has poems published in *Sheffield Thursday*, *Angel Exhaust*, *Connections*, *Borderlines*, *Iota*, *Other Poetry*, *The Yellow Crane*, *Poetry Nottingham International*, *Poetry Monthly* and elsewhere. She has also been published in many anthologies, including *Her Mind's Eye* and *Contemporary English Poetry*. Her book, *Edith Sitwell: The Forgotten Modernist*, was published in 1996. She recently won a diploma in the *Scottish International Open Poetry Competition* for her poem 'Gentle Song'. She has performed her work at venues in England and Scotland. Forthcoming poems will appear in *The Interpreter's House*, *Never Bury Poetry*, *Various Artists* and elsewhere.

Glenn R. Wilkinson received his PhD from the University of Lancaster in 1994 and currently teaches History at Mount Royal College in Calgary, Alberta, Canada. He is working on a book concerning Edwardian cultural attitudes toward war and the origins of the First World War to be published by Palgrave.

Introduction

The past two decades have brought profound changes both to our understanding of the Great War as a cultural event and to our conception of what we mean by, and include in, the term 'war literature'. Twenty years ago, the critical gaze of British and North American literary scholars seldom wandered beyond the works of the English 'war poets' or the prose literature of so-called 'disillusionment', texts such as *All Quiet on the Western Front, A Farewell to Arms, Good-bye to All That* and – as the single female contribution to a supposedly masculine genre – Vera Brittain's *Testament of Youth*. Today, a far more complex, varied and contradictory assemblage of works confronts us, as the designation 'war literature' has moved beyond the battlefield to include the creative expressions (whatever their rhetorical context or ideological orientation) of anyone, soldier or civilian, man or woman, who struggled to interpret the unthinkable. Divided more or less evenly between poetry and prose, between essays that examine such canonical figures as Wilfred Owen and Siegfried Sassoon and those that recover literary voices long ignored, and comprised, again virtually in equal measure, of contributions from male and female scholars, this collection presents the myriad faces of Great War literary study at the close of the twentieth century.

As intended, the book reflects a wide range of theoretical sensibilities and examines an equally diverse assortment of genres, nationalities and conclusions regarding the war, some condemnatory, others seemingly propagandistic. Nevertheless, we have divided the 15 essays that follow into five areas of critical inquiry – with, of course, some inevitable overlap. Part I, 'Textuality and War', presents two essays that expand textual analysis in directions virtually inconceivable twenty years ago, applying to non-fictive discourses – in this case, the supposedly 'factual' memoirs of a celebrated fighter pilot and the war-related reportage and advertising of pre-1914 British newspapers – methods of textual analysis once reserved for fiction, drama, poetry. Indicative of the work now being done in the emergent field of Cultural Studies, both pieces proceed from the notion, articulated by Aram Veeser in his introduction to *The New Historicism* (1990), that 'literary and non-literary "texts" circulate inseparably', and that techniques of close reading may be applied to both areas with equal benefit (xi).

The scholarship in Part II, 'Beyond the Trenches', reflects a similar rethinking of traditional demarcations, particularly the gendered dichotomy between 'soldiers' (who alone, presumably, become 'war writers' or 'war poets') and 'civilians', a dichotomy that has long served to marginalize the literary responses of women to a war whose unprecedented horrors touched everyone. Stella Benson, May Sinclair, Edith Sitwell, H.D., Harriet Monroe – these authors, and others, emerge at last as profound interpreters of total war through four essays that build on such major feminist studies as the first volume in Sandra Gilbert's and Susan Gubar's *No Man's Land* (1988), Claire Tylee's *The Great War and Women's Consciousness* (1990) and Sharon Ouditt's *Fighting Forces, Writing Women* (1994). The largest of the five sections, Part II reflects the veritable sea change that feminist thought has produced in Great War criticism, especially over the past decade, a revitalization analogous to the concurrent, and equally fecund, impact of postcolonial theory on Conrad studies.

Also concerned with issues relating to gender, two of the three essays in Part III, 'Nationality and Response', carry the volume beyond the geographical boundaries that so often circumscribe English and American study of the Great War: here, the wartime poetry of French women, a subject neglected even in France, receives a detailed analysis; so too do the works of women novelists in the British Dominions, a literary landscape virtually undiscovered until recently. The third essay 'breaks new ground' of a different kind, unearthing in American narratives once dismissed as mere propaganda a surprisingly significant exploration of cultural interchange between the old world and the new and the birth of a distinctly American wartime mythos.

Few readers will already be acquainted with the works considered in the first three sections; more than anything, the scholarship included here is meant to suggest the variety of literature(s) spawned by the war, a variety that researchers have come to perceive largely through the growth of essentially anti-canonical, 'decentring' critical orientations, especially new historicism and feminist theory (in its many forms).

Indeed, what separates the essays in Part II, for example, from Paul Fussell's *The Great War and Modern Memory* (1975) or Bernard Bergonzi's *Heroes' Twilight* (1965) is less the assumption, frequently expressed by the contributors, that ignoring women writers creates an invalid version of literary history, than the shift in critical Zeitgeist since the 1970s that enables such an assumption to be conceptualized and articulated. It is perhaps helpful to remember that Fussell's study, which remains the most frequently cited analysis of Great War literature ever written, appeared four years before Sandra Gilbert and Susan Gubar's virtual christening of American feminist criticism in *The Madwoman in the Attic* (1979), one of the first studies to reveal the potentialities of interpreting writing as a gendered act. To read the first nine essays in this collection is to appreciate how dependent subjects are on the approaches used to frame them – what Hayden White has called 'the content of the form' – as well as the extent to which critical works, like the texts they analyse, are determined by their intellectual milieu.

The essays in Parts IV and V provide, in contrast, a sampling of current criticism on topics that have attracted intense discussion ever since the fiftieth anniversary of the Armistice – namely the relationship between the Great War and Modernism and the work of two English war poets, Wilfred Owen and Siegfried Sassoon. The former topic is addressed, first, in an essay whose examination of avant-garde painting and poetry, both before and during the war, reminds one of such cross-national, interdisciplinary studies as Modris Ekstein's *Rites of Spring* (1989) and Jay Winters' *Sites of Memory, Sites of Mourning* (1995). Further insight into 'Modernists at War', the title of Part IV, appears in the second essay in this section, which offers perhaps the most incisive analysis to date of e. e. cummings' *The Enormous Room*, a profound and often neglected Modernist response to the Great War.

Part V, 'Revising the War Poets', illustrates how two poets – each a virtual icon of the trench war on the Western Front and among the most anthologized English writers of the period – have fared amid the current climate of revisionism and canon reformulation. The first two essays present antithetical responses to Wilfred Owen, one stressing Owen's ultimately attractive struggle with class prejudice, the other casting a cold eye – in a manner similar to Adrian Caesar's deconstructive analysis of Owen in *Taking It Like a Man* (1994) – on the popular claim that Owen had become, by the time of his death, an 'anti-war' writer. Suggestive of the increasingly complex and ambivalent picture of the war poets that has emerged in the 1990s, these two pieces are followed by a pair of analyses that reflect Siegfried Sassoon's growing reputation as a poet of considerable variety and depth. Each essay, in its own way, indicates how far Sassoon has come in recent criticism from his image, still found in anthologies or reference works, as a mere mouthpiece for front-line angst. The penultimate essay considers Sassoon's 'Repression of War Experience' in light of the poet's homosexuality and exposure to psychoanalytical theory, while the final piece forms an appropriate coda for the collection, tracing Sassoon's growing fears of another world war through his poetry of the 1920s and 1930s – a body of work that has only begun to attract appropriate critical scrutiny.

As with any collection, this book represents hard choices: in particular, our decision to present so many pieces devoted to English and American women's literature, and to devote an entire section to Owen and Sassoon, made it impossible to represent as wide a range of continental writers as we would have liked. Here the collection differs from Holger Klein's excellent 1976 anthology, *The First World War in Fiction*, which includes analyses of English, American, French, German, Italian and Austro-Hungarian works. Yet coverage in one area is always detrimental to another: consistent with the definition of 'war literature' operative in its day, Klein's collection does not address a single woman writer, nor does it rescue any unfamiliar, non-canonical texts from obscurity.

Morever, we compiled this collection not only to illustrate the fresh perspectives brought to Great War scholarship in recent years, but to suggest promising new areas of research. Indeed, many of the omissions in this volume reflect less the preferences of its editors than the work still required if we are to understand the cultural impact of the Great War in all its facets. Historical writing about the Great War, for example, has yet to be considered through the kind of textual analysis presented in Part I of this collection. Likewise, the works of continental and colonial witnesses to the conflict remain – despite the progress made in comparative studies such as Holger Klein's collection or Frank Field's *British and French Writers of the First World War* (1991) – unfamiliar territory to most English and North American scholars (in fact, only a handful of essays on non-English or American writers were submitted for our consideration). Here, the exploratory scholarship of Nancy Sloan Goldberg and Donna Coates, included in Part III, could well serve as a model. And, finally, the recovery of works by English and American women writers, though currently a field of intense scholarship, remains far from complete. As we hope this collection makes clear, Great War literary study has recently occupied territory all but ignored twenty years ago; however, for the scholar drawn to this tragic crucible of twentieth-century history, there is more than one no man's land left to document and to interpret.

PATRICK J. QUINN
STEVEN TROUT

Part I
Textuality and War

1
Beyond Fiction? The Example of *Winged Warfare* (1918)

Chris Hopkins

The project of this volume is to look afresh at the literature of the Great War from the perspectives of the twentieth century's end. The new perspectives that have become possible recently include the development of both new critical approaches and new areas of interest which have come into being since the publication of the standard works of the 1960s and 1970s (such as Bernard Bergonzi's *Heroes Twilight – A Study of the Literature of the Great War* in 1965, Holger Klein's edited collection of critical essays *The First World War in Fiction* in 1976, and Paul Fussell's *The Great War and Modern Memory* in 1979). The new critical approaches and methodologies are, of course, part of the general interest in the insights of theory across all areas of literary studies. The new focuses of interest are also related to this development, particularly as it touches questions about the canon and the construction of literary history. Thus both popular fiction/culture about the War and fictions by women have received an increasing amount of attention. My own project in this essay belongs to the second of these two types of new perspective – it seeks to explore the possibilities of a new area, brought to light at least in part by some recent critical developments. Within that, though, it looks at an area which, while lying solidly within the ambit of traditional interest in the Great War, has been oddly neglected.

The project is an apparently simple one, focusing on a shift from literature of the Great War to narratives of the War. The newness of this move arises from a willingness to read new kinds of text and from a new sense of the possible relationships between literature, narrative and history. There has been a general sense that literature may not be as distinct from other kinds of writing as once seemed axiomatic. Thus cultural critics (such as Anthony Easthope in *Literary into Cultural Studies*, 1991) have argued that literary texts should not be the sole focus for study and have promoted the study of a wider range of texts and ultimately a shift in attention from literature to culture. Other critical developments have supported this move away from the uniqueness of literary texts. The work of Hayden White has suggested that the distinction between fictional and factual kinds of writing are not simply given – so that historiography can be seen as deeply informed by patterns of narrative which do not just arise from the data. Other kinds of non-fictional works have received similar attention, notably autobiography. These approaches (which do not, of course, exhaust related developments) imply that all texts can be studied, that non-fictional texts use narrative devices and, overall, that culture itself is the textual arena which critics should read. There have been (and are) various debates and responses to these kinds of development within literary and cultural studies. My reference to these issues is not, however, just a general point about all literary study, but has a particular bearing on literature and the Great War. For while a range of new critical developments has been applied in this field, there has been a tendency to retain to a surprising degree a focus on literary texts. Thus even a critic like Paul Fussell, though very open to discussing non-literary and uncanonical works and concerned to give a wide-ranging cultural history of the War, is still much more interested in discussing fully works which have already been classed as 'classic' and hence *literary* narratives.

The literary focus seems surprising in this field of study in particular for a number of reasons. From the very beginning, critical reactions to writing about the War have been concerned not only with texts as 'literary works' in a separate aesthetic sphere, but with their connection to political, cultural and social issues. The reasons for this are self-evident – the War was generally perceived as a turning point or crisis in European history, and as the first 'mass war' it was a common experience for whole populations (in varying ways), so that accounts of it were not necessarily regarded as specialist testimony so much as witness to a shared experience. Thus the literariness (or not) of novels or other accounts of the War was not always the main issue. Klein puts this very clearly in the Introduction to *The First World War in Fiction*:

> If war literature was committed, was of necessity political, so was criticism at the time. The cataclysm and its consequences could not be pushed aside. And the political considerations impinged heavily on the aesthetic ones. War literature was in effect mostly treated as separate from other sorts of literature. Rarely does one come across a remark like H. M. Tomlinson's: 'The test for a book about the War is

the same as for any other book'...Fiction here had an immediate factual correlative of which millions were aware, and the overriding criterion applied to war fiction was truth.

(4)

This sense that writing about the War was not just 'writing' (i.e. was not in a separate artistic sphere from everyday experience) has continued in the critical treatment of its fiction. Here there is, of course, an interest in literary questions (the deployment of formal features, use of literary modes and models and so on), but this has always been accompanied by an interest in historical and cultural questions (what cultural factors created particular ways of describing the War? how did the experience of War modify literary responses? what impact did War fiction have on postwar history? and so on).

But despite this sense of history (predating a more general critical turn towards history), the main focus has remained on works which are – or which can be said to be – literary or fictional. Such a focus can be justified in various ways (probably mainly by arguing for the superiority of literary accounts), but justification of this kind is particularly problematic for fiction of the Great War, because a large number of the texts which have come to form a canonical corpus are, in fact, not obviously fictional at all. There is in various ways a quite clear awareness of this problem among critics. Klein's Introduction says:

These studies are concerned with war fiction. In view of the vastness of the material selection is necessary. And one of the principal non-national categories for comparative work is genre. Fiction offers itself particularly as it continued to be used longest by war writers, no doubt because prose narrative...is especially suited to the full re-creation of historical events and states of society. Moreover, as prose is the most frequently read genre in the modern era, this is the medium in which the war had its widest impact on the reading public.

(4)

Klein is well aware of a certain problem in matching the selection of texts (fictions only) with the more wide-ranging reasons for studying writing about the War. A little earlier in the Introduction he says that 'the War fundamentally affected...man's outlook on the world. This accounts for the permanent interest...it holds' (2). The mismatch here is between studying the representation of the War for its vast cultural impact and studying its representation in fiction. The paragraph quoted above tries to mediate between the two aims, but soon runs, I think, into problems. There is a notable slippage between different terms used to indicate the kind of texts being studied: 'fiction', 'prose narrative', 'prose'. The terms do not by any means necessarily indicate the same kind of writing: 'prose' seems to be much wider than 'fiction', and 'prose narrative' does not clearly signify a fictional work. Selection is said to be necessary because of the vast amount of material – the material in this case being all possible kinds of accounts of the War. This is certainly no understatement, as the catalogues of books dealing with the War cited by Klein and others of his contributors suggest. Thus for Britain there is Sir George Prothero's *Analytical List of Books Concerning the Great War* (London, 1923 – published, interestingly, by the Foreign Office) and for France there is Jean Vic's *La Litterature de Guerre*, 5 vols (Paris 1918–24). Other combatant nations have their own equivalents (see Klein, notes, 211). The reasons given for selecting fictionality as the criterion for choice are not entirely convincing though. Prose is undoubtedly 'the most read genre in the modern era', but not necessarily *fictional* prose. The texts which I shall discuss below were all books which remained in print for a long period and sold in large enough numbers to influence public attitudes towards the Great War. But none were obviously classifiable as fiction. In fact, a good number of the books discussed in *The First World War in Fiction* are not self-evidently fiction either (many could be – and have been – called autobiography).

This problem is certainly not Klein's alone, but is part of a more general problem. George Parfitt acknowledges the difficulties of selection and the particular problem that autobiographical modes of writing were common responses to the War:

> [There is a] difficulty in defining the limits of the subject. There is no adequate bibliography of fiction of the war and this hints at the problems of defining which novels should be included and which should be excluded, some of these problems being more formidable than others. At what point does a novel which takes account of the war become a novel of the war? When does a novel become a memoir?
>
> (2)

Parfitt refers, like Klein, to the problem of selecting texts, though he restricts himself without further discussion to novels. However, he immediately acknowledges that many texts of the War are not indisputably novels at all, and that novels and memoirs in this particular field often have a blurred boundary between them.

This uncertainty is not a general one in criticism of the novel – there is little dispute about whether most Victorian novels are novels or memoirs. It is a specific problem for fiction of the War, because actual involvement was so widespread and because 'factual' (or quasi-factual) accounts of personal experience came to seem the most obvious way of writing about the War. Though in one way a problem, in another way this is an opportunity. If the autobiographical accounts of Robert Graves or Ernst Junger can be the subject of criticism, then perhaps so can those of other writers who have not so far become canonical writers of the War.

Critics of the Great War have not, in fact, been wholly resistant to broad canons, because of their implicit engagement with history. Thus Bergonzi has a whole section on 'Autobiography'. It is notable, though, that it deals mainly with the canonical writers who are often regarded as novelists or honorary novelists: Blunden, Graves, Sassoon, Manning. He does, though, also discuss briefly the autobiographical works of Frank Richards (*Old Soldiers Never Die*, 1933) and Cecil Lewis (*Sagittarius Rising*, 1936). Both of these are quite often referred to by critics but rarely discussed in much detail. Indeed, it seems clear that Bergonzi discusses them so much more briefly than he does Graves or Sassoon because they are silently categorized as less complex and, in fact, non-literary works. This relative simplicity may, of course, be the case and Bergonzi is more inclusive than Klein or Parfitt, but the treatment of these texts on the margins of Great War literature is significant of the general tendency. Critics agree that the literature of the War has curiously blurred boundaries but, in fact, the field still retains a strong focus on works which have become seen as literary. And they may, indeed, be exceptional works. Nevertheless, the reasons for undertaking criticism of the writing of the War seem subject to a lack of clarity which has oddly delimited the writing studied.

Bergonzi in this 'Autobiographies' section makes two further useful and connected points which have still not been much developed due to the silent assumptions of many critics. He observes that 'there had been a steady trickle of war books appearing from 1919 onwards, ranging from artless personal narratives to official histories of regiments or campaigns, which had attracted dedicated readers' (146), and that 'there were other kinds of war in 1914–1918 from that of the trench-fighters, even though their experience was predominant' (168). The first comment draws attention to the quantity of critically unexplored autobiographical narratives of the War, and also points towards another assumption in the main critical focus – that of the periodization of war writing. Most critics concentrate on the apparent resurgence of War books in the period 1928 to 1930 – but there were earlier accounts, and the date of publication of a text may, of course, contribute much to what it has to say and how it says it. The comment about 'artless personal narratives' is also suggestive of relevant issues. However artless or unliterary, all narratives must have some principles of organization, and questions about how far 'literary' and less (or un?) literary narratives of the War differ may be interesting ones in terms of cultural history. Neglected narratives of the war may offer the history of different constituents of a culture, or may confirm certain shared conceptions of the unprecedented experience of modern war. This takes us on to Bergonzi's second point. There were, indeed, other experiences of the War from that of the trenches – because it *was* a world war and a modern war. But the trenches do dominate the critical literature to the point where other aspects of the War seem to have no (literary?) history. Thus narratives of the naval war, the intelligence war or the War in Africa (for example) are rarely mentioned in critical works (though such narratives exist and were widely read in the 1920s and 1930s). Even some aspects of the War on the Western Front have received little attention – including narratives of prisoners of war and narratives of the wholly new experience of the war in the air. Lack of attention to the impact of aerial warfare seems particularly surprising, since it is part of the application of science and industrial production on a massive scale to warfare which characterizes the 1914–18 War, and because it might seem to offer an alternative sort of imagery of the war from the mudbound immobility of the trenches. This selective critical memory is not necessarily false to the general collective memory of the War. The domination of representations of the War by the trenches is not coincidental, but part of a metaphorical sense of the significance of the War, where the unprecedented mobilization of the three most industrially advanced nations in the world resulted in millions of men living in mud holes and counting progress in terms of yards of mud won (Cecil Lewis gives a striking version of this figuring of the War, and particularly the war in the trenches, as an absurd development of modernity in *Sagittarius Rising*, 103). Nevertheless, a genuine history of the representation of the Great War should take some note of other accounts and of their narrative forms and cultural impact: how, for example, did pilots represent their war, and how did they compare their experience with that of those fighting below them in the trenches? (Bergonzi, again, does take note of some of these other kinds of experience, discussing Cecil Lewis's *Sagittarius Rising* (1936) and Francis Brett Young's *Marching on Tanga* (1917) which deal with the war in the air and in East Africa respectively. See *Heroes' Twilight*, 168–70.)

This essay then will suggest that some attention be given to other writings of the War – autobiographical texts dealing with aspects of the War which have not become part of the literary/cultural history of the Great War in the same way that the trenches have. In some ways its project is like that of critics who have studied the neglected stories of women's experience of the War, though the material itself is very different, being still firmly located in the 'masculine' sphere of military service. Sharon Ouditt's *Fighting Forces, Writing Women – Identity and Ideology in the First World War* (London, 1994) is in some ways closest in its approach in that it discusses literary and other kinds of writing with equal attention. Other studies such as *Women and World War I*, ed. Dorothy Goldman (1993), have discussed women's experience of the war but with a dominant focus on literature (though many of the writers it discusses are far from canonical). Having discussed the problems which critics have had in selecting Great War texts and in justifying their selection, I must now face the same problem myself. I have chosen to discuss one text in some detail: William Bishop's *Winged Warfare of 1918*. It is an autobiographical and in that sense non-fictional narrative dealing with the war in the air, and I have chosen it partly because it seems particularly unliterary and unsophisticated and because its early date differentiates it from most of the classic narratives of the War. If it can be read in a critically useful way, then so too, I feel, can a large number of other narratives of a broadly similar non-fictional kind. Furthermore, *Winged Warfare* was reprinted by Penguin in 1937, and therefore was quite widely read in the 1930s as well as on its first publication. Given the apparent emergence of a set of rather different classic narratives of the War in the 1930s, the existence of this alternative kind of account in a popular edition seems of interest. I will explore ways in which this narrative can be read and what it can add to critical readings of the cultural history of the War.

There was, of course, no obvious pre-existing literary model for narratives concerning air warfare. But, as in the case of trench war, different narratives do seem to display related patterns based on the sequence of events which lead to the presence of the narrator at the Front. Thus *Winged Warfare* (like Cecil Lewis's *Sagittarius Rising*, 1936) recounts how the narrator came to join the Royal Flying Corps, the rite of passage involved in learning to fly, progression towards a front-line aerodrome and then the experience of air combat itself. (It is notable how closely a fictional text which has been read over a longer period – Captain W. E. Johns's *Biggles Learns to Fly* (1935) – matches these two autobiographical accounts; Johns says in the preface to an edition of 1955 that 'as the reader may guess, the writer's own experiences were much the same as those described therein' (5). William Bishop became the most decorated and most famous Canadian flyer of the war. He received the MC, DSO, DFC and VC and was acknowledged as having shot down 72 German aircraft. As noted above, *Winged Warfare* was sufficiently well-known to be reprinted by Penguin in 1937 (their listing included it under 'Travel and Adventure', together with Blunden's *Undertones of War* and Von Rintelen's *The Dark Invader*). The narrative opens with an explanation of how he came to be a flyer – such an explanation being necessary presumably because it was an unusual choice. The explanation focuses on a major attribute – symbolic and literal – of the trenches: 'It was the mud, I think, that made me take to flying' (21). However, all is not quite as it appears. Bishop is not referring to the mud of the trenches, but to the somewhat less baleful (?) mud of a cavalry camp in England, his first posting on arrival with the Second Canadian Division. Nevertheless, his treatment of the contrast between mud and air draws on the complex of meanings which other texts, including C. E. Montague's *Disenchantment* (1922) and *Sagittarius Rising*, drew from the trenches more directly. Bergonzi comments on a chivalric theme in both of these writers:

> There were other kinds of war in 1914–18 from that of the trench-fighters, even though their experience was dominant. One of them, C. E. Montague, deploring the decline of chivalry during the struggle, had wistfully reflected that only amongst the airmen had the traditional habits of chivalry remained possible. This theme was enlarged upon in *Sagittarius Rising*...
>
> (168)

Bishop too creates his version of this contrast between the dirt of the earth and the cleanliness of the sky:

> Everything was dank, and slimy, and boggy. I had succeeded in getting myself mired to the knees when suddenly, from somewhere out of the storm, appeared a trim little aeroplane.
>
> It landed hesitatingly in a near-by field as if scorning to brush its wings against so sordid a landscape; then away again up into the clean grey mists.
>
> ...I knew there was only one place to be on such a day – up above the clouds and in the summer sunshine. I was going into the battle that way. I was going to meet the enemy in the air.
>
> (21)

The patterns of imagery are clear – while the struggling cavalry man is muddy, encumbered and static, the aeroplane is trim, able to move as it wishes, has choices and volition (as even the 'hesitatingly' suggests), and is associated with the natural world of the air (the phrase 'to brush its wings' images it as like an insect). Even the grey mist becomes 'clean' to sustain the figuring of the aerial domain. Like C. E. Montague and Cecil Lewis, Bishop links the aeroplane to the idea of chivalry – but his position in a muddy cavalry camp gives his connection an interestingly literal edge: 'I had fully expected that going into battle would mean for me the saddle of a galloping charger, instead of the snug little cock-pit of a modern aeroplane' (21). Chivalry has moved, in effect, from the muddy cavalry to the 'clean' aircraft, with the addition of modern comforts (the discourse here shifts towards something suspiciously like that of advertising). This compares interestingly with the paragraphs from *Sagittarius Rising* quoted by Bergonzi:

> It was like the lists of the Middle Ages, the only sphere in modern warfare where a man saw his enemy and faced him in mortal combat, the only sphere where there was still chivalry and honour. If you won, it was your own bravery and skill; if you lost it was because you had met a better man.
>
> You did not sit in a muddy trench while someone who had no personal enmity against you loosed off a gun, five miles away, and blew you to smithereens – and did not know he had done it! That was not fighting; it was murder. Senseless, brutal, ignoble. We were spared that.
>
> (168–9)

Both writers have a sense of the freedom of the war in the air, associated with cleanliness and with a personal, individual control over their fate. This, indeed, seems to be the basis of the link made between chivalry and air warfare: fighting becomes personal (again), an activity where the individual does count. This is what the mobile and free activity of *Winged Warfare* can give.

Chivalry, in this sense does, indeed, seem to be a key theme of *Winged Warfare*. However, Bishop's narrative makes this possibility of 'freedom' into a much more aggressive individualism than Lewis does. The positive values of the cleanliness in the opening anecdote about mud are part of a network of values in the narrative which prioritize notions of singleness and detachment. While in the process of transferring to the Royal Flying Corps, Bishop reflects, 'A few more days of cavalry mud and I was convinced that to be an observer in the air was far better than commanding a division on the ground' (23). The narrative is a markedly individualist one, and, as in this quotation, tends to shun any social organization or sense of social grouping. While trench narratives may often be preoccupied by comradeship and/or modern mass warfare, this air narrative focuses obsessively on the first person narrator. At first trained to be an observer, Bishop represents himself as always aiming at the supreme experience of being a lone fighter pilot:

> But all the times I was observing I wanted to be fighting. Whenever I saw one of the small, swift, single-seater machines, which were just then coming into vogue for fighting purposes, my resolve to become a fighting pilot would grow stronger and stronger.
>
> (24)

Being selected for training as a pilot makes Bishop 'happier than I can express' (31) – it is as if flying alone is the fulfilment of the real value of flight, the escape from the social dependency of the ground.

Bishop's account goes on to detail every flight he makes alone, explaining that he conceived the ambition to become an 'ace', and in particular to approach the 'record' of Captain Albert Ball. He has a liking for flying alone when he can (rather than with a patrol), putting in as much unofficial overtime as possible:

> Some days I could have been accused of violating all the rules of a flying men's union (if we had had one). I would fly as much as seven and a half hours between sunrise and sunset...The more I flew the more I wanted to fly.
>
> (91)

His ambition is strongly associated with a strikingly individualist obsession with German two-seater aircraft:

> Along with the new ambition there was born in me as well a distinct dislike for all two-seated German flying machines! They always seemed so placid and sort of contented with themselves. I picked a fight with the two-seaters wherever I could find one, and I searched for them high and low. Many people think of the two-seater as a superior fighting machine because of its greater gun-power. But to me they always seemed fair prey and an easy target. One afternoon, soon after this Hun hatred had become a part of my soul, I met

a two-seater. As bad luck would have it ... the enemy escaped. Much disgusted, I headed away homeward, when into my delighted vision there came the familiar outlines of another Hun with two men aboard ...

(92)

The text seems unable to offer any consistent motive for this dislike – slipping here between ruthless functional arguments (they are easy prey) and idiosyncratic emotions (they annoy him!). It seems possible that enemy two-seaters are seen as a betrayal of the individualist destiny of the airman, which Bishop is striving to bring to perfection by equalling the victories of the then supreme British flyer, Captain Ball. Certainly, the hostility towards two-seater here seems more than tactically motivated – Bishop in the next paragraph machine-guns the second two-seater after it has landed – a tactic represented in some other accounts as barbarically infringing a well-understood chivalric code. (Similar behaviour by a German pilot forms the substance of the penultimate chapter of Captain W. E. Johns's *Biggles Learns to Fly*. The behaviour of the pilot is regarded with horror, and its deviancy is clearly understood from the chapter title, 'The Yellow Hun' (141–51).)

As this incident may suggest, it is not easy for a modern reader to like the persona of Bishop. Indeed, his representation of combat and of the Germans is often vicious, as when he talks of the pleasure of being sure you have killed an enemy pilot when you see a plane go down in flames ('You know his destruction is absolutely certain', 89). This clinical sense of certainty and purposiveness is a notable feature of the text, very different from the futility and impersonality in many trench narratives, and it is linked to the text's focus on Bishop as lone fighter. He seems to have only a minimal social context – no friends or comrades are named, and there is relatively little account of any activity on the ground (apart from an allegedly hilarious episode when his squadron paint ducks and pigs to resemble aeroplanes ... , 169–72). The narrative derives almost all its pleasure from the detailed description of aerial combat after aerial combat – the experience which Bishop seeks like an addictive drug (he regards leave as a rather unwelcome interruption). In the main the only sense of a social grouping beyond the individual is that provided by national type – the German airmen do not play fair and are unwilling to leave the safety of their own lines, while individual but unnamed officers from the British Dominions are particularly noted for bravery (a dying Australian pilot is said to have come half way round the world to fight, a New Zealander helps Bishop against the enemy even though his machine gun has jammed, and Canadians are said to be extremely keen to come to Europe to fight – 111, 179, 22).

I have so far not discussed a major part of the context for this text's difference from more familiar writings of the War – its original wartime publication date of 1918. This may immediately suggest why its differences exist – it may be a work of propaganda more than anything else. This certainly helps to account for the narrative's wish to minimize regret and to maximize a sense of purpose, satisfaction and fulfilment of individual destinies. It may also help to explain a lack of any perspective beyond the immediate – its function is to sustain morale and commitment to the War now. However, these factors do not mean that there is nothing for critics to say about this text. Nor do they necessarily make it an entirely different kind of text from later and more 'literary' ones, though they do offer some clearly different representations of the War. Propaganda or not, a number of established myths or representations of the War are already here. Though in a rather inexplicit way, there is a sense of the War as a destruction of individuality in the very insistence on the individualism of *Winged Warfare*. When Bishop sees those fighting on the ground he has difficulty believing in their reality or individuality, and though at times this is presented in a propagandist way as a testament to efficiency, it is more often a sign of the difference between the mass war below and the airman's strange remoteness from normal human life. Thus a sequence beginning with praise of efficiency and nonchalance soon modulates into something less under control:

> From the air it looked as though they did not realise that they were at war and were taking it all entirely too quietly. That is the way with clock-work warfare. These troops had been drilled to move forward at a given pace . . .
>
> Suddenly over the top of our parapets a thin line of infantry crawled up and commenced to stroll casually toward the enemy. To me it seemed that they must soon wake up and run; that they were altogether too slow; that they could not realise the great danger they were in. Here and there a shell would burst as the line advanced . . . Three or four men near the burst would topple over like so many tin soldiers . . . I could not get the idea out of my head that it was just a game they were playing at; it all seemed so unreal. Nor could I believe that the little brown figures moving about below me were really men – men going to the glory of victory or the glory of death. I could not make myself realise the full truth or meaning of it

all. It seemed that I was in an entirely different world, looking down
from another sphere on this strange, uncanny puppet-show.

(85–6)

These men seem to lack all the qualities which Bishop as airman has –
they are unaware, lack speed, do not react and have no overview. There is
a genuine bewilderment here, though also a sense of superiority, which
reinforces itself against the anonymity of those below. This is not
exactly a straightforward piece of morale-boosting – even for those who
imagine themselves as pilots. The puppets below reinforce the individuality of the observer above, but only if his sensibility shares a remoteness
and detachment akin to that ascribed to them. The text does, at such
moments, have a kind of (limited) self-awareness resulting in a certain
bewilderment.

The text, though keen in some ways to present war in the air as
a liberating game, also shows some explicit sense of the mental strain
which it involves:

When I left for my leave in England I was not very keen on going.
The excitement of the chase had a tight hold on my heartstrings, and
I felt that the only thing I wanted was to stay right at it and fight and
fight and fight in the air. To me it was not a business or a profession,
but just a wonderful game. To bring down a machine did not seem
to me to be killing a man; it was more as if I was just destroying
a mechanical target, with no human being in it. Once or twice the
idea that a live man had been piloting the machine would occur and
recur to me, and it would worry me a bit. My sleep would be spoiled
perhaps for a night. I did not relish the idea even of killing Germans,
yet . . . it seemed more like any other kind of sport . . .

When I reached England, however, I found I was in a very nervous
condition. I could not be still. After a week there, in which I enjoyed
myself tremendously, I found I was getting quieter, and realised that
my leave was probably doing me a world of good . . . to make it still
more ideal, I did not have the usual dread of going back to France – I
was looking forward to it. I realised that this short rest had quieted
my nerves and had left me in a much better state of health.

(141–2)

As when the narrative deals with the troops in the trenches, this attempt
to deal with the mental strain of the War is extremely uneasy. On the
one hand it tries to sustain the sense that shooting down German

planes is just like a game, but, at the same time, there is a strong awareness that this cannot be maintained without implying the utter callousness of the narrator. He therefore has to show some sensitivity towards human life while not allowing this to dilute keenness for the War. This produces a kind of split personality on which killing has partly a highly disturbing effect, and partly no effect at all. Both effects are needed for the narrative to fulfil its function as *acceptable* propaganda. But instead of remaining silent about this split, the text draws attention to it by what seems to be an explanation of, or, anyway, a circumstance accompanying, this state of mind. Thus, despite the denial of anything more than the loss of a night's sleep, there is next the introduction of Bishop's hitherto unacknowledged mental condition. In fact, his discovery of his 'very nervous condition' only when he arrives in England suggests precisely that he has been concealing some part of his experience in France from himself. However, this symptom must also, of course, be disposed of so that he can return to the keenness with which this particular sequence began.

For a reader disturbed by this inability to construct a coherent or normal attitude to the experience of War (especially disturbing when 'Winged Warfare' itself is seen as having a specific potential for the satisfaction of the individual), the passage may open up other sustained uncertainties about the capacity of this autobiographical narrative to understand its own story. Thus if Bishop's keenness here begins to seem pathological, perhaps there is a more general way in which youthful eagerness and trauma are blurred in the book. Perhaps the pigs and ducks painted with aircraft markings and the continuous obsessive hunting for aircraft to shoot down (especially two-seaters) does, despite the book's clear function of encouraging war as a way to personal health, nevertheless point to a traumatic inability to pursue this desired satisfaction without areas of numbness and confusion. Bishop's keenness on the War appears, even in the narrative's own terms, as a species of mania.

I have little doubt that *Winged Warfare* could suitably be put into the category which Bergonzi calls 'artless narratives'. It is not an obviously sophisticated piece of writing, and has little sign of contact with any literary culture or even any clear sense of what an autobiography is (other similar kinds of text, including *Sagittarius Rising*, are, however, much more conscious of both autobiographical and literary conventions). What, then, is the advantage in spending critical effort on non-fictional texts of this kind? Firstly, as argued at the opening of this essay, if we are really interested in the cultural history of the Great War, then literary value may not be the only concern. Indeed, texts with little awareness of literary culture may have new things to tell us, or may confirm the extent of the myths and representations with which we are already familiar. Secondly, these texts *are* criticizable – however artless, they do reveal aspects of the War's impact, and can contribute to an understanding of the problems of representing that crisis point in European history. Thirdly, they can help to give access to representations of the War at periods other than in the classic 'war books' resurgence period of 1928–30. Finally, readings of such neglected texts may help to remind us that the War was not received and interpreted during the 1930s solely through works such as *All Quiet on The Western Front* and *Goodbye To All That*, but also through other widely read accounts, such as *Winged Warfare* (1918), A. J. Evans's *The Escaping Club* (1921), Captain Von Rintelen's the *Dark Invader* (1933) and Cecil Lewis's *Sagittarius Rising* (1936) – all of which were available in popular and large editions.

Works cited

Bergonzi, Bernard. *Heroes' Twilight – A Study of the Literature of the Great War.* London: Macmillan – now Palgrave, 1965.

Bishop, William. *Winged Warfare.* Harmondsworth: Penguin, 1937 (Folkestone: Bailey & Swinfen, 1975).

Evans, A. J. *The Escaping Club.* Harmondsworth: Penguin, 1921.

Fussell, Paul. *The Great War and Modern Memory.* Oxford: Oxford University Press, 1975.

Johns, W. E. *Biggles Learns to Fly.* London: Hodder & Stoughton, 1935.

Klein, Holger (ed.) *The First World War in Fiction.* London: Macmillan – now Palgrave, 1976.

Lewis, Cecil. *Sagittarius Rising.* Harmondsworth: Penguin, 1936.

Parfitt, George. *Fiction of the First World War – A Study.* London: Faber & Faber, 1988.

Von Rintelen, Franz, *The Dark Invader.* Harmondsworth: Penguin, 1933.

2
Literary Images of Vicarious Warfare: British Newspapers and the Origin of the First World War, 1899–1914

Glenn R. Wilkinson

Introduction

The literature of the First World War has become an area of study which has encompassed many diverse disciplines. Fields such as poetry (whether good or bad, personal or epic), the diaries and journals of participants (both the famous and the ordinary), autobiography (including the non-fiction and the fictional versions), short stories and novels (written by both participants and non-combatants), and letters (to and from the front) have been studied under the rubric of First World War literature. It seems almost any form of writing now can be considered 'literature'. However, newspapers appear to remain excluded from this literary clique. This is indeed a pity, for newspapers as a historical source are unequalled in this period. They also contain within their pages all of the elements of war literature. Newspapers published poetry, mostly of the bad variety, spontaneously submitted to the local and national press during times of martial activity. Diaries, memoirs and short stories written by soldier or war correspondent observers were often serialized and read with interest. Letters to and from the front were sent to the editor and published either to condone or condemn a particular issue the newspaper had championed. The press, then, can be used to ascertain the literary perception of warfare held by contemporaries.

However, for those looking back from a late-twentieth century perspective, the strongest images of 1914 are those contained in news reports, photographs and early films showing a great mass of people, mostly men, who crowded around recruitment offices early in August 1914

soon after the announcement that war had broken out. This phenomenon can be compared to the image we have of what war was like on
the Western Front, with its muddy and damp rat-infested trenches, the
constant fear of raids and the omnipresent stench of death. It seems
difficult to understand why people would *willingly* and *enthusiastically*
want to be a part of this nightmare. However, this is the image of the
First World War given to us by Robert Graves and Erich Maria Remarque,
soldiers who were reflecting on their war experiences in the 1920s and
1930s. It was not necessarily the image of war held by the Edwardians as
they crowded around the recruitment stations or sent their menfolk
marching off to war.

It is, then, valuable to examine newspapers in order to determine
what exactly were the current attitudes and perceptions towards warfare
before the First World War. These attitudes must be seen as a fundamental
element in the origin of the war and its longevity. It would have been
difficult, if not impossible, to wage war without the active support, or at
least the acquiescence, of the civilian population who either became
soldiers themselves or encouraged others to volunteer. It is, as James Joll
states, *attitudes* which make war possible, and therein lies an explanation
for the origin of the war (Joll, 1984, 194). An examination of the ways
in which *actual* warfare was vicariously experienced by readers of newspapers would go some way to explain the popular response to the call
to arms. If warfare was seen as something beneficial, exciting, fun and
not too dangerous, then volunteers would not necessarily have to think
very hard about becoming soldiers and fighting for their country.

Newspapers are valuable as a historical source to access these attitudes
of actual warfare for many reasons. Firstly, the development of the press
in the latter half of the nineteenth century led to a more commercial,
reader-oriented form of communication. The press was seen less as
a means to educate and mould readers than as a means to entertain and
advertise products of mass consumption. With the decline of the pulpit
and pamphleteering, and before the development of other mass media
such as radio or, to some extent, film, newspapers were the main point
of contact with the outside world (Koss, 1981, 9).

Secondly, the many inherent qualities of newspapers as a form of
communication lend themselves to encourage the use of the press as
a source. For example, newspapers have to be seen as a two-way form of
communication, not as editors and owners of the press imposing their
beliefs on a 'tabula rasa'. The act of buying a newspaper on a regular
basis meant that readers reinforced the images they saw, indicating that
the relationship was more than simply readers being told what to think

or see. Certainly newspapers set the agenda, but the way in which that agenda was discussed had to be in a language understood by readers. Therefore, an examination of the imagery and language used to describe warfare in the press will go some way to indicating the perception of war held and reinforced by Edwardians. In addition, newspapers had to relate to their audiences immediately; they could not wait to be 'discovered' by future audiences like works of great literature. Nor could the press have an eye for posterity or future reputation, unlike diaries or public documents.

Yet, in order to make sense of the imagery contained in newspapers, it is necessary to put those findings within their historical context. Developments in cultural perceptions and practices must be kept in mind and connected to images. Movements such as those directed towards national efficiency and the fear of physical/racial degeneration informed images of the soldier/warrior and the use of martial force. Developments in sporting culture and the entertainment industry helped to foster images of war as a sporting activity or game and as a form of theatrical spectacle. Lastly, the increasing cultural denial of death encouraged the depiction of warfare as an activity which held few deadly consequences. It is these areas that will be examined by using illustrations and written images contained in the coverage of six wars published in representative Edwardian newspapers.

Images of the Soldier/Warrior

The nineteenth century saw the development of what John Mackenzie has called 'the favourable and acceptable face of the soldier everywhere', as the soldier became not only popular hero, but also harbinger of civilization. Early nineteenth-century images of the soldier, those whom Wellington referred to as 'the scum of the earth', were based upon soldiers who were used to quell civil unrest, such as the 'Peterloo' riot in 1819, were billeted on an unwilling and resentful civilian population and were poorly treated by their officers. With the creation of a civilian police force, the image of 'Christian' soldiers derived from the Indian Rebellion (1857–58) and the army reforms instituted by Edward Cardwell in the 1870s, the image of the soldier improved (Mackenzie, 1992, 1, 4).

By the beginning of the twentieth century, soldiers had come to be seen in the press as harbingers of civilization, due mostly to the perceived benefits of Western Imperialism and to the impression that soldiers represented order, justice and reason. Yet they also were seen to act as gauges to the process of becoming 'civilized'. The soldiers which best exemplified this 'civilizing process' were the Japanese, who had demonstrated their martial prowess by soundly defeating the Russians in the Russo-Japanese War (1904–05). The image presented here in the *Illustrated London News* was that the Japanese had gone from the barbarism of pre-Western contact to a modern, civilized (i.e. westernized) state in a matter of a generation, and that their martial development was a sign of this. Indeed, the newspaper press in Britain emphasized the connection between the Japanese adoption of European drill and uniforms through military reform and the process of becoming 'civilized'. While there was an element of favouritism for a formal ally, reports repeatedly stressed the degree of martial development as a sign of the progress of 'civilization' (*Illustrated London News*, 16 January 1904, Supplement VII).

Depictions of the Use of Force

For the Edwardians, military activity was not only seen as a means to demonstrate a level of 'civilization', it was also perceived as a natural and beneficial activity. Anti-war sentiment was seen as a 'blindness to elementary human nature' and doomed to failure (*Illustrated London News*, 3 February 1900, 142). The benefits of warfare related to the perception of it acting as a bulwark to racial degeneration and being a positive and medicinal activity.

Part of the presentation of war as a natural activity centred around the perception that war was an acceptable component of the human condition, a natural and expected form of personal interaction. In addition, this image of war can been viewed as reinforcing particular forms of masculinity and countering the 'infection' of effeminate values of peace and cooperation. These elements can be observed in a *Punch* cartoon published during the Boer War, entitled 'Plain English' (*Punch*, 11 October 1899, 175). War, like a fist-fight among men, was an acceptable means of regaining 'prestige' and 'honour' for the wrongs inflicted upon the protagonists. It was a method of showing the prewar tensions and the wartime conflict, and, like fist-fighting, was acceptable and legitimate when all other options had been explored.

Fist-fights also establish and maintain aspects of masculinity which were strongly associated with warfare. Both were seen as gendered spaces and means of asserting masculine domination over the feminine 'other'. The *Daily Mail*, for example, felt that war was not only a gender-defining activity, but was the sole factor in preventing women from gaining equality with men. In an article, 'Women and War', the paper noted the female voice of 'rage and fury' raised against war, which was seen by women as pure 'folly'. Yet this voice of opposition to warfare, while initially futile, signified what the paper called 'the subtle infection of womanishness which is bringing nearly the whole of the world's manhood to womanish points of view on manly matters'. This 'infection' of anti-war sentiment, symbolized by the Hague Conferences, would not only end war, but would emasculate men by reducing the significance of their gender role and end their 'superiority' to women. For when women stopped war, they would gain true emancipation, 'for they will have annihilated the only thing that bars them from equality or perhaps superiority to the fighting man' (*Daily Mail*, 24 October 1912, 7). The desire to see the end of war was seen to be set against the nature of masculinity; men defined themselves in terms of participation in warfare, a rite of passage and that which separated them from the feminine 'other'. Attempts to end warfare were perceived to be not only undesirable, but also contrary to nature.

One of the more obvious ways in which military activity was seen as beneficial was that it prevented the further degeneration of the race by promoting physical activities, encouraged the martial spirit and fostered patriotism. However, a more subtle benefit of warfare was that it was good for the enemy. Here, military activity was associated with the medicinal properties of pills and, if necessary, full-scale medical operations. This tendency can be seen in a cartoon published in the *News of the World*, just prior to the outbreak of the Boer War in October 1899. In this cartoon, entitled 'Violent Diseases Require Violent Remedies', in which Colonial Secretary Joseph Chamberlain was portrayed as a doctor holding a large pill labelled 'reforms' taken from the 'cabinet meeting pill box' and offering it to his patient, President Paul Kruger. The patient, surrounded by medicines and looking nervous, said, 'Why Doctor, that's a much bigger pill than the one I wouldn't swallow last week!', to which the Doctor replies, 'Yes, I know, but your case is getting worse, and unless you swallow it at once, it may mean an operation' (*News of the World*, 1 October 1899, 1). Thus the reforms demanded by the British government to allow equal rights to the Uitlanders were portrayed as a bitter, almost impossible pill for the Boers to swallow, as to acquiesce to the demands would cause more disruption than they were willing to sanction. The threat of war, neatly referred to by both the medical and the military term, 'operation', was seen as the only alternative to the ill-health of the Boers. In this way, war was linked to a positive undertaking, a necessary medical operation rather than to a negative destructive military campaign.

War as Sport/Game

The anti-war campaigner Norman Angell noted in 1910 that the British saw 'the spectacle of war [as] even more attractive than the spectacle of sport. Indeed, our Press treats it as a sort of glorified football match.' In doing so, Angell touched upon not only the common perception of warfare as a game, but also the role of the newspapers in propagating that image (Thompson, 1992, 184). The increasing use of images of war as a sporting practice during the nineteenth century was encouraged by developments in sport and the reporting of it in the press. The middle-class move to codify the rules and regulations of traditional sports can be seen as analogous to similar attempts to remove the excessive barbarities of armed conflict. The result was a move towards agreement on rules of warfare which culminated in the Hague Conferences of 1899 and 1907. By the end of the nineteenth century, coverage of sport increased in the non-specialist daily and, in particular, the weekly press. These utilized an average 10 per cent or more of available news space in daily papers like the *Daily Mail*, and up to 14 per cent in Sunday papers such as the *News of the World*. This attention to sporting news led to the development of the sports page and the sports editor, both of which became almost universal by 1900, with *The Times* the only notable exception (Mason, 1988, 47–9).

While forms of language used sporting imagery to convey warfare, one of the most striking depictions of war as a game occurred when papers published actual war game boards of a current conflict. The *Illustrated Mail* and the *Daily Mirror* both published one of these 'War Games', the former during the Boer War and the latter for the Russo-Japanese War (*Daily Mail*, 12 October 1899, 3; *Daily Mirror*, 11 February 1904, 8–9). Yet other, more upmarket papers discussed or illustrated their pages with ironic references to these games, suggesting that their readers were also keen game players, or at least knew about the practice. These references also include evidence to suggest how this method of following the course of war was a family event, with children and women actively involved. Interviews with wives of men in South Africa showed that not only children were playing soldier-games, but that whole households were active. One wife was found to have tacked up a map of the war area and was 'evidently taking the cheeriest interest in the grim game at the Cape' (*Daily News*, 27 January 1900, 6).

The middle-class ideal, found in the full-page *Illustrated London News* drawing 'Follow the Flags', where father reads dispatches while the children eagerly place flags on a mounted map, was the object of parody by *Punch* in cartoons entitled 'The Enthusiast' and 'The War Game and How it is Played' (*Illustrated London News*, 16 December 1899, 869; *Punch*, 16 March 1904, 187; 20 April 1904, 285). These illustrations demonstrate that the practice of following troop movements on a board-mounted map was widespread, at least among certain classes, for they could not have been successfully depicted or ridiculed if the 'game' had been unusual or uncommon. In addition, it was seen as a 'game' where readers became involved in the strategic nature of conflict, but were able to avoid the 'bludgeon work' of actual combat themselves.

War as Theatre

The use of the term 'theatre' in describing warfare has become so common as to be unremarkable. Terms such as 'Pacific Theatre', 'European Theatre' or 'Theatre of Operations' to denote an area of conflict have become acceptable and have acquired their own legitimacy. Theatrical metaphors used in newspapers can be seen as more than simply figures of speech, for they can be used to determine a particular mind set or *mentalité*. The very ubiquity of stage and spectacle imagery in the press before 1914 indicates their importance and utility as a means to determine how Edwardians experienced war. Both the theatre and the press underwent significant changes in the last decades of the nineteenth century which enabled them to be seen as important cultural venues, and led to the ready use of theatrical imagery to describe warfare.

In the 1880s there occurred a movement towards 'naturalism' in acting, where actors expressed themselves in ways appropriate to setting and dialogue rather than through a stock set of facial or arm gestures. Concomitant with this tendency was the increasing 'realism' of sets and props, which made theatre more convincing (Jackson, 1989, 153). Yet despite this trend towards increasing 'realism' in some aspects of the stage, popular demand still required what James Woodfield has identified as the prevalence of 'unreflecting optimism', happy endings and the avoidance of 'psychological truth'. For Woodfield, the increasing respectability of the theatre contributed to the 'falsification of life on stage', and a presentation which was 'more refined, but only offered an escape from life not an examination of it' (Woodfield, 1984, 16, 3, 18, 19). Indeed, J. C. Trewin has suggested that the Edwardian theatre represented a time of 'unrepentant make-believe' (Trewin, 1976, 3). Thus the theatre represented not so much 'reality' but more 'realistic' illusions.

Newspaper images included references to warfare as a stage play, soldiers as actors and war correspondents describing themselves as 'theatre critics'. While the mere use of these images adds weight to the contention that warfare was depicted as a theatrical entertainment, scene–curtain–audience images also indicate a certain distancing of readers from the realities of warfare. The 'curtain' represents the 'fourth wall' through which audiences watch the action on stage. It reminds them that the performance is illusory, no matter how realistic it appears, and that when the entertainment ends, they will resume their ordinary routine. Percy Fitzgerald mentioned the significance of the 'curtain' in his book *The Art of Acting*, written in 1892, suggesting that it represents 'the barrier between the real and the ideal world' (Jackson, 1989, 219). The naturalness of theatre imagery as applied to war reporting suggests that the same ideas apply: that if the readers are the 'real' world, the war on the other side of the curtain is the 'ideal' or 'unreal' world. This indicates then that not only was war an entertaining piece of theatre which moved its audience, it was also not real. The 'actors', unlike the 'audience', inhabited an ephemeral, unreal world which lasted only as long as the 'curtain' remained up.

These theatrical images, of course, required an area on which to be staged. In this way, the 'theatre of war' became more than just an area of military operations, it was a term to denote the physical place encompassing the 'sets', the 'acting' and the 'audience' mentioned in war dispatches. War correspondents even made specific comparisons to particular theatres, such as Ellis Ashmead-Bartlett's reference to the assaults on Port Arthur, which were so perfectly staged that they 'could not have been better witnessed had they been mounted at Drury Lane' (*Black and White*, 10 September 1904, 358; Ashmead-Bartlett, 1906, vii).

The visual representations of warfare in the form of cartoons utilized a wide range of these images to portray warfare as theatrical entertainment. Anticipating the war correspondent George Lynch, who saw the Battle of Elandslaagte as an intricate 'military tableaux', *Punch* depicted Field Marshal Kitchener as 'stage manager' of the 'Theatre Royal, S. Africa, Feb. 1, 1901'. He was portrayed in top hat and tails at the edge of the stage and in front of the curtain, saying to the 'audience', 'Ladies and Gentleman, on account of the elaborate preparations for the final tableaux, I must request your kind indulgence while the curtain remains down.' The different phases of the war were thus represented as different music hall tableaux, and the British public or 'audience' were asked to remain patient while Kitchener's blockhouse and flying column system was put into place (Lynch, 1903, 34; *Punch*, 6 February 1901, 117).

Images of Death

In examining descriptions of dying in British literature, Garrett Stewart suggests that death is the ultimate fiction, an event which can only be described by those who have not experienced it. Descriptions of death are thus much more dependent on cultural perceptions and the imagination of the writer than other literary events (Stewart, 1984, 4–5). Newspaper representations of death on the battlefield similarly must be, by their nature, fictional. While the act of dying is a fictional event for authors, the way that death was portrayed in the press reveals much about Edwardian perceptions of warfare. If the reality of death and wounding were denied, suppressed or glossed over, the impression of readers that war's sporting, entertaining and adventurous qualities were not diminished by its horrors would be reinforced, and the positive images of war would remain.

Ways in which the cultural denial of death became manifest were through the replacement of direct images of death, such as skulls, bones and cadavers in contemporary sepulchres, with classical allegorical allusions, such as empty or cracked urns, willows and broken columns. Jennifer Leaney believes that this change of imagery in the late-nineteenth century represented a 'desire to swathe the reality of decomposition in a romantic aura, masking and denying the actuality of death'. In addition, she suggests that this denial was extended further through the use of 'decorous language', where the word 'dead' was rarely found and replaced by euphemisms such as 'passed on', 'passed away' or 'gone to God' (Leaney, 1989, 131).

Warfare was portrayed by the press as being 'more humane' than earlier nineteenth-century conflicts in the manner that death occurred. Lyddite, the new explosive developed by the British, was said to be humane because it killed virtually painlessly (*Daily Mail*, 2 June 1904, 4; 4 January 1905, 5; 15 December 1899, 5), while the new aerodynamic ammunition was not an efficient 'man-stopper', in that it did not expand inside the body on entry nor cause horrendous powder burns (*Daily Mail*, 18 December 1899, 4).

The most emotive event depicted in photographs was perhaps the aftermath of the Oasis Massacre where photographers took pictures of dead and wounded Arabs, attacked by Italian troops in 1911. The *Illustrated London News* published several photographs showing these scenes, including a collection of four photographs entitled 'War As It Is: Dead Arabs in Heaps in Tripoli', which utilized the belief in the ability of the camera to eschew manipulation and show the realities of war – war 'as it is'. These photographs were not in close-up, were indistinct and the wounds inflicted upon the Arabs were not shown, nor was there much indication of blood on their bodies. They were seen, as the title suggests, as 'heaps' of bodies, looking more like piles of clothing rather than distinct individual soldiers (*Illustrated London News*, 11 November 1911, 770–1). Thus the dead and wounded were not shown clearly and distinctly in photographs, despite their unique suitability as subjects that did not move and could be easily approached.

The illustrations in advertisements displayed a similar tendency to deny the reality of death and wounding, as these would naturally associate products with the negative and suppressed aspects of warfare. Yet advertisements often did utilize images of actual warfare, but ones in which the beneficial qualities of the product were presented. The first ever use of aerial bombardment, which occurred in the Turco-Italian War, inspired the advertisement of 'Pergen – The Ideal Aperient'. The product was depicted as bombs being dropped from an aeroplane onto bell tents marked 'Constipation', 'Ill Health' and 'Loss of Appetite' in the same manner that the Italians dropped bombs on Turkish camps. The casualties suffered in these bombing raids, their negative effect, were hidden and denied, as the targets were not soldiers but tents representing disease rather than life, the destruction of which was a beneficial objective (*Illustrated London News*, 17 February 1912, 268).

Advertisements played upon this idea by associating their products with regenerative qualities which aided in the recovery of the wounded. Bovril, for example, ran a half-page advertisement in the *Illustrated London News* which claimed that 'Bovril gives life to the soldier faint from loss of blood'. It showed a wounded soldier with one arm in a sling, signifying a minor wound, looking healthy, strong and in no pain while drinking a cup of Bovril. Here, the advertisement implied that wounds inflicted in war were minor and painless, and that because they were so, they could be treated through consuming 'liquid life' Bovril (*Illustrated London News*, 24 February 1900, 275).

Conclusion

It is obvious from the perspective of the Edwardians and their vicarious experience of warfare that the prospect of war in 1914 did not seem all that onerous. Indeed, the idea that warfare defended 'the race' from physical and moral degeneration suggested just the opposite. By seeing soldiers as the harbingers and measurement of 'civilization' with warfare as a natural, masculine-defining activity, the image of military violence was quite beneficial. In addition, the images of war as a sporting pastime and as a theatrical entertainment encouraged these positive impressions of warfare to be current in Edwardian culture. Moreover, images of the negative consequences of warfare, namely death and wounding, did not act to dampen these positive perceptions. Death remained hidden and the pain and agony of the wounded was denied.

While our impressions of war on the Western Front remain essentially vicarious, we at least have Graves and Remarque to tell us of their experiences. The Edwardians in 1914, all those young men and women who shouted and cheered for war, did not. It is clear, then, how those young people could willingly and enthusiastically want to be a part of the experience of war. It is equally clear that these vicarious and tragic literary perceptions contributed to the outbreak of the First World War and to its horrific longevity. Perhaps in order to avoid the same fate, we should bear in mind our own perceptions of warfare when next we willingly and enthusiastically wish to engage in an act of military aggression.

Works cited

Newspapers

Black and White
Daily Mail
Daily Mirror
Daily News
Illustrated London News
News of the World
Punch

Articles and Books

Ashmead-Bartlett, Ellis. *Port Arthur*. London, 1906.
Jackson, Russell. *Victorian Theatre*. London, 1989.
Joll, James. *The Origins of the First World War*. London, 1984.
Koss, Stephen. *The Rise of the Political Press in Britain*, vol. I. London, 1981.
Leaney, Jennifer. 'Ashes to ashes: cremation and the celebration of death', in Ralph Houlbrooke, (ed.), *Death, Ritual and Bereavement*. London, 1989.
Lynch, George. *Impressions of a War Correspondent*. London, 1903.
Mackenzie, John. *Popular Imperialism and the Military, 1850–1950*. Manchester, 1992.
Mason, Tony. *Sport in Britain*. London, 1988.
Stewart, Garrett. *Death Sentences: Styles of Dying in British Fiction*. Cambridge, 1984.
Thompson, Paul. *The Edwardians: The Remaking of British Society*. London, 1992.
Trewin, J. C. *The Edwardian Theatre*. Oxford, 1976.
Woodfield, James. *English Theatre*. London, 1984.

Part II
Beyond the Trenches

3
Encoded Enclosures: the Wartime Novels of Stella Benson

Debra Rae Cohen

In her 1990 survey of British women's First World War writing, *The Great War and Women's Consciousness*, Claire Tylee announces her intention of identifying the 'women's myth' of the Great War – a myth notably excluded from standard literary surveys of the period. Written partly as a corrective to Paul Fussell's influential *The Great War and Modern Memory*, Tylee's work is part of a recent attempt by feminist critics and historians to extend the traditional definitions of war to accommodate female experience. As Margaret Higonnet points out, war itself is a highly gendered concept; 'commonplace definitions of war draw a gendered boundary' between 'battlefield' and 'home front', 'combatant' and 'non-combatant' ('Cassandra', 145–6). As war changes, the military must continually redefine the combat zone as 'wherever "women" are not' (Enloe, 15). Focusing on female war experience leads to an awareness of war as less firmly bounded in both space and time than conventional historiography would have it; for women, as Cynthia Enloe has argued, war is less a circumscribed physical event bounded by treaties than an ideological, economic and psychological struggle experienced over an extended period of time (cited in Higonnet, 'Helix', 46). 'We must move beyond the exceptional, marked event, which takes place on a specifically militarized front or in public or institutionally defined areas,' states Higonnet, 'to include the private domain and the landscape of the mind' (46).

Tylee's work brilliantly traces the ideological currents that marked women's writing about the First World War, highlighting in her treatment of 'the landscape of the mind' the self-censorship and euphemism, the verbal proprieties and 'mental petticoats' that led many women to accede to 'illusion, often self-administered ... a kind of propaganda-induced cataract that corrupted their imaginative vision' ('Petticoats',

136–7). Yet in her analysis of those works that tore down the 'verbal screens', evading the evasions of bourgeois proprieties and propaganda, she grants primacy to the impressionistic narratives of nurses at the front and to works, like Rose Macaulay's *Non-combatants and Others* and Mary Hamilton's *Dead Yesterday*, which explicitly mirror the poltical debates and ambivalences of the home front. In doing so, she short-changes the extent to which narratives of evasion, those that depict and enact the re-encoding of war into euphemism, can themselves sub-versively denaturalize hegemonic discourse, utilizing 'ironic devices of translation and substitution to expose the ideological underpinnings of the rhetoric of war' (Higonnet, 'Not So Quiet', 222).

In particular, Tylee, like other feminist revisionists, overlooks the work of Stella Benson, whose wartime novels illuminate the workings of conflicting ideologies on the home front by means of a complex inter-play of realism and fantasy. Benson, a popular novelist in Britain after the war who died young in 1933, was known throughout her career for books whose dreamy heroines tried on identities like clothes. In her wartime novels, though – written when Benson was only in her mid-20s – fantasy elements are promoted from the level of metaphor to play an active role. In one novel, witches rub shoulders with war-workers; in the other, childhood utopias interpenetrate the London slums. Magic and fantasy intrude themselves into realistic narrative, interrogating the orderly processes of the 'rational' world. This genre-mixing, which, I suspect, has eliminated Benson from serious consideration as a novelist, actually renders her books more useful for exploring exactly that construction of myth with which Tylee concerns herself. Although her idiosyncratic faux-naif style led puzzled reviewers to compare her works to Kipling's fairy tales (quoted in Bedell, 41), Benson, despite her often cloying whimsicality, has less in common with Edwardian fantasists like Barrie than with later political allegorists such as Rex Warner and Sylvia Townsend Warner, the latter of whom, Jane Marcus has argued, 'transforms the fantastic into a kind of superrealism' ('Alibis', 285). In *This Is The End* (1917) and *Living Alone* (published in 1919), Benson externalizes as genre elements (sacred spaces, magical personalities, fairy children) those sites of ideological dispute which in conventional narrative are merely thematized. In doing so she makes explicit a pat-tern which distinctively marks home-front novels written by young middle-class women during the war: these novels are characterized by a series of evasions and exclusions, in which the imaginative claims of young heroines coping with the reality of the war vie with the rhetoric of the bourgeois society that created the war. In a sense, these novels (although they articulate these concerns very differently) represent the home-front experience as a battle of enclosures: the fantasy structures the young protagonists use to encode and thus cope with war are set against the hegemonic system of exclusions that make the war possible. Although the fantasy structures rarely survive for the length of the novel, they undermine and denaturalize bourgeois structures, often by way of involvement with elements abjected from bourgeois society – outlawry, transgressive sexuality, the poor. The home front is thereby represented – and all very neatly within the provisions of the Defence of the Realm Act – as a site of self-deconstructing rhetorics, unstable gender and pervasive doubt. By utilizing the structures of fantasy to express and interrogate the terms of wartime rhetorics, Benson can engage in a coded debate without fear of prosecution or suppression.

Jay, the heroine of *This Is The End*, has run away from her family and its genteel restrictions to live, simultaneously, in the 'Brown Borough' slums of London and the Secret World of her imaginings. Working in uniform as a bus conductor, she sends long, descriptive letters back to her relatives, which they attempt to analyse for clues to her location. But Jay's letters chronicle life in her Secret World, in the idyllic House by the Sea; as ciphers, they conceal not her location, but her conscious-ness of the war, restating it in bearable terms: 'There is an aeroplane at this moment – dim as a little thought – coming between two turrets of cloud. I suppose it is that I can hear, but it sounds like the distant singing of the moon' (23). For Jay, this is an escape, not away from reality, but to a less contingent, 'realer', reality ('How can you tell it's not 1916 that's the ghost?' she asks the ageing dreamer Mr Russell (214)).

Jay's world of retreat is highly overdetermined, an enclosure coded as commentary on various contemporary ideological renderings of sacred space. The rhetoric of the war years utilized the trope of edenic space in a number of ways. On the one hand, the perception of the war as a sudden shattering of 'Beauty and Certainty and Quiet' (Dangerfield, 441–2), as a bomb in the garden party, led to the retrospective reconfig-uration of prewar England as a prelapsarian state from which 'one swung off into space, into history, into darkness, with every lamp extin-guished and every abyss gaping', as an overwrought Henry James put it early in the war (qtd in Buitenhuis, 59). On the other, in its reliance upon the evocation of England's 'green and pleasant land' as the essence of what the troops were fighting for, wartime rhetoric made reference to a notion of England as an enclosed, inviolate garden that had existed as part of the national mythology since the time of Spenser (Stallybrass, 204–5). In the prewar years, this idea of England as sacred soil was encapsulated most clearly in Kipling's *Puck of Pook's Hill* and *Rewards and Fairies*, which linked the continuity of English history to a sense of sacred responsibility and inheritorship and 'that spirit of place which, according to Conservative philosophy', says Raphael Samuel, 'is the touchstone of "true" national feeling' ('Preface', xi). That Jay's Secret World is connected to this latter notion is made clear when her brother, Kew, at an ancient place of power (probably Shaftesbury Ring), recognizes it as 'the nursery of all Secret Worlds'; the fact that Benson is interrogating rather than accepting the concept as a motivating factor in war emerges when the narrator, immediately afterwards, mourns the knowledge of the spirit of the place as 'what . . . these two years have taken from us, what . . . we have lost' (76, 77).

Jay's retreat also interrogates the 'prelapsarian' myth of prewar England, a myth predicated on nostalgia for a time before 'all the world [turned] topsy-turvy' (Macdonald, 69), when men were men and women were women. As a young woman described (like Benson herself) as 'suffragetty' and 'rather too apt to swallow this Socialist nonsense' (109, 6), Jay is in withdrawal from (in both senses of the phrase), rather than nostalgic for, traditional constructions of gender and class; her retreat to a pre-gendered 'long secret childhood' (198) where she and her Secret Friend live in a brother/sisterhood of perfect equality[1] parallels her move away from abstracted, distanced charity to share the war deprivations of the Brown Borough slum dwellers.

In declaring to her brother Kew that she wants to do 'not work for the poor, but work with the poor' (29), Jay is coding herself in opposition to those middle- and upper-class 'tourists' of the East End who arrived in motor cars to see the results of air raids and munitions plant explosions (Pankhurst, 193; Woollacott, *On Her*, 85), as well as to the charitable and regulatory workers, usually middle-class women, whose work on behalf of working-class families often involved a profound misunder-standing of the nature of their lives, and the attempted imposition of bourgeois moral values (Braybon, 141–9; Woollacott, *On Her*, 168–9).[2] In abandoning her expected role as a lady, Jay transgresses both class and gender lines.

Benson contrasts Jay's attitudes toward war, class and gender with the jingoistic platitudes of her Cousin Gustus and the crafted sentiments of his wife, the novelist. Mrs Gustus, ironically dubbed 'Anonyma', is a skilled purveyor of 'word-vignettes', who commodifies fantasy into saleable dollops of predigested nostalgia. An avid consumer, as well as producer, of bourgeois rhetoric, she believes her own discourse, even as the text itself denaturalizes it, reveals it as fictive: 'The self that she shared so generously with others was . . . not founded on fact, but modelled on the heroine of all her books' (44).

In creating herself, Mrs Gustus reinscribes the norms of femininity with almost parodic verve, self-consciously larger than life: 'Anybody but Mrs Gustus would have been drowned in her clothes. But she was conceived on a generous scale, she was almost gorgeous, she barely missed exaggeration. In her manner I think she did not miss it' (8). It is this sort of rearticulation that Judith Butler sees as potentially the occasion for the 'critical reworking' (x) of gender norms. But Mrs Gustus's parody, far from subverting hegemonic norms, invokes womanliness as a kind of fetish in the service of bourgeois expectations, recapitulating the way propaganda mobilized traditional images of femininity in the service of the war (Ouditt, 16, 47). Thus Mrs Gustus uses her 'womanly charm' (19) to manipulate Kew into trying to bring Jay back to fulfil her role as a 'lady'. Haranguing a Quaker pacifist, she appeals to the plight of women 'born to put up with second bests' and 'superfluous' in wartime to shame him into playing the man (165). Similarly, she invokes womanhood to position herself in relation to the poor – 'dear fellow-woman', she describes herself appealing to a working-class Londoner in one of her 'word-vignettes'. The term ostensibly registers identity, but emphasizes only distinction: 'lady' is the word that it conceals.

Mrs Gustus's 'war work' involves sentimental writing about the inhabitants of the Brown Borough slums: 'You would never guess how much insight into the souls of the poor, four hours a week can give to a person,' the narrator comments dryly (41). By rendering the poor picturesque, Mrs Gustus underscores their status as Other, as subject of abjection and nostalgia, and normalizes that status as a necessary condition of wartime experience. The word 'vermin', with its associations of filth and disease, serves in both of Benson's wartime books to link all those whose abjection makes possible the functioning of the war society. It is used to refer to the poor (Jay is excoriated for her desire to 'bring vermin into the house' – i.e. adopt Brown Borough babies (17)), and also the enemy – 'vermin' is the term of opprobrium in Benson's rendering of the propaganda rhetorics of the war (*Living Alone*, 145). In his final words to Jay from the trenches, her brother denaturalizes this rhetoric by recognizing its reversibility. Hit by a sniper's bullet at the end of the book, Kew sends her a message by a friend:

> He wandered a little, I think, because he seemed worried about the rats that might be caught in the trap he had set. He seemed to mix up the rats and the Boches. He said that these creatures didn't know

they were vermin, they just thought they were honest average animals
doing their bit, and then suddenly killed by a malignant chaos.

(228)

The word 'vermin' comes by extension to mean all those in the trenches,
undermining the structure of abjection and thus the rationale for the
war itself.

Doing 'war-work', in Benson's use of the word, seems to involve the
reiteration of such terms of abjection and the reinscription of bourgeois
norms. Certainly this is supported historically in the hysterical reaction
by both the government and the middle-class public to the prospect of
women workers and soldiers' dependents free to spend their wages or
allotments. According to Sylvia Pankhurst, 'alarmist morality-mongers
conceived monstrous visions of girls and women, freed from the control
of fathers and husbands who had hitherto compelled them to industry,
chastity and sobriety, now neglecting their homes, plunging into excesses,
and burdening the country with swarms of illegitimate infants' (98).
Patriarchal and class ideology configured unsupervised women, particularly working-class women, as a threat to the nation. As Lucy Bland and
Philippa Levine have detailed, the women police became, largely, the
policers of women; the state, in the persons of welfare supervisors and
the Ministry of Pensions, became the soldier's surrogate, using the
threat of abjection to discipline his wife, and penalizing her for behaviour
deemed inappropriate (Pedersen, 1000). Benson highlights and ironizes
this situation: Sarah Brown, the middle-class protagonist of *Living Alone*,
does war-work 'collecting evidence from charitable spies about the
Naughty Poor' (77).

Benson makes clear that abjection *is* indeed war-work, in the sense
that it constructs the society that makes war possible: she says of Sarah
Brown's committee, 'all six women were there because their country
was at war, and because they felt it to be their duty to assist it to remain
at war for the present' (4). So it's telling that Jay, in *This Is the End*,
describes in similar terms the gendered expectations she has abandoned,
prospective marriage to a 'most respectable young man': 'She wrote to
me that she couldn't keep up that engagement,' says Kew. 'Not even by
looking upon it as War Work' (18). Sharon Ouditt has described the way
popular images of the war appropriated romance as a necessary adjunct
to patriotism: 'if women were to keep the home fires burning, that fire
was to be as alive in their hearts as it was in their hearths' (89). In her
rejection of class and gender norms, Jay is resisting the appropriation of
femininity for the uses of war.

By opting for not the 'war-work' of romance, but the more public work of the bus conductor, Jay at first seems to ally herself with the enthusiastic troops of young middle-class women for whom the war offered a patriotic excuse to 'cast off the old ways and enter public space without fear' (as Martha Vicinus has written of the suffrage movement, 256). But for Jay, the bus is less a triumphant vehicle of liberation (as Virginia Woolf makes it in *Mrs Dalloway*, linking Elizabeth's ride down the Strand with her sense of potential and possibility) than a means of repositioning herself. Living in the Brown Borough, working among the crowds, Jay is re-enacting the two elements that Eric Leed identifies as characteristic of the 'liminality' of the trenches – pollution and invisibility (19). Against 'Anonyma', a self-consciously feminized bourgeois individualism configured as spectacle, she constructs herself as 'anonymous': transgressively unnoticeable, transgressively degendered. Her work in uniform as a bus conductor codes her in opposition to the war by rendering herself sexually ambiguous, a person-in-uniform, rather than either (in Mrs Gustus's terms) soldier or superfluous woman. Encountering Jay in London, unbeknownst to the rest of the family, Kew is profoundly shaken not by Jay's residence in the Brown Borough, but by the apparition of his sister in uniform, 'a kilt and yards of gaiters...a hat like a Colonial horse marine'. 'It seems curious', the narrator notes, 'that he should deplore the fact that Jay had turned into a 'bus-conductor more deeply than he had deplored her experiments in sweated employment' (127, 131).

The root of Kew's anxiety is sexual; he dwells on the image of Jay being asked out by 'trousered bus-conductors' – overtly an image of cross-class sexual transgression. But the slippage of class here conceals a slippage of genders: 'trousers' are no longer a trustworthy marker for masculinity, when women are already wearing the kilt (itself, of course, male dress). Judith Butler's terms prove useful here again: by wearing the uniform skirt, Jay parodically overinscribes the marker of femininity, which only serves to destabilize and unsettle it *as* a marker (is it a skirt? or a kilt?). Such destabilization affects Kew's own sexual identity: 'The only difference between us used to be her skirt,' he mourns, 'and now she has gone a good way towards discarding that' (142). The trousers of the bus conductor, then, may signify Brown Borough 'vermin' – or, in the words Mrs Gustus uses to dismiss peace supporters, 'women in either sex' (165).

For Jay herself, however, the sexual indeterminacy of uniform is an extension of the anonymity of the job, anonymity which allows her, unexamined, to go through the motions of fare-taking while simultaneously living in her Secret World. The conditions of her labour, encoded by fantasy, are reflected there in a deeper, purer anonymity: 'The best part about Secret Friends is that they will never weary you by knowing you. . . . Your unnecessary identity is tactfully ignored, and you know the heaven of being dispassionate and detached among the things you love' (6). A pre-sexual paradise, a 'long secret childhood' (198), the Secret World resists both the depredations of war-in-time and the expectations linked to gender. Although 'Story' exists there, it is positioned as pre-linguistic, and thus resistant to the Law; rhetoric is subsumed into the song of the roses and the confusion of the sea: 'The Law cleared its throat, and looked nervously at the schooner, and at the sun, and at the other boat, and at the Secret Friend. The Law likes to be argued with. Take away words, and where is the Law? Silence always annoys it' (57).

'Don't tell me facts, because I know they will bar me for ever out of my House by the Sea,' Jay tells Mr Russell. 'Facts are contraband there' (213–14). But it is the imposition of facticity on Jay's Secret World that eventually destroys it; specifically, the 'facts' of sex and death. Insisting on his link with Jay, Mr Russell declares his love, imposing on the Secret World the demands of adult sexuality, a threat to Jay's idyll that she only resists by interpreting it as pre-sexual: 'Surely no friend ever loved her friend as I love you, and surely there never was as little room for sin and disappointment in any love as there is in ours. Surely there are no tears in the world any more, and no Brown Borough, and no War' (223). This is a last-ditch effort on Jay's part to resist the breaking of her 'bubble enchantment'; on her return home a friend brings her the news of Kew's death in the trenches, a 'fact' her Secret World cannot survive.

Whereas facticity shatters the Secret World, illusion undermines Jay's other retreat to reality; her parallel withdrawals from wartime propaganda into communion with childhood and communion with the working class falter due to their incompatibility. Like the aristocrat's landscape garden, which used enclosure to create an illusion of nature, sculpting an image of freedom through the exclusion of the 'disgustful' and the working class (Franklin, 144, 146), Jay's Secret World is constructed by repressing the Brown Borough around her. At several points in the text, Benson makes it clear that Jay's 'work with the poor' and her friendship with her working-class neighbours has resulted in only an incomplete communion, and that she is less free from the 'forced fidelity' of bourgeois ideology that she thinks herself to be (29). One episode implies that Jay has been affected not just by the wartime construction of the past as an idyllic space, but by the propaganda rhetoric that she consciously disavows. Trying to comfort a soldier's wife, Jay buys her a copy of Dürer's engraving of 'St. George', which looks 'rather like [her husband], if it wasn't for the uniform'; looking at it, Mrs Morgan doesn't recognize the saint, but reads his armour as a respirator, and 'blast[s] the war that made it necessary to wear them' (61–2). Coded in this incident is Jay's continued vulnerability to the ideology of chivalry that presented the war as a 'Christian crusade against the barbaric Hun' (Tylee, 57). In this iconography St George played a prominent and publicized part: in the wartime tale of the 'Angels of Mons' (originally an obvious fantasy by Arthur Machen that was picked up, exaggerated and spread – and believed – as gospel), St George appears in the sky over the Belgian town, and calls up angelic bowmen to help an embattled British force rout the Germans. The witnesses know it is St George because they recognize his face from the English sovereign coin (Buitenhuis, 103–4). The presence of St George in the incident from *This Is The End* emphasizes the distance that separates Jay from her working-class neigh-bours, even as she reaches out to them: not only does Mrs Morgan see past the chivalric sentimentality of the image to the real war it euphem-izes, but the fact that she fails to recognize St George underscores the dif-ference between 'work[ing] with' the poor and actually *being* poor – there aren't too many sovereigns circulating in the Brown Borough.

'When you find that your entrance no longer fills a Brown Borough room with sudden silence, you may be glad and know that you have ceased to be a lidy [*sic*] or a toff,' comments the narrator of Jay's attendance at a neighbourhood gathering (185–6). But despite her seeming assimi-lation, Jay is nevertheless set apart. Angela Woollacott has commented on the way middle-class women who policed women workers during the war misunderstood the public nature of working-class life (*On Her*, 178), the degree to which privacy is itself a facet of bourgeois individu-alism. In *This Is The End*, Jay uses the working-class crowd to secure herself middle-class privacy, sitting with the crowd in the pub while alone in her Secret World. Her anonymity is the anonymity of the ostrich. Indeed, her separateness is confirmed by the very job to which she looks to keep her unnoticed:

''Bus-conductors don't know nothink,' said the Chap from the Top Floor in a loud belligerent voice, illuminated by an amiable smile. 'I orfen look at 'bus-conductors, an' think, "Pore devils, they don't know 'arf of life, not even a quarter. They only meets the haristoc-racy wot 'as pennies to frow about, they never passes the time of day with a plain walkin' feller like me wot ses 'is mind an' never puts on no frills. 'Bus-conducting oughter be done by belted earls an' suchlike,

it ain't a real man's job. Pore devils," I ses, lookin' at em bouncin'
along, doing the pretty to all the nobs, wivout so much as puttin'
their toe in the mud. "Pore devils."'

(188 9)

In one anarchic burst, the Chap from the Top Floor serves to destabilize once more ideological positions, rendering Jay's destabilizing of
bourgeois norms itself uncertain. Is the bus conductor's uniform really
a site of transgression if it can be semiotically linked to the belt of an earl? Is
Jay re-encoding gender if bus-conducting isn't 'a real man's job' anyway?
And is she really at one with the poor (identified in *Living Alone* as the
inhabitants of 'Mud Street'[3]) if she never puts her toe in the mud? Benson
comically forces us to recognize the tenacity of ideology, the degree to
which Jay is irrevocably marked by the bourgeois training from which
she is trying to disengage. We are forced to wonder if, as Jane Marcus
has posited, 'the "highbrow" adoption of popular culture is merely
a "democratic" effort' consciously adopted 'for the duration' ('Afterword',
475) – thus configuring it, despite Jay's anti-propaganda position, as
a patriotic gesture. For despite her avowed goal of avoiding the 'bird's-eye
view' (29), Jay *has* positioned herself atop the bus, in a role that allows
her simultaneously to embrace the poor symbolically and exclude them
imaginatively.

In a sense, Jay has appropriated the East End as a 'Room of One's
Own', securing the freedom to free herself imaginatively from bourgeois
constriction by using the working class as a backdrop to the construction of bourgeois subjectivity. This is enclosure configured as 'the defensive side of individualism' (Samuel, 'Introduction', xxxix). In her final,
futile attempt to recolonize her imaginative space, the Brown Borough –
along with the war, along with sexuality – is part of what she explicitly
excludes from the Secret World. Indeed, class and sexuality are mutually
encoded in this rejection. Earlier, Jay claimed identity with the working
class by telling a sweat-shop operator that 'ladies and women had
exactly the same sort of inside' (32) – an offence against bourgeois
propriety in its acknowledgement of the presence of *bodies* (and thus,
implicitly, also, against the euphemisms of war rhetoric). Now, in
excluding bodies from the Secret World, Jay renders this parity of needs
and desires 'unspeakable' as well – and by extension, surrenders to the
exclusionary rhetoric of war.

Leaving the sexless, genderless anonymity of the Secret World, Jay
re-enters the marriage plot; unable to resist the 'reality' of the war, and
of the demands of class and gender, she picks up her abandoned

'war-work' and marries the respectable young man. The bleakness of this ending is emphasized for us by Mrs Gustus's summation: 'our little Jay has at last found [capital R-] Romance' (241). But as Meredith Bedell has pointed out, the finality of *This Is The End* is undercut by the narrator's insistence at the outset that she (one assumes) is presenting only 'the end, for the moment' and that 'system is a fairy and a dream'. The fantasy-embracing narrator subjects the entire text of the novel to destabilizing uncertainty: 'this is my unfinal conclusion,' she announces. 'I feel no security in facts, precedent seems no protection to me' (1). The word 'precedent' here is important; the slogan-loving Cousin Gustus is 'never at a loss for a precedent' (17). It is precedent which, in Judith Butler's formulation, makes the law possible, through appeal to an authoritative chain of citation: 'The performative speaking of the law . . . works only by reworking a set of already operative conventions. And these conventions are grounded in no other legitimating authority than the echo-chain of their own reinvocation' (107). To cast doubt on precedent is to subvert the citation of the law, resignifying it as it is restated, undermining its very Law-ness. The narrator's insistent uncertainty opens out the ending of *This Is The End*; is the war won? *Has* the war won? We don't really know.

Throughout the novel, Benson subjects bourgeois truisms to denaturalizing parody by calling attention, by capital letters, to the very process of citation:

> The fundamental facts that you and I accept from our youth upwards, like Be Good and You Will Be Happy, or Change Your Boots When You Come In Out Of The Wet, or Respect Your Elders, or Love Your Neighbor, or Never Cross Your Legs Above The Knee, did not impress Jay.
>
> (2)

Jay and her brother Kew distinguish between capital-letter and small-letter sentiments, configuring the former as tired sloganeering: '"Why is it that faith with a little F is such a perfect thing, and yet Faith, grown-up Faith in Church, is so tiring?" "Perhaps one is overworked and the other isn't," suggested Kew' (36–7). When Kew is shot, he attempts to break the citational chain that will construct his death as sacrifice:

> . . . he said he could lie to Anonyma and your cousin vicariously through the War Office, which would write to them about Glory, and Duty, and Thanks Due. But he wanted me to write to you, and

tell you how it happened, and tell you that death was just an ordinary old thing ... without a capital letter ...

(226)

Yet understanding how citation operates to lend authority to language and naturalize ideology does not free one, the book leads us to suspect, from their effects. Jay and Kew, after all – J and Q – are themselves both capital letters, and thus, like capital-F Faith and capital-R Romance, implicitly bourgeois constructions. While *This Is The End* presents Jay as herself questioning and defusing wartime rhetorical structures, our final – or 'unfinal' – impression is of Jay herself as a battlefield of ideologies, herself a synecdoche of home-front debate.

In *Living Alone*, her second wartime novel, Benson continues to interrogate the rhetorics of Law and propaganda; but here, instead of making her heroine a battlefield, she further externalizes the strands of ideological debate, using the figures of witches and wizards to denaturalize social practice. She defines these magical figures as 'those who are born for the first time' (27); throughout the book, their naive restatement of bourgeois truisms renders those truisms absurd, breaking the citational chain that vests them with 'natural' authority. ('How can two people be righteously scourging each other at the same time?' asks the witch in response to propaganda. 'It is like the old problem of two serpents eating each other, starting at the tail. There must be some misunderstanding somewhere' (147)). Magic is presented in *Living Alone* as the antithesis of the law, as everything the abjection of which makes the law possible. Indeed, in this novel magic is *literally* abjected: after a witch invades her war-work committee, and under the influence of a magic sandwich, the 'Sandwich of Knowledge', Sarah Brown abandons her office, in an antic version of the end of *Paradise Lost*, pursued by 'the spirits of parsons and social workers with flaming swords, pointing at the door' (94).

Whereas *This Is The End* alternates between elegy and sarcasm, *Living Alone* is altogether more arch, wild and hectic in tone, as if Benson's narrative were showing the strain of two more years of war. And the 'battle of enclosures' it chronicles doesn't offer a childhood paradise as an alternative to war-rhetoric; here, the two alternatives seem equally bleak. Like Jay, Sarah Brown finds respite from the world in fantasy; unlike Jay, she 'sleep-walk[s]' through her waking life. Like Mrs Gustus, she scripts her own identity; unlike her, she can never quite believe her own story.

Perhaps because the novel's fantasy elements are located outside her, elements of her experience rather than her construction, Sarah Brown

is a less sympathetic figure than Jay. Without even a Secret Friend to
share her inner life, her closest companion is her dog; a trope on the
classic figure of the eccentric British spinster, Sarah Brown is fashioned
as a deliberately indigestible lump, a reification of the 'problem
of the superfluous woman' which began to occupy journalists and
pundits again as the war drew to a close. Assumed to be object, not subject, the 'superfluous woman' was discussed as human excess, that
which must be abjected for the good of the community, as in Lady Bruton's
emigration scheme in *Mrs Dalloway*. Writing in late 1917, essayist
Mrs Alec-Tweedie demonstrates the degree to which superfluous
women were configured as another variety of 'vermin': 'One shudders to
think of a future with a large part of the world populated by women.
Women are made to mate with men and men with women. It may
take a whole generation to stamp out the surplus of women and begin to
adjust society again' (162).

As if conscious of 'superfluously' taking up space, yet unapologetic,
Sarah Brown lives almost entirely within her own mind, barely impinging
on the world:

> Men and women have given me everything that such as I could
> expect. I have never met with reasonless enmity, never met with
> meanness, never met with anything more unbearable than natural
> indifference, from any man or woman. I have been, I may say,
> a burden and a bore all over the world; I have been an ill and fretful
> stranger within all men's gates; I have asked much and given nothing;
> I have never been a friend.
>
> (35–6)

Unlike Jay, she opens the novel as a self-isolated, passive tool of 'war-
work', mouthing the jargon of categories and exclusions. The 'war-work'
world is depicted as one hyperconscious of degrees of entitlement. Even
the dead from a nearby crypt (risen in error when they mistake an air
raid for the Last Trump) are only concerned with establishing precedence
over each other: 'Do you suppose the sheep will be allowed to hear
the trial of the goats,' asks one ladylike resurrectee, 'or will the court be
cleared?' (120). Benson continually juxtaposes fine shades of social
judgement with the bluntness of magic which renders them idiotic:
when the witch herself makes her first, tempestuous appearance in Sarah
Brown's committee-room, the narrator dutifully records that 'her clothes
were much too good to throw away. You would have enjoyed giving
them to a decayed gentlewoman' (5).

The witch's entrance disrupts the workings of Sarah Brown's committee, which literally disciplines the bodies of the poor by controlling access to food grants and allotments; by unsettling the relationship between a body and its name, the witch immediately destabilizes this process. 'How'd you mean – real name?' she asks. 'You see, the truth is, I was never actually christened. . . . I was born a conscientious objector' (12). Throughout the book, those who are close to magic stymie and frustrate categorization, undermining the bureaucracy that supports the war. Peony, whom Sarah Brown meets when she moves into the boarding house run by the witch, the House of Living Alone, is to the charity officials exactly that monstrous woman run amok whom they have anticipated in an atmosphere of 'moral panic' (Pedersen, 996). She is a symbol of irremediable excess – the recipient of a 'half-pint of milk daily, regardless of the fact that last month she had received a shilling's-worth of groceries from the Parish' (79). Like many of the former inhabitants of 'Mud Street', stigmatized as the 'Naughty Poor', Peony escapes the bureaucracy that seeks to contain her; a nexus of magic, Peony is pregnant with a fairy child who has been visiting her for years, and whom she only realized was magic because he never grew old enough to be conscripted. As that transgressive oxymoron, an 'unmarried wife' (83), Peony represents an uncontainable excess of desire.

As the antithesis of the law, magic is a locus not only of desire, but of gender confusion. The wizard Richard, Peony's True Love (and the father picked out by her fairy child), is continually identified as somehow not a real man (thus configuring him in opposition to that early war rhetoric which presented the battlefield as the site of masculine rite of passage). 'It is true that Rrchud [*sic*] isn't like other women's boys,' admits his mother, Lady Arabella. 'Do you know, I have only once seen him with other boys, doing the same as other boys, and that was when I saw him marching with hundreds of real boys . . . in 1914. . . . It was the happiest day I ever had, I thought after all that I had borne a real boy' (48). At the book's end, when Lady Arabella laments the advent of a 'faery grandson' (255), her rhetoric explicitly links magical and sexual transgression. The witch, similarly, is continually misidentified by the representatives of the Law as a 'male in female disguise' (224).

The war bureaucracy naturally resists such destabilizing forces: Richard finds that 'in France the smallest pinch of magic seems to make the N.C.O. sick, and that's why I never got my stripe' (108). The witch's attempt, while in a dogfight over London with a German counterpart, to explode propaganda rhetoric rather than bombs earns her a charge under the

Defence of the Realm Act for 'obstructin' 'Is Majesty's enemies in the performance of their dooty' (225).

Abjected by the bourgeois structures of the war bureaucracy, magic nevertheless reappears – as Peter Stallybrass and Allon White have described in relation to the carnivalesque – in the return of the repressed. Each member of the war-work committee, convinced that the witch's magic speaks uniquely to him or her, sneaks off to the House of Living Alone – slumming – to try to acquire what each thinks she has to sell. At the book's end, they indulge in a bourgeois orgy of magic that, echoing the violence of the war itself, ends up destroying the House.

Sarah Brown, in all this, is less the battlefield than a peculiar no man's land, continually defined by what she is not. She is vulnerable to magic, the narrator suggests, because she is 'not a real woman', 'only half a woman' (188, 84). Terms that condemn her according to bourgeois gender norms are here reinscribed as paradoxically empowering (similarly, she 'hears' magic better because of her deafness). Sarah Brown, then, responds to the denaturalization of propaganda which the witch's presence implies; infected by magic, she is unable to continue her 'war-work'. Yet just as Jay cannot merge with the working class because of the impossibility of purging oneself of ideology, Sarah Brown can never actually *become* magic. As in *This Is The End*, there is an incomplete communion: Sarah Brown, attempting to save the witch from prosecution, makes her leave with her for America. But in doing so, she reveals herself as still operating within the constraints of bourgeois ideology; in running from the law, she grants it power. The witch understands that there is no reason to flee from the law, or from the war – indeed, it's the constitutive abjection of magic that makes the society that makes war possible. Magic must struggle where war *is*. The witch leaves Sarah Brown to enter America – an 'unmagical' land – alone. Unable to aspire to magic, Sarah Brown nevertheless firmly resists further appropriation by the Law, declaring herself, as she arrives in America, to be deaf to its language. Sarah Brown, unlike Jay, ends the novel with enclosure intact; in leaving the arena of war, she carries with her the 'greater House of Living Alone' (264). Rather than a magical realm, this is a sort of ideological halfway house, a bourgeois enclosure defined in opposition not to the working class but to the entire world; confirmed in her isolation, Sarah Brown is less a 'superfluous woman' than one for whom the world is superfluous.

In a sense, the non-endings of these wartime novels may only reflect the pervasive recognition that all endings must be tenuous so long as the war lasts – a more problematic version of the novel's jingoistic conclusions 'now we must gird our loins for the future' conclusion. But their resistance to closure bespeaks a broader and more subversive resistance as well. Even though the transgressive positionings of both protagonists are undercut, their stance against wartime rhetoric thrown into question by their continued vulnerability to bourgeois ideology, Benson's endings leave open the possibility of further subversion, denaturalizing even themselves. Just as Jay's re-entry into the marriage plot in *This Is The End* is undermined by the narrator's insistence on radical indeterminacy, Sarah Brown's loss of magic in *Living Alone* is contradicted by the self-defining implacability of her deafness, her emphatic refusal, as she enters America, to 'hear' the discourse of the law. Nancy Huston has argued that men have made war into 'the paradigm of all narratives' (278) predicated on the construction of women as audiences; refusing to hear its discourse, refusing to accept 'fact', becomes a strategy for rewriting the paradigm. In resisting closure Benson continues to emphasize war as an ideological struggle, written beyond its own 'ending', and helps to dismantle the neat dichotomies of battlefield and home front, war and peace.

Notes

1. Utopia is thus not merely pre-sexual, but positioned before the awareness of gendered expectations; I am reminded here of Lady Bruton's dreams of childhood in *Mrs. Dalloway*. According to Claire Tylee, it was 'by comparison with their brothers, their imagined "comrade-twin," to use Adrienne Rich's epithet, that girls learned their own inferior and dependent role' (244). Angela Woollacott has analysed the powerful symbolic role played by brothers in women's literature of the Great War ('Sisters and Brothers in Arms'); certainly Jay's brother Kew serves that function here, first abetting the survival of her 'Secret World' and then contributing, by his death, to its downfall.
2. By having Jay live in the Brown Borough (probably Hoxton, in the East End, where Benson herself went to live and work), Benson is aligning herself with Sylvia Pankhurst, who broke with her mother Emmeline and sister Christabel over the issue of the war, condemning militarism as she continued to work for the rights of East End women. Benson was clearly aware of this controversy and the very public presence of former suffragettes in war-work; her first novel, *I Pose* (1915) was concerned with the suffrage movement.
3. Benson's continued use of the word 'mud' in connection with the poor, like her use of the word 'vermin', shows her awareness of the overlapping bourgeois construction of working-class life and the war as inappropriate sites for 'ladies'. At this time 'mud' was an inevitable reminder of the Western Front, itself configured as a no woman's land; Cyril Falls dismissed the very notion of women's Great War writing with the words 'really, it is not the place of women to talk of mud' (qtd in Beauman, 128).

Works cited

Alec-Tweedie, Mrs. *Women and Soldiers*. London: John Lane, The Bodley Head, 1918.

Beauman, Nicola. '"It is not the place of women to talk of mud": some responses by British Women Novelists to World War I', *Women and World War I: The Written Response*, ed. Dorothy Goldman. London: Macmillan – now Palgrave, 1993.

Bedell, R. Meredith. *Stella Benson*. Boston: Twayne, 1983.

Benson, Stella. *Living Alone*. London: Macmillan – now Palgrave, 1919.

——. *This Is The End*. London: Macmillan – now Palgrave, 1917.

Bland, Lucy. 'In the name of protection: the policing of women in the First World War', *Women-in-Law: Explorations in Law, Family and Sexuality*, eds Julia Brophy and Carol Smart. London: Routledge, 1985, 23–49.

Braybon, Gail. *Women Workers in the First World War: The British Experience*. London: Croon Helm, 1981.

Buitenhuis, Peter. *The Great War of Words: British, American, and Canadian Propaganda and Fiction, 1914–33*. Vancouver: University of British Columbia Press, 1987.

Butler, Judith. *Bodies That Matter*. New York: Routledge, 1993.

Cooke, Miriam and Angela Woollacott (eds). *Gendering War Talk*. Princeton, NJ: Princeton University Press, 1993.

Dangerfield, George. *The Strange Death of Liberal England*, 1935. New York: Capricorn, 1961.

Enloe, Cynthia. *Does Khaki Become You? The Militarization of Women's Lives*. Boston: South End Press, 1983.

Franklin, Jill. 'The Liberty of the Park', in Samuel (ed.), vol. 3, 141–59.

Higonnet, Margaret R. 'Cassandra's question: do women write war novels?', in *Borderwork: Feminist Engagements with Comparative Literature*, ed. Margaret R. Higonnet. Ithaca, NY: Cornell University Press, 1995, 144–61.

——. 'Not so quiet in no-woman's-land', in Cooke and Woollacott (eds), 205–26.

Higonnet, Margaret R. and Patrice L.-R. Higonnet. 'The double helix', in *Behind the Lines: Gender and the Two World Wars*, eds Margaret R. Higonnet et al. New Haven: Yale University Press, 1987, 31–47.

Huston, Nancy. 'Tales of war and tears of women', *Women's Studies International Forum*, 5.3 / 4 (1982): 271–82.

Leed, Eric J. *No Man's Land: Combat and Identity in World War I*. Cambridge: Cambridge University Press, 1979.

Levine, Philippa. '"Walking the streets in a way no decent woman should": women police in World War I', *Journal of Modern History*, 66 (March 1994): 34–78.

Macdonald, Nina. 'Sing a Song of War-Time', in *Scars Upon My Heart: Women's Poetry and Verse of the First World War*, ed. Catherine Reilly. London: Virago, 1981.

Marcus, Jane. 'Afterword', *We That Were Young*. By Irene Rathbone. 1932. New York: Feminist Press, 1989, 467–98.

——. 'Alibis and legends: the ethics of elsewhereness, gender and estrangement', *Women's Writing in Exile*, eds Mary Lynn Broe and Angela Ingram. Chapel Hill: University of North Carolina Press, 1991.

Ouditt, Sharon. *Fighting Forces, Writing Women: Identity and Ideology in the First World War*. New York: Routledge, 1994.

Pankhurst, E. Sylvia. *The Home Front*, 1932. London: Cresset Library, 1987.

Pedersen, Susan. 'Gender, welfare, and citizenship in Britain during the Great War', *American Historical Review*, 95 (1990): 983–1006.

Samuel, Raphael. 'Introduction: exciting to be English', in Samuel (ed.), vol. 1, xviii–lxvii.

—— (ed.) *Patriotism: The Making and Unmaking of British National Identity*, 3 vols. London: Routledge, 1989.

——. 'Preface', in Samuel (ed.), vol. 1, x–xvii.

Stallybrass, Peter. 'Time, space, and unity: the symbolic discourse of *The Faerie Queene*', in Samuel (ed.), vol. 3, 199–214.

Stallybrass, Peter and Allon White. *The Poetics and Politics of Transgression*. Ithaca, NY: Cornell University Press, 1986.

Tylee, Claire M. *The Great War and Women's Consciousness: Images of Militarism and Womanhood in Women's Writing, 1914–64*. Iowa City: University of Iowa Press, 1990.

——. 'Verbal screens and mental petticoats: women's writing of the First World War', *Revista Canaria de estudios ingleses*, 13–14 (1987): 125–52.

Vicinus, Martha. *Independent Women: Work and Community for Single Women 1850–1920*. Chicago: University of Chicago Press, 1985.

Woollacott, Angela. *On Her Their Lives Depend*. Berkeley: University of California Press, 1994.

——. 'Sisters and brothers in arms: family, class, and gendering in World War I Britain', in Cooke and Woollacott (eds): 128–47.

4
The Self in Conflict: May Sinclair and the Great War

Terry Phillips

The re-evaluation of attitudes to the Great War which began in the 1960s has contributed to a privileging of certain kinds of writing and the neglect of others. In the case of May Sinclair, the modern unpopularity of her pro-war stance is compounded by her gender. Claire Tylee has pointed out that only from the late 1970s has what she calls the '"men-only" construction of the Great War' been challenged. As long as the notion of 'war-literature' was confined to the battlefield, women would be automatically excluded (Tylee, 8–9). Sinclair's stance also excludes her from any consideration of women writers under the general category of pacifist women, while her belief that the War was more important than the suffrage campaign, of which she had been a supporter, has contributed to her neglect by modern feminists. For example, Laura Stempel Mumford argues that Sinclair's privileging of the war over the suffrage movement 'relegates the very movement she has championed ... to a position of triviality' (Mumford, 179). In this chapter I intend to argue that Sinclair's writing is worthy of attention. She was no unthinking jingoist. She opposed the extremes of war enthusiasm in a letter to the *Manchester Guardian* (Zegger, 16), and after its conclusion campaigned on behalf of the civilian population of Germany (Sinclair, 'Worse', 147–53). Her war writing is largely a product of her inability to believe, without benefit of hindsight, 'anything that's been thought and written (within the last twenty years, anyhow) more important than the winning of the War!' (Boll, 111). It expresses one woman's attempt to face up to the challenge of what war meant to her as an individual, a writer and a woman, and should not be dismissed because of its failure to conform to end-of-century ideological consciousness.

The novelist May Sinclair (1863–1946) was well-known in her own day as a novelist, literary critic, Idealist philosopher, advocate of women's suffrage and proponent of psychoanalysis, although she is today known only by the three novels republished in recent years: *The Three Sisters* (1914), *Mary Olivier: A Life* (1919) and *Life and Death of Harriett Frean* (1922), notable for their concern with female identity and their literary experimentation. Among Sinclair's prolific output, including 24 novels, are four texts largely relating to the Great War. The first of these, *A Journal of Impressions in Belgium*, published in 1915, recounts Sinclair's experiences between 25 September and 12 October 1914 as the secretary and reporter attached to a field ambulance in Belgium based in Ghent. The publication of *A Journal* was followed a year later by *Tasker Jevons: The Real Story*, which in its final parts draws closely on Sinclair's 17-day experience in Belgium. The year 1917 saw the publication of *The Tree of Heaven*, which debates in fictional form the issues, rather than the experiences, of *A Journal* to produce a complex war novel. Finally in her 1920 novel, *The Romantic*, Sinclair returned once again to the material of *A Journal*. Some of her later work, particularly *Anne Severn and the Fieldings* in which a character returns from the front with shell-shock, make incidental use of the war experience.

Theophilus Boll recounts the broad facts of Sinclair's expedition to Belgium (Boll, 106–7). The Commandant referred to in *A Journal* was Dr Hector Monro, who like Sinclair herself was a member of the Medico-Psychological Clinic of London. It would appear that Monro regarded Sinclair's appointment as not altogether satisfactory, since after her departure for England for further fundraising he requested the War Office not to allow her to rejoin his ambulance.

A knowledge of Sinclair's life and work, particularly her autobiographical novel *Mary Olivier: A Life*, makes clear that one of her central concerns was the establishment of her own identity as an independent, thinking woman against the repressive values of society, her family and particularly her mother. By 1914, Sinclair had successfully established herself, not only in career terms as a writer, but as someone who felt her identity intact. It is arguable, and *A Journal* provides support for such a view, that although her intellect assented to the war it did challenge her hard-won sense of self in three main ways.

First, she recognizes the necessity for military authority and discipline, which counters her modernist concern with the primacy of the self. *The Three Sisters*, published in the months immediately prior to the outbreak of war, demonstrates Sinclair's Idealist belief that alongside preservation of individual identity there must come a recognition of the legitimate

demands of others, which may on occasion demand the sacrificial surrender of the self to the higher demands of a transcendent Reality. Having
accepted that the war represents a legitimate call to sacrifice, *A Journal*
shows Sinclair's struggle to live with the consequences. The issue is
sometimes made quite explicit. On the day of the arrival of the Ambulance Corps in Ghent, she surveys the membership and attitudes of the
corps, commenting:

> We have visions of a relentless discipline commanding and controlling
> us. A cold glory hovers over the Commandant as the vehicle of this
> transcendent power...If nothing can be found for our women in
> the Hospital they will be sent home.
>
> (*Journal*, 26–7)

Interestingly, in view of her philosophical opinions, she employs
transcendence as a metaphor to express the claims of military discipline so great as to override even her precious individuality. It is also
worth remarking that she foresees the demands of that military
authority as likely, not to force her into a situation of which she is
afraid, but on the contrary to deny her insistent desire to be involved
in action. Indeed this desire for action, at the risk of insubordination,
was probably the reason for her banishment. The childish desire for
excitement in some parts of the narrative is redeemed by Sinclair's
self-awareness and recognition of the tension between the acceptance
of her obligations to her fellow human beings and her own individual
desires:

> But now that I realise what the insatiable and implacable Self is after,
> how it worked in me against all decency and all pity, how it actually
> made me feel as if I wanted to see Antwerp under siege, and how the
> spirit of adventure backed it up...'
>
> (*Journal*, 156–7)

There are I think two other crucial ways in which Sinclair found her
sense of self threatened by the war: her gender and her occupation. The
commonly held view that the position of women was advanced by
the war is in some respects undeniable but nevertheless it presented
those women like Sinclair who did not feel they could join the battle for
peace with the fact that they could not fully participate in 'the biggest
fight for freedom' (*Tree*, 277). As Tylee points out, 'It remained fundamental to the English woman's conception of herself that women do

not kill' (Tylee, 254). The following comment testifies to such a sense of exclusion:

> It is with the game of war as it was with the game of football I used to play with my big brothers in the garden ... The big brothers let their little sister kick off; they let her run away with the ball; they stood back and let her make goal after goal; but when it came to the scrimmage they took hold of her and gently but firmly moved her to one side.
>
> (*Journal*, 122)

The modern reader can no longer call war a game, even in metaphorical terms, yet recognizes the burning envy and frustration which lies behind the comment. Unable, because of her convictions, to take the route of feminist pacifist resistance which others took, the result is a certain ambiguity, a tension between Sinclair's desire for action and her recognition of its unsuitability. Thus, on the occasion of one of her many disputes with Tom the chauffeur, she gives way and gets out of his ambulance car, recognizing that Tom, like Lord Kitchener, cannot be elevated 'above the primitive plane of chivalry' (*Journal*, 236–7). The reference to the 'primitive plane of chivalry' leaves the reader in no doubt about Sinclair's own views, but in accordance with her expressed belief that the war is more important than anything, she has no choice but to leave the feminist battle to a later date.

The third challenge which the war makes to Sinclair is one familiar to artists in any time of crisis. Her response is uncompromising. She recognizes none of the tensions between obligations to her art and obligations to the contemporary crisis, but rather places her art at its service, commenting on the occasion of meeting an old friend, an American sculptor: 'In the world that makes war we have both entirely forgotten the world where people make busts and pictures and books' (*Journal*, 106). The failure to assign a privileged position to her art leaves her, however, feeling doubly weakened. Not only is she a woman but she cannot even do a woman's war-work, regretting 'for the hundredth time that I had not had the foresight to be trained as a nurse when I was young' (*Journal*, 313).

A Journal of Impressions in Belgium is a distinctive and very personal narrative, written sometimes with a degree of humour to which I have not done justice. Some of the issues it raises reappear in *Tasker Jevons: The Real Story*, begun shortly after Sinclair's return from Belgium and published in 1916. It is a fictional account of a writer whose extraordinary adventures while in sole command of a scouting car under the auspices of the Belgian Red Cross earn him a heroic reputation and the respect of those who previously despised him. Jevons can in some ways be seen as wish fulfilment on Sinclair's part, playing the role that she would like to have played, but her actual self is represented by two other characters, the narrator and Jevons's wife, Viola – by the writer and the woman. The writer-narrator plays only an insignificant role in Jevons's shadow while Viola is only reluctantly allowed to take part, against Jevons's better judgement. *A Journal* and its crude fictionalization in *Tasker Jevons* demonstrate Sinclair's struggle with the tension between her need to preserve the self and her recognition in a time of war of the demands of the group, her role as a writer and the role of women.

The Tree of Heaven, published in 1917 marks a considerable advance in Sinclair's war writing. No longer dependent on a reworking of the novelist's own experience, this novel takes for its subject the more general field of the war, while debating through a range of characters the questions which Sinclair's own experiences had raised. It tells the story of the Harrison family, Frances and Anthony and their daughter Dorothea and three sons, Michael, Nicky and John, from the time when the children are little until 1916, when Michael, Nicky and Dorothy's fiancé Frank have lost their lives in the war. It is a pity that critics have tended to dismiss this novel as sentimental (Zegger, 93) for it is more complex than such a description allows. It is very much a dialogic novel in which a variety of voices debate issues, many of which can be traced back to Sinclair's account of her experiences in Belgium: the relationship of the autonomous individual to the war effort, the human cost of the war, the role of the artist and the role of women.

The novel is divided into three parts, the second of which is entitled 'Vortex'. This word comes to stand for any kind of group or popular movement which threatens the individual self, Sinclair's familiar concern. Michael Harrison stands most strongly against such influences and his stand initially causes him to reject the war:

> Michael . . . was afraid, not of the War so much as of the emotions of the War, the awful, terrifying flood that carried him away from his real self and from everything it cared for most.
>
> (*Tree*, 286)

Indeed, although a certain amount of irony is directed against Michael, he is nevertheless given a powerful voice to argue against capitulation to the mass emotion:

> He objected to being suddenly required to feel patriotic because other people were feeling patriotic, to think that Germany was in the

wrong because other people thought that Germany was in the
wrong, to fight because other people were fighting...

(*Tree*, 287)

It is not simply his attempt to remain rational in the face of collective
emotion which makes Michael a powerful anti-war figure for much of
the novel. In spite of Sinclair's own support for the war, she does give
voice to the view which declares that the cost is too high, partly
through the character of Michael who shows an awareness of the suffering
which war inevitably brings. Having lived in Germany himself, he
points out, again with some justification: 'I don't want to make dear old
Frau Henschel a widow, and stick a bayonet into Ludwig and Carl, and
make Hedwig and Lottchen cry' (*Tree*, 284). Michael is not alone,
although he is the most favourably treated of the characters who speak
out against war. In the early chapters of the novel, Frances's brother,
Morrie, an incorrigible failure and consequently a dependant on
Anthony, is sent out to fight in the Boer War. He returns a broken man
and finds it difficult to get anyone to listen to his vivid description of
wartime conditions. Although the character is not very attractive, and
perhaps by implication not strong enough to face the horrors of war,
rather like the young George Wadham who, later in the novel goes out
to the front talking of the 'Great Game' and comes back a broken man
(*Tree*, 326), the horror of warfare is inescapably presented to the reader
through Morrie's account.

The presence of Wadham in the novel indicates that although Sinclair
apparently sentimentalizes Nicky in opposition to Michael, she is aware
of some of the more shallow manifestations of war enthusiasm. Nicky,
however, is clearly presented as something different. It is the representation of Nicky which causes most difficulty for the modern reader,
as it did for some of Sinclair's contemporaries. For example, Herbert
Seligman argues that Sinclair sentimentalizes Nicky and that Michael is
'misrepresented and misunderstood' (Robb, 222). Some of Sinclair's
other writing expresses a strong sense of a transcendent Reality which
she refers to on occasions in *A Journal*, when for example she speaks of
her sense that 'something had been looking for you, waiting for you,
from all eternity out here' (*Journal*, 80). Something of this is represented
in the account of Nicky's experience. Just as Michael represents from
his childhood a rejection of the 'collective soul', so Nicky manifests an
almost joyous acceptance of the unfairness of life, dismissing childhood
punishments, a false accusation at Cambridge, his being beaten to the
idea of the 'Moving Fortress' by Frank Drayton as 'jolly sells' (*Tree*, 172).

Like Michael, his character is formed before the war, not by the war. They represent two of Sinclair's preoccupations about the nature of identity: Michael clearly stands for the preservation of the self while Nicky stands for the willing surrender of that carefully preserved self to the greater good, often seen by Sinclair as transcendent Reality.

The novel clearly argues that at the moment of 'going over the top', Nicky experiences that transcendent Reality (*Tree*, 323). However, true to the dialogic nature of the novel, other arguments are presented and the reader is left free to read against the text. Certainly the modern reader, carrying too many images of the horrors of the Great War, finds Nicky's ecstatic description of 'going over the top' contained in a letter from the front to his second wife Veronica hard to take. However, if Nicky is unaware of the sort of psychoanalytical research which might be brought out against his view, his creator certainly is not and the letter continues to open up the debate, albeit in the form of a rejection of counter arguments, referring to one of Nicky's comrades:

> He says he feels the ecstasy, or whatever it is, all right, just the same as I do; but that it's simply submerged savagery bobbing up to the top – a hidden lust for killing, and the hidden memory of having killed, he called it. He's always ashamed of it the next day, as if he had been drunk.
>
> (*Tree*, 323)

He adds that his sergeant-major more prosaically attributes it to a 'ration of rum'. True to Sinclair's Idealist philosophy, Nicky has the last word, dependent on a moral distinction:

> They're all wrong about it, because they make it turn on killing, and not on your chance of being killed. That – when you realise it – well, it's like the thing you told me about that you said you thought must be God because it's so real. I didn't understand it then, but I do now. You're bang up against reality – you're going clean into it – and the sense of it's exquisite. Of course, while one half of you is feeling like that, the other half is fighting to kill and doing its best to keep on this side of reality. But I've been near enough to the other side to know.
>
> (*Tree*, 323–4)

This element in *The Tree of Heaven* is undoubtedly the least satisfactory for the modern reader, even allowing for Sinclair's expressed awareness of other possible explanations for the 'ecstasy', both here and in *A Journal*, such as the footnote reference to the views of 'a distinguished alienist' on the battle experience (*Journal*, 170). Tylee comments that 'Sinclair continued to preach the Victorian message of the spiritual value of war' (132), while Rosa Maria Braccio remarks of Sinclair and others, 'the social judgements and analyses of these writers rested very often on spiritual tenets' (45). I think such comments distort Sinclair's position. What she is discussing is not the value of war but the preparedness in any situation to surrender one's own will, and if necessary one's own life, in accordance with one's conscience, which she saw as submersion in a greater Reality. Where the position can legitimately be criticized is not on these grounds but what Tylee describes as her failure to fathom 'the drawn-out strain that front-line soldiers had to endure, or the deep trauma of killing' (Tylee, 133), which in turn has much to do with her inevitable exclusion from the war as a woman.

The other source of Michael's opposition to the war, which reflects another of Sinclair's own concerns, is his position as an artist: 'This is the end of all the arts. Artists will not be allowed to exist except as agents for the recruiting sergeant. We're dished' (*Tree*, 253). *A Journal* would suggest that Sinclair accepted the view of the arts in war which Michael clearly opposes. In the closing sections of the novel, Michael, persuaded by a number of events, but most particularly by his brother Nicky's death, also enlists. Ultimately, and with a certain logic, once he has accepted the necessity for war, like his creator he accepts the subservience of art. The last letter he writes home raises the issue of the role of art in war. After writing that he too, like Nicky, experiences what he sees as 'the point of contact with reality', he continues:

> Of course we shall be accused of glorifying War and telling lies about it. Well – there's a Frenchman who has told the truth, piling up all the horrors, faithfully, remorselessly, magnificently. But he seems to think people oughtn't to write about this war at all unless they show up the infamy of it, as a deterrent . . .
>
> To insist on the world remembering nothing but these horrors is as if men up to their knees in the filth they're clearing away should complain of each other for standing in it and splashing it about.
>
> The filth of War – and the physical torture – Good God! As if the world was likely to forget it.
>
> (*Tree*, 348)

It seems to me that this is a very important passage. Michael does not suggest that the unnamed Frenchman should not have written as he did in case he demoralizes the allied populations, a suggestion which would have been an attack on artistic integrity. The ground of his opposition is not what the Frenchman writes but the Frenchman's insistence that no one should write anything else. In other words, it is Michael, writing now from a pro-war position, who defends artistic integrity. Michael does not deny the horror and suffering of war. Modern readings of texts such as *The Tree of Heaven* tend superficially to dismiss them as glorifying or sentimentalizing war because they do not acknowledge that artistic integrity demands the right to record other emotions. From the privileged standpoint of 80 years on, I do not myself regard the Great War in the way that Sinclair regarded it, but I recognize *The Tree of Heaven* as an important representation of one aspect of wartime experience.

It should not escape the reader, however, that it is wartime experience from the perspective of the home front. Sinclair, having expressed the tension between women's desire for involvement and the restrictions imposed by contemporary constructions of femininity in *A Journal* and *Tasker Jevons*, endorses the more conservative view of women's role in *The Tree of Heaven*. Dorothy, the eldest of the Harrison children, who belongs to a whole series of strong independent women in Sinclair's fiction, has an involvement with the movement for women's suffrage which eventually leads her to imprisonment in Holloway Prison, a year or so before the outbreak of war. Dorothy has resisted the advances of the worthy Captain Frank Drayton on the grounds that he cannot accept her involvement in the suffrage movement, but the outbreak of war radically changes the position. In the event, Drayton's sudden call-up prevents even their hastily arranged marriage. Before they part, however, Dorothy gives up her intention to join an ambulance corps in Belgium. The independent-minded Dorothy accepts the primacy of Drayton's the soldier's wishes over her own. On this issue the novel is uncompromising:

> But it won't make it easier for us to win the War. You can't expect us to fight so comfy, and to be killed so comfy, if we know our women-kind are being pounded to bits in the ground we've just cleared.
>
> (*Tree*, 274)

Dorothy accepts the argument with only a tiny regret that she can't do anything for 'those Belgian women' (*Tree*, 274). As with other issues in the novel, the issue of women is with ruthless logic made subordinate to the greater issue. It is worth commenting here that what this section does do is call into question that rather unfair castigating of women who encouraged men to enlist by writers such as D. H. Lawrence, Richard Aldington and e. e. cummings. Pacifists have long unfairly blamed women for their powerless position so effectively dramatized in the 'Women of England Say: Go' poster, a position in which they are after all only objects of the male gaze.

What a perusal of *The Tree of Heaven* does is make clear the connection between support for the war and the inscription of women within a patriarchal ideology. The independent Dorothy only agrees to marriage after the declaration of war. Her sister-in-law Veronica, Nicky's second wife, is represented in the conventional guise of the 'Woman of England': 'I am thinking of her. You don't suppose Veronica'd stop me if I wanted to go? Why, she wouldn't look at me if I didn't want to go' (*Tree*, 256). Veronica is frequently contrasted with two other women: her mother Vera, who has worked her way through one husband and two lovers and left Veronica to be brought up by the Harrisons, and the faithless Phyllis Desmond, Nicky's first wife, who marries him only to give a name to her unborn child. It is not altogether surprising therefore to find Vera and Phyllis, in their different ways, making what may be regarded as anti-war statements. What is interesting is that these two women, both outside the conventions of patriarchal order, are given a voice to make important comments which cannot be lightly dismissed. In relation to Nicky and Frank Drayton's moving fortress, in conversation with her lover Alfred Orde-Jones, Phyllis makes the perceptive comment:

> 'How funny they are! Frank wouldn't hurt a fly and Nicky wouldn't say "Bo!" to a goose...and yet they're only happy when they're inventing some horrible machine that'll kill thousands of people who never did them any harm.' He said, 'That's because they haven't any imagination.'
>
> (*Tree*, 178)

Although Michael's letter, quoted above, suggests the text's final verdict that war must be undertaken even in the full knowledge of its horrors, Orde-Jones nevertheless makes the trenchant comment that lack of imagination plays its part in what becomes the irreversible movement towards war. Vera's contribution is even more revealing. She attempts to prevent her lover, Lawrence Stephen, from enlisting and, after pointing out the undeniable truth that had he succeeded in fighting for Ireland, he would have been hung by the government he now wishes to fight for, is told: 'It's women like you that are the traitors. My God, if there was a Government in this country that could govern, you'd be strung up in a row, all of you, and hanged' (*Tree*, 300). Small wonder, then, if such comments reflect anything of the reality of life in wartime England, that the women for the most part said 'Go!' The conversation continues:

> 'Men don't want to be loved that way. That's the mistake you women will make.'
> 'It's the way you've taught us. I should like to know what other way you ever want us to love you.'
>
> (*Tree*, 301)

Vera has made her point. Women who don't say 'Go!' are obeying instincts which the men who now reject them have been only too anxious to cultivate in times of peace.

I wish to add only a short postscript on the subject of the last of Sinclair's war texts, *The Romantic*. The novel is focalized through its central character, Charlotte Redhead, who with her fiancé, John Roden Conway, and two companions takes a field ambulance to Belgium. Once again the same dates and the same villages are the subject of the narrative. This time, however, Charlotte is forced to realize that her 'lover' is a coward who is quite prepared to place her in danger. After his death, Dr Donald McClane, the leader of a rival ambulance, who is clearly modelled on Hector Monro, explains in what seem to be rather crude psychoanalytical terms that John's cowardice is linked to his impotence, and that he is 'an out and out degenerate' (*Romantic*, 244). *The Romantic* represents a partial reassessment of Sinclair's war writing. There is a much greater concentration on the sufferings of the wounded, sometimes quite graphically represented, rather than on the exhilaration of chasing out to various villages. Moreover the plot itself, and the title of the novel, throws into question the sort of romantic war enthusiasm which is only mildly criticized in *The Tree of Heaven*. Charlotte loses patience with John's 'romancing' and towards the end of the novel says to a third member of the ambulance, Billy Sutton: 'All that war-romancing. I see how awful it was. When I think how we went out and got thrills. Fancy getting thrills out of this horror' (*Romantic*, 237). The words may be taken as a comment on Sinclair's own writing, and indeed that of many of her contemporaries. It is reasonable to suppose that, while not necessarily completely revising her view on the war, she may have come to a new estimate of its cost.

Literary studies are beset by the dangers of categorizing and Sinclair's writing on the war, particularly *The Tree of Heaven*, has suffered from being dismissed as simply sentimentalizing, romanticizing or glorifying war. It is my contention that her war writing should be read in the context of all her work, as reflecting her preoccupations with identity, gender and the transcendent rather than as a simple response to war propaganda. Moreover her writing is complex. *The Tree of Heaven* in particular gives expression to a variety of voices, male and female, which reflected the reactions of groups and individuals to the national crisis surrounding them. In particular it gives due weight to the complexity of women's position in the war and provides evidence of the 'double-bind' in which women found themselves, blamed whether they supported or discouraged their menfolk.

Works cited

Boll, Theophilius M. *Miss May Sinclair: Novelist*. Rutherford, NJ: Fairleigh Dickinson University Press, 1973.
Braccio, Rosa Maria. *Merchants of Hope*. Oxford: Berg, 1993.
Mumford, Laura Stempel. 'May Sinclair's *The Tree of Heaven*: the vortex of feminism, the community of war', *Arms and the Woman*, edited by Helen M. Cooper, Adrienne Auslander Munich and Susan Merrill Squier. Chapel Hill: University of North Carolina Press, 1989.
Robb, Kenneth. 'May Sinclair, an annotated bibliography of writings about her', *English Literature in Transition*, 16 (1973).
Sinclair, May. *Anne Severn and the Fieldings*. London: Hutchinson, 1922.
———. *A Journal of Impressions in Belgium*. London: Hutchinson, 1915.
———. *Life and Death of Harriet Frean*. London: Collins, 1920.
———. *Mary Oliver: A Life*. London: Cassell, 1919.
———. *The Romantic*. London: Collins, 1920.
———. *Tasker Jevons: The Real Story*. London: Hutchinson, 1916.
———. *The Three Sisters*. London: Hutchinson, 1914.
———. *The Tree of Heaven*. London: Cassell, 1917.
———. 'Worse Than War', *English Review*, 31 (August, 1920): 147–53.
Tylee, Claire. *The Great War and Women's Consciousness*. Basingstoke: Macmillan – now Palgrave, 1990.
Zegger, Hrisey D. *May Sinclair*. Boston: Twayne English Author Series (192), 1976.

5

'Lives Mocked at by Chance': Contradictory Impulses in Women's Poetry of the Great War

Deborah Tyler-Bennett

In the poem 'Clown's Houses', Edith Sitwell creates a barren urban landscape where youthful lives are 'mocked at', and realities of existence outside the city are hidden from a generation conditioned to react only to fantasy (Sitwell, 1920, 36–8). Typically, Sitwell uses folk tale genres to inform her text for, as with E. T. A. Hoffmann's Nathaniel and his encounter with the spectacles of Dr Coppelius, youth's vision of the world is corrupted by 'star bright' masks (Sitwell, 1920, 37; Hoffmann, 1952, 53). In this poem, a new generation is beguiled into a life of hedonism, whereas within the city's 'paper thin' houses, old 'shades' weep for some calamitous past event (Sitwell, 1920, 37). As with many of the poetic landscapes created by Robert Graves, Sitwell's terrain works via contrasts (the orange heat of the sun compared to pale and brittle urban architecture, or youth's gaudy dress as contrasted to old shadows or 'blind' houses) (37). Yet the device which unifies these paradoxical images is perhaps the most chilling reminder of how the 'Great War' affected the course of Sitwell's aesthetic, as both youth and age are depicted as being little more than marionettes in the hands of an unseen state. It is interesting to note that, despite the power of poems like 'Clown's Houses', Sitwell remains best known for works written during the Second World War, such as the elegiac 'Still Falls the Rain: The Raids, 1940. Night and Dawn' (Sitwell, 1946, 15–16). This is due to the fact that although many early poems (1914–26) contain images taken directly from the poet's experience of the First World War, they are not categorized as 'war poems' due to her use of abstract titles, folk tale settings, colourful commedia costumes and figures, and metres which are derived from those of nursery rhymes. Despite this, poems contained in early volumes, such as *The Wooden Pegasus* (1920), are saturated by war imagery, containing as they do repeated references to dead youth, stifled parental grief and the image (frequently associated with works by male poets such as Wilfred Owen) of blinds being drawn. Indeed, while 'Clown's Houses' appears to be critically accepted as a fine war poem, many other references to war in Sitwell's early poetry seem to go unheeded.

Sitwell's works appear to be an appropriate place from which to begin discussion of women's poetry of the Great War, as recognized ideas of what constitutes a 'war poem' do not appear to be geared to embrace abstract or allegorical poems by women. Indeed, the explanation of an existing critical preference for elegies, the poetry of incident or poetic 'testimonials' could be regarded as canonical in origin. Early anthologists like Brian Gardener, although including poets such as Sitwell, Eleanor Farjeon and Laura Riding in biographical notes, defined the poetry of the First World War as being chiefly a male preserve and, despite their additions of a few women, subsequent anthologists appear to have endorsed this traditional view (Gardener, 1964). Anthologies published in the 1980s and 1990s thus appear to select poems by women via the suitability of the genres which they chose to write in as companion pieces to works by male contemporaries such as Sassoon, Owen, Rosenburg and Gurney (Parsons, 1987; Vansittart, 1983). For example, in 1987 the anthologist I. M. Parsons included Charlotte Mew's poignant poem concerning divisions between public memorial and private testimony, 'The Cenotaph', as the single representative of women's war poetry, while Peter Vansittart's 1983 text employs uncompromisingly testimonial works by Marie Tsvetayeva and Anna Akhmatova (Parsons, 1964, 174; Vansittart, 1983, 54, 14). If separatist anthologies, such as Catherine Reilly's *Scars Upon My Heart* (1981), indicate that women wrote a variety of good war poems, women's poetry has yet to be featured in mainstream collections (Reilly, 1981). Also, despite presenting an impressive array of women's writing, from the jingoistic verses of Jessie Pope at the beginning of the war to elegies by Vera Brittain and Eleanor Farjeon and the angry outpourings of May Wedderburn Cannan who despaired at the war's continuation, Reilly's collection might also be regarded as concentrating on the familiar genres of elegy, testimony and incident. Poets who use allegorical, mythical or fantastic narratives to critique the impact of war (such as Sitwell, H.D., Iris Tree, Phyliss M'egroz, and Jane Barlow) are largely neglected in collections of war poetry, both male and female, yet their contribution to women's war poetry is both significant and astonishing.

One could argue that the use of mythic, folk or fairy tale narratives, adopted to explore contemporary issues, represented an aesthetic which was developed by writers such as Sitwell, Tree and H.D. from works by Victorian women poets like Christina Rossetti, Mary Elizabeth Coleridge and Isa Craig. Also, this strategy had been further politicized when used by 'suffrage' poets such as Eva Gore Booth, Sylvia Pankhurst and the Holloway Prison 'jinglers' of 1912 (Norquay, 1995, 120, 172; Tyler-Bennett, 1998, 117–18). However, before considering how women poets writing during the First World War adapted their predecessors' use of the fantastic for their own pacifist or politicized purposes, it is necessary to combine critical strategies.

It remains significant that, while new texts on women's writing during the period frequently emerge, few of them consider the impact of poetry by women on how the First World War came to be perceived. Both Claire M. Tylee's excellent study on images of 'militarism and woman-hood' in the Great War, and Sharon Ouditt's incisive analysis of crises concerning identity and ideology during the period, focus mainly on prose works (Tylee, 1990; Ouditt, 1994). However, Ouditt's distinctions between ideological constructs of 'femininity' and women's first-hand experiences of both bereavement and war-work (which she depicts as an uneasy liaison between 'romance and realism') can be adapted to the study of women's poetry, as can Tylee's question as to whether women's writing can be regarded as 'mythopoeic' (Ouditt, 89–130; Tylee, 1990, 15). Tylee's assertion that 'women's written memory was not homogeneous' and her desire to discover whether there exists an 'imaginative memory of the First World War which is distinctly women's' can, likewise, be deployed in the exploration of poetry (Tylee, 1990, 15). In order to distinguish how 'imaginative memory' is recorded in poetic works using structures derived from folk-narratives, one can twin Tylee's questions about mythopoeic writing with Marina Warner's definition of fairy tales as 'reverberative historical documents' where 'evidence of conditions from past social economic arrangements coexist with the narrator's innovations' (Warner, 1994, xix). Warner's insistence on folk/fairy tales as reflectors of 'lived experience', particularly recording the 'tribulations of women', can be used, in part, to explain why poets such as H.D. turned to fantastic narrative structures in order to frame wartime experiences (Warner, 1994, xix).

As with Sitwell's works, H.D.'s poetry is often described as being politi-cized during the blitz. In fact, during the First World War H.D. was still seen to be a member of the Imagist School, a product of Ezra Pound's tutelage. Yet, when turning to the early volume *Sea Garden* (1916), one is struck (as with Sitwell's *The Wooden Pegasus*) by the sheer volume of war myths conjured by the poet (H.D., 1975). The setting for much of H.D.'s early work is Hellenistic, thus comparisons between poems published in 1916 and the war raging in Europe are often presented as secondary to her classical sources. Thus the Trojan wars are foregrounded at the expense of the 1914–18 war, a conflict which isolated H.D. from her husband, the writer and editor Richard Aldington, and destroyed the lives and aspirations of many of her peers. Although a few of the works published in *Sea Garden* may have been written prior to the war, her 1916 collection's overriding themes appear to be concerned with the fragility of youth and the desecration of young male bodies by instruments of war. In 'Loss', the young female speaker is glad that her lover has drowned, rather than going to fight in a conflict which has maimed and destroyed his contemporaries, transforming them into a phantom army (H.D., 1975, 21).

The concept of a phantom army has its origins in ancient sources, but was also a feature of much of the iconography emanating from the First World War; as Mark Girouard indicates, ghostly icons included the 'angels of Mons' who were featured on postcards and elsewhere as watching over England's soldiers, and the spirits of chivalric Pre-Raphaelitic knights depicted on stained glass memorials and postcards early in the war, while many upper-class letters, speaking of the deaths of public-school educated boys, such as Julian and Billy Grenfell, describe them as joining a ghostly legion (Girouard, 1981, 287–8). Thus H.D.'s phantom army, her 'ghostly host', can be perceived as achieving double resonance, as the image refers both to her Greek source and the 'ghostly host' of contemporary war dead. Indeed, the concept of a young body uncorrupted by war, as was depicted on many early memorials, could not be maintained throughout a conflict where disfigurement and injury became increasingly visible. In much of H.D.'s poetry, beauty in death is displaced, visible only on the corpse of a young man who dies quickly, before he gets to fight. Yet other mythopoeic descriptions of war do not concentrate on the image of an embodied 'death of spring' but, like Sitwell's vision of masked youth, attempt to encapsulate public delusions concerning the young.

For many women poets who develop narratives which attempt to explore why, at the outset of war, people are so inclined to follow jingoists, or who attempt to contrast this behaviour with postwar public attitudes, the folk-tale narrative provides a powerful aesthetic strategy. It is worth recalling how popular chivalric narratives were during the First World War, being used in epic stage productions such as *Where the*

Rainbow Ends (which began in 1912 and ran throughout the war), and in novels such as Henry Newbolt's *Happy Warrior* (1917) (Girouard, 1981, 2). Also, it is important that one recognizes the variety of mythic narratives adapted as sources for war poetry by women, as some of these (such as H.D.'s 'Loss') are derived from classical mythology, while others come from European folk traditions, such as the startling 'Danse Macabre' by the undeservedly obscure Phyllis M'egroz.

M'egroz, about whose biography I have been able to discover little, is listed in the British Library Catalogue as having produced a single volume of poetry, *The Silver Bride* (1924). Despite this slender output, she was obviously a well-respected poet in her day, publishing in Orage's *New Age*, *The Fortnightly Review*, *The New Statesman*, *Voices*, *The Bookman* and various other journals and anthologies. Her poems often contain a wry Georgianism, with overtones of De La Mare at his least nostalgic and most chilling, and blend skeins of Northern, Western and Eastern European folk narratives with a sense of the gothic derived from French symbolism and British decadence. For example, 'Danse Macabre' bears overtones of Wilde's 'The Harlot's House' (1885), while retaining the grim quality of British and Irish folk tales where unfortunate young men are 'danced to death' by fairy women (Wilde, 1977, 789–90; Briggs, 1990, 88–9). Yet, M'egroz's subject is the Great War and her music is no fairy reel but the sound of the 'Fox trot, murry roll, three step, or jazz' (M'egroz, 1924, 16). Dance music such as this was popular both during the war and afterwards and M'egroz, like many of her contemporaries, appears to have believed that frenetic dancing and party-going were means by which to forget the carnage. Unlike Mew's cenotaph, where the war dead are commemorated wholly in terms of inaction and typified by 'some young, piteous murdered face', M'egroz's wild dance of death springs the dead from their graves, creating the impression of the violent war ballet defined by Modris Ekstein (Mew, 1921, 59; Ecksteins, 1989, 199). The poem deliberately under-cuts old assertions that dance is symbolic of pleasure, and that 'youth is made for dancing', as M'egroz's young bodies 'dance' to the bullet's whine (M'egroz, 1924, 16). Here, female figures are depicted via the iconography of the 'angels of Mons' and carry death within their breasts, despite their victorious outward trappings of 'rose crowns' and 'glittering girdles' (M'egroz, 1924, 17). M'egroz leaves the reader in no doubt that, at the climax of the dance, those war memorials which Mew outlined in terms of passive female sorrow, will crack open bringing forth a legion of dead souls who mock the very notion of youth. The poem's last stanza is uncompromising, suggesting one bleak cry: 'We seem to hear dead, twisted lips again /Utter a thin uncadenced sound of pain – '(17).

If a single theme is shared by M'egroz, H.D. and Sitwell, it is that of unforgivable waste. Yet, no matter how similar the contents of works by the three remain, mythopoeic structures employed by them are diverse. Sitwell's sterile city exists in contrast to H.D.'s sun-drenched Aegean landscape, exteriors which could not be inhabited by M'egroz's Western European wraiths. Curiously enough, these poetic myths are not located within the Keatsian terrain of Wilfred Owen's 'Strange Meeting' a poem which, for all its mythological flourishes, remains firmly fixed in the landscape of the trenches (Owen, 1987, 360–1). It is also significant that most of the poets under discussion were not involved in types of war-work such as nursing or voluntary services undertaken by Vera Brittain and others. Also, Sitwell, H.D. and M'egroz all defined themselves as poets by profession, unlike some women who found inspiration during wartime and then never wrote again. Specific differences exist between approaches to war poetry by professional poets and the latter, as women who wrote only for the war's duration tended to locate their work very strongly within traditions of memorial, recorded incident or patriotic narrative. Contextually, such poems were frequently published on postcards sold to raise donations for the Red Cross or Soldier's Funds. Poets working to this format often fixed themselves within a local area, thus many of their works are more often discovered in County Record Offices than in library collections or anthologies. Two such poets are Annie Price from Nottingham and Leicester's Marianna Laura Jones (Price, L. 981; Jones, P77/4). Thanks to the efforts of Jones's grandson, Ross Wolfendon, her poetic output is well documented, and it can be perceived that, while sticking to a chiefly patriotic format, Jones's poetry maintains a surprisingly broad outlook which is refined as the war develops (as, although never losing her jingoistic tone, Jones's emphasis changes from pure patriotism to documentary, which highlights the impact of women's work on the course of the war). However, while pursuing works by local war poets in libraries and record offices in Britain, Scotland and Ireland, I have yet to find a poet like Jones using either mythological or folk genres to create aesthetic structures, as most local poets appear to stick to those immediate, semi-journalistic devices employed by Jones, Price and others. Thus, within the wide area of women's war poetry, contradictory impulses appear to be at work, namely the strategy of using plain incident, emotion and location (which could be adapted to encompass either jingoism or pacifism), or the contrasting desire to develop a mythic/

folkloric context for tales of loss, anger and betrayal such as the Great War occasioned.

One of the only poets who appears to have intertwined both strategies is Sitwell's compatriot, Iris Tree. Tree's work is almost forgotten today, ignored by academic studies and anthologies alike. Yet, she was to produce some of her most haunting works during, and shortly after, the war. Also, as her volume *Poems* (1920) demonstrates, the experience of war shaped Tree's poetic output as a whole. Tree was the daughter of Maud Holt and Herbert Beerbohm Tree (and thus niece to Max Beerbohm), and a friend to both Sitwell and Nancy Cunard with whom she exchanged poems. Her work appeared in *Poetry*, *Vanity Fair* and Sitwell's anthology cum journal, *Wheels*. All pieces included in *Poems* are dated, thus Tree indicates to the reader not only what poems were written during the 1914–18 war, but also at what stage of the war they were composed. Many of these poems are untitled, a piece of 1918 which begins 'we are the caretakers of empty houses' combines realism (carefully describing the dusty perimeters of a locked and shuttered house) with a fantasy concerning the house's ghostly occupant (Tree, 1920, 12). Likewise, in another piece dated 1918, a rain storm echoes with sounds of battle, where wolves howl, bones rattle and a red sunrise figures a slaughterhouse (17). This poetic landscape combines testimony of lived experience (hearing the guns from France) with a common folkloric setting (a moonlit forest circled by wolves). In a poem of 1917, Tree (then aged twenty) depicts herself as living with ghosts of dead friends, relatives and lovers, and this indicates why she chooses to blend folk narratives with a testimonial aesthetic (19).

In my opinion, Tree's masterpiece of the war years is one combining the familiar source of Browning's 'The Pied Piper of Hamelin' (1845) with the British folk stalwart of the phantom drummer, used by both 'Thomas Ingoldsby' and Edith Sitwell (Browning, 1909, 166–74; Ingoldsby, *c*. 1870, 339–51; Sitwell, 1958, 110–12). The poem (contained in the section 'Smoke' and prefaced by a Curtis Moffat woodcut of No Man's Land) uses a lone drummer as a Pied Piper figure. The drummer is initially depicted in flashback, riding into a rural town 'wearing a gaudy costume and with banners dancing' (Tree, 1920, 56). As with Browning's piper, the drummer enraptures those in the crowd who are child-like, figures who race to follow him: 'They left their lovers and their mother's lap,/ Their homes demolish' (56). In folk style, the gaudy drummer later returns as a ragged version of himself, emerging 'palsied', 'drear', his bent limbs banging a bone on a soundless barrel (56). This poem of 1914 appears to present one answer to Tylee's question concerning women's mythopoeic writing, as Tree's myth is used early in the war to convey with immediacy the possible after-effects of jingoism. Ouditt's assertion that much women's writing emanating from the conflict interwove personal experiences of despair with the desire to record public behaviour is borne out by the conclusion of Tree's poem, where she questions 'war fever', by asking where marching men might end up (57). Just as Browning's narrative ends with Willy, the lame child who could not follow the piper, mourning his fellows, so Tree concludes with an image of war fever giving way to individual loss, urging the reader (just as Browning urges Willy to keep his promise) to place a ribbon on a soldier's grave (Browning, 1909, 174; Tree, 1920, 57).

Another poet adapting a Browningesque framework for war poetry is the Southern Irish writer Jane Barlow. Barlow's 'The Irish Archangel: Michaelmass, 1915' is a monologue spoken by Theresa Nolan, a mother 'heart scalded' by a war which has struck 'thousands dead, and each a mother's son' (Barlow, 1916, 4–5). Both Barlow and Tree could, therefore, be regarded as adapting a mythopoeic framework in order to critique the war as, at one juncture, Barlow's Michael literally becomes an archangel, the living embodiment of a figure on a war memorial. Also, although mentioning collective mourning for thousands, the archangel figure points to Nolan's feeling of imaginative isolation.

Although I have subtitled this piece 'contradictory impulses' in women's writing of the First World War, it must be noted that such impulses are often stylistic, as even a jingoistic poet like Jones acknowledged the terrific scale of human loss during the war years. The impulse to write for a market aimed chiefly at working people leads both Price and Jones to choose a format of commemoration, whereas, for Barlow, the Browningesque monologue enables her to take recorded memory and endow it with symbolic resonance. For Tree, M'egroz and Sitwell, poets writing for both a commercial readership and the avant-garde, the fantastic enables a recording of loss via experimentation with form: Sitwell with patterns in sound and syllabics; H.D. via imagism and classical reference; Tree with irregular metrics; and M'egroz within the tonal arrangements of Georgian poetry. It is worth noting how broad the mythological spectrum used by these poets is as, although all writing memorably about the war, H.D. refers to the battle of Troy in order to frame her tales of loss and betrayal, while Barlow uses the symbolism of Catholic liturgy to tell similar stories. One could also suggest that via her use of Catholicism, Barlow critiques the Catholic church's role in sending young Irishmen to war.

However, no matter what the mythological framework of these poems, a common bond between them is the way in which they convey international social changes via fantastic narratives. After M'egroz's dance of death there can be no return to tranquillity, nor can the grieving shadows who inhabit Sitwell's shuttered rooms emerge into the sunlight. If Sitwell and Tree depict women as individually grieving, they re-figure the aesthetic used by Charlotte Mew, the eldest poet of the three. For, if Mew's view of the cenotaph contrasts the obscenity of how the commercial values of a bustling marketplace displace the history of the war memorial which also stands there, then it also presents an image of groups of women united by sorrow (Mew, 1921, 59). Such passive unification is questioned by Tree, H.D., M'egroz and Sitwell, as personal losses are described by them in terms of utter isolation. What unites these poets is, in the end, the desire to create mythic narratives which convey loss, while mediating between past aesthetics and emergent modernism.

Acknowledgements

Dr Martyn Bennett for reading the text, Mrs D. and Mr J. Tyler for providing useful sources and comments, Staff at the Angel Row Library, Nottingham, the Leicester County Record Office, the National Library, Ireland, the British Library, National Archives, Ireland, the Edinburgh Poetry Library, the Scottish National Library, Wood-End Museum, Scarborough.

Works cited

Barlow, Jane. *Between Doubting and Daring: Verses*. Oxford: Blackwell, 1916.

Briggs, Katherine. *A Dictionary of Fairies*. Harmondsworth: Penguin, 1976; London: Black Swan, 1990.

Browning, Robert. *Dramatis Personae and Dramatic Lyrics*. London: Chatto & Windus, 1909.

Cecil, David. *Max: A Biography* London: Constable, 1964.

Ecksteins, Modris. *Rites of Spring: The Great War and the Birth of the Modern Age*. Boston: Houghton, 1989.

Gardener, Brian (ed.) *Up the Line to Death: The War Poets 1914–18*. London: Methuen, 1964.

Girouard, Mark. *Return to Camelot: Chivalry and the English Gentleman*. New Haven, CT: Yale University Press, 1981.

H.D. *Sea Garden*. London: St James's Press, 1975.

Hoffmann, E. T. A. 'The Sandman'. *Eight Tales of Hoffmann*. London: Pan, 1952, 53.

Ingoldsby, Thomas (Rev. Richard Harris Bareham). *Ingoldsby Legends: Or Mirth and Marvels*. London: Frederick Warne & Co., *c*. 1870s.

Jones, Marianna Laura. Leicester County Record Office. P77/4.

M'egroz, Phyllis. *The Silver Bride*. London: Selwyn & Blount, 1924.

Mew, Charlotte. *The Farmer's Bride* London: Poetry Bookshop, 1921.

Norquay, Glenda (ed.) *Voices and Votes: A Literary Anthology of the Women's Suffrage Campaign*. Manchester: Manchester University Press, 1995.

Ouditt, Sharon (ed.) *Fighting Forces, Writing Women: Identity and Ideology in the First World War*. London: Routledge, 1994.

Owen, Wilfred. *The Oxford Library of Poetry*, Vol 3. Oxford: Oxford University Press, 1987, 360–1.

Parsons, I. M. (ed.) *Men Who March Away: Poems of the First World War*. London: Hogarth Press/Chatto & Windus, 1987.

Price, Annie. *Angel Row*. Library Local Authors Collection, L. 981.

Reilly, Catherine (ed.) *Scars Upon My Heart: Women's Poetry and Verse of the First World War*. London: Virago, 1981.

Sitwell, Edith. *Collected Poems* London: Macmillan – now Palgrave, 1958.

——. *The Song of the Cold* London: Macmillan – now Palgrave, 1946.

——. *The Wooden Pegasus*. Oxford: Basil Blackwell, 1920.

Tree, Iris. *Poems*. London: John Lane/Bodley Head, 1920.

Tylee, Claire M. (ed.) *The Great War and Women's Consciousness: Images of Militarism and Womanhood 1914–26*. London: Macmillan – now Palgrave, 1990.

Tyler-Bennett, Deborah. 'Suffrage and poetry: radical women's voices', in *The Women's Suffrage Movement. New Feminist Perspectives*, eds J. Purvis and M. Joannu. Manchester: Manchester University Press, 1998.

Vansittart, Peter (ed.) *Voices From the Great War*. Harmondsworth: Penguin, 1983.

Warner, Marina. *From the Beast to the Blonde: On Fairy Tales and Their Tellers*. London: Chatto & Windus, 1994.

Wilde, Oscar. *Complete Works*. London: Collins, 1977.

6

'The Huge Gun with Its One Blind Eye': Scale and the War Poetry and Writings of Harriet Monroe

Allesandria Polizzi

According to Nosheen Khan in *Women's Poetry of the First World War*, the writing of women during the time between 1914 and 1918 is 'a hitherto neglected part of the huge literature inspired by the war' (1).[1] Despite being an influential woman of this time period, Harriet Monroe presents us with one of those figures overshadowed by this tradition of ignorance.[2] Khan's choice of the adjective 'huge' and my use of the metaphor of shadow and light are most fitting here because they demonstrate one of the binary qualities prevalent in many considerations about the First World War and shown quite clearly in Monroe's poetry and editorials. This issue is scale or what George Lakoff and Mark Turner call an 'image-schema' of 'bounded' (and therefore, unbounded) space. 'A bounded space with an interior and an exterior,' they tell us, 'is an image, but an extremely skeletal and schematic image.... In physical domains, image-schemas have two roles. First, they provide structures for rich mental images.... Second, image schemas have an internal logic that permits spacial reasoning' (97–9). In the framework of this consideration, the vastness of the First World War, the Great War, the war to end all wars, is coupled with the minuteness of peace wavering as a tiny speck of possibility in the distance of the future and a tiny speck of memory in the distance of the past. This pattern of scale can be found in many concerns at this time, particularly in reference to the place of women: the place of women during wartime, the place of women in the developing modernist literary tradition and the place of women's work as artists, activists and employees.[3] In the metaphorical context of scale, women's experiences and voices were on the fringe of the great male war. Women were on the horizon while men were in the foreground. Scale is therefore an illuminating lens through which we can view the writings during the First World War.

Harriet Monroe's work elucidates the scale of the time period, particularly within the context of the social and literary sentiments of the developing modern era. Strong and feminine, insightful and emotional, 'Monroe was feared in some quarters as an Amazon leading women to take over American poetry' (Drake, 73). Julian Symons demonstrates Monroe's importance most fittingly. Within the 'Founding Fathers' section of his book *Makers of the New*, Symons has a chapter entitled 'The Men (and a Woman) of 1912'. The naming of Monroe as a 'Founding Father' not only shows her impact on American literary modernism but demonstrates how stubbornly some critics maintain the masculine, 'boys' club' vision of our literary past. To go so far as to relegate Monroe to a parenthesis, as an aside, marginalizes her even further.[4]

Women have been minimalized in our literary and historical consciousness, but they were stronger than our selective literary history would lead us to believe. Among others, the authors in *Rereading Modernism: New Directions in Feminist Criticism* are quite successful in proving this point. 'What is particularly surprising about this selective canonization,' writes Lisa Rado in the collection's introduction, 'is that, perhaps to the greatest extent in history, modern women authors played a pivotal role in shaping the aesthetics of their time. . . . [They] not only participated in the modernist project, but actually shaped it' (4–5). Women were leading the literary frontier as both editors and founders of the 'Little Magazines' that made the modernist literary movement, as well as poets in their own right. Women were also a strong contingency in wartime politics as they organized, according to Mark Van Wienan, 'the first American demonstration against war' 'donned [in] black and march[ing] to the beat of muffled drums down New York's Fifth Avenue' (688). Such a fervour of active women, in conjunction with the first wave of feminism, has led many critics to argue that modernism was deeply impacted by these 'new' women.

As the founder and long-time matriarch of *Poetry* magazine, Harriet Monroe may have personified the fear many men had of a female warrior class. According to Michael Castro and many other critics of the modernist era, '*Poetry* was the most influential poetry journal of the day . . . ,' and as editor and founder of this influential magazine, Monroe was quite powerful (18). 'She was a born fighter,' writes Eunice Tietjens in *The World at My Shoulder*, 'as many a man discovered to his discomfort, a little dynamo of determination. Her crisp incisive prose attacks on careless or prejudiced thinking with regard to the poets, who were always her darlings, have done much for the cause of the art in America' (31). As a woman of authority, Monroe was able to promote poets of either gender, and she had equal respect for them both. While she did much to support the male elite who still fill anthologies under the title of modernism, Monroe also supported women poets' 'frank sincerity of their revelation of the feminine point of view. The women poets of our time,' Monroe said with potency in her book *Poets and Their Art*, ' . . . have been content to be women.' (141). She was what male writers feared most, a warrior ready to claim the poetic world of the feminine, a world that to most men at the time would be the truest wasteland if overpopulated with what Havelock Ellis described in *The New Spirit* as 'women [who] are comparatively free from "genius"' (10).

It was feared that the lush mountains of men's works, the bulking mass in the forefront, would lie hidden behind the oaks of these 'new' women. Gilbert and Gubar explore this idea as well: 'To poet-critics from Lawrence, Eliot, Pound, and Williams, to Ransom and Blakmur, a literary landscape populated by women . . . may have seemed like a no man's land, a wasted and wasting country . . . ' (155). Men feared that women would take over their place as poets, that they would invade what 'by and large remained (and may have been unconsciously designed as) a men's club' (Gilbert and Gubar, 156).[5]

As with their understanding of poetry and modernism, to many critics, literary historians and modernists, the First World War was an experience shared only among men. The outbreak of the Great War seemed to serve as a leveller of any possible female domination. If war literature is, as stated by Evelyn Hinz in 'An Introduction to War and Literature', 'a transcript of historical battles, a verbal imitation of what happened', then most women writers are excluded from this experience and therefore this literary inspiration and movement (vii). The impact of this war on the increasing strength of women, whether through women's suffrage or through literature, is worth noting. Norman Cantor points out that western culture was faced with what may be described as a reformation, a convergence of the old and the new:

> The old culture in 1914 was threatened by cultural revolution. . . . The First World War could be seen as a desperate, although largely unconscious, effort of the old order to save itself. The path of self-preservation for the old culture ran through war. For the war reasserted nationalism, historical traditions, male chauvinism, social

hierarchy, and the ideological Christianity. The First World War was
the way used by the old culture to stave off the advent of the new.

(131)

In reaffirming these aspects of the old order (particularly, for my purposes,
male chauvinism), the First World War did much to silence women
authors, in what Lisa Rado calls a 'massive cultural "forgetting"' (4). As
Jane Marcus puts it, 'all wars destroy women's culture, returning
women to the restricted roles of childbearing and nursing and only that
work that helps the war effort' (249). Through war's phallocentricism,
its exclusion of women, men once again gained the upper hand; men
were centred in the expansiveness of war while women were subjugated
to the periphery.

But as critics such as Khan have shown us, women *were* motivated to
write by the First World War. Their contribution to our understanding
of this event is enhanced by looking at it within the context of scale, for
while women were not involved as combatants in the tremendous
battlefields, women were on the fringe, distanced from battle but affected
nonetheless. 'Women read such books as outsiders, as beholders of the
opposite sex' (Tylee, 225). If men's experience is the centre, the interior,
then women make up the exterior, however invisible they may have
seemed. Their perspectives, therefore, give balance to our understanding
of literary history.

Harriet Monroe was one of these women. In fact, the war so deeply
affected Monroe that she wrote about it quite often. In her preface to
The Difference and Other Poems, for example, she attributes the great
change in her development of poetic insight to the war. In writing of
herself as a young poet, she describes a woman who 'grew up in a world
which appeared to her not only warless but dedicated to a wise future
of peaceful development. ... War was not a reality, but a legend, to her
consciousness' (1).[6] Portraying herself thirty years after this time of
peaceful ignorance, Monroe describes a woman who 'shows not only
a change of opinion and feeling from youth to middle-age, but the
terrible enforcement of that change through the immense and wasteful
disaster of the World War' (1–2). This change, caused by a disaster
which is 'immense', has, in Monroe's eyes, made the scale of life expand.
'A century ago each man's world was small, each neighborhood
supplied of its own needs. ... Today each man's world is enormously
enlarged, each village makes demands to the ends of the earth, and
governmental issues seem to outgrow the capacity of the individual
human brain' (2).[7] War stretched the imagination and the impact of

action. It moved Monroe's consciousness (and as she proposes, the consciousness of all) outward.

While she saw her consciousness as becoming enlarged, of encompassing the vast world, Monroe recognized that her place was more strongly diminished by its confinement and movement inward. This is shown quite clearly in Monroe's poem, 'On the Porch'. Here, the speaker begins by describing her place, 'roofed in, screened in'. The poem's movement inward demonstrates the minimalization of her place. The speaker is hidden and constricted as the roof pushes her down and the screen squeezes her in. While she is small, the world, particularly the male world of war, is large.

While this minuteness is exclusionary, it is also protective. It keeps her 'From the pattering rain. . . . I lie / Snug and dry, / And hear the birds complain.' She is compartmentalized and socialized to remain separate from the difficult, morally shattering experiences such as war. She is, in fact, physically kept from them, but although her body is constricted, her spirit is not so easily minimalized. It is like the birds she hears complain, free to flutter but distanced from her. The next stanza in the poem is like the song of those birds carrying the reader to the visions of the speaker, a song which breaks free from constraints and gives the reader visions and images of a war women are supposed to be protected from. The small scale of her body and of her place in society, her place as a woman far from battle and yet emotionally affected by it even in that distance, diminishes even further as her mind and spirit travel past these limitations. She experiences the emotions of war, what Monroe called 'the feeling of blank amazement and rebellion which is a sudden shattering of hope' (Poet's, 341). Yet she is only able to hear the rain and birds, unable to touch war but still touched by it. It is ironic that the further she seems from war, the closer she comes to the experience. For, as the lines fall back in place, as she lies roofed in, the seas of war wash over her with increased strength.

Once the poem turns to the images of war, of 'the huge gun with its one blind eye', the speaker experiences the vast glories of war and the immense horror of death while leaving the small woman behind as a faint memory of her confinement beneath the roof and surrounded by the cage of the screened porch. Although she glorifies this picture with images of an 'army proudly swinging / Under gay flags', this immediately turns to bitter irony as the army marches past 'the glorious dead heaped like rags'. In fact, we know from Monroe's writings that she was concerned with the poetic tradition of glorifying the images of war in contradiction to her own repulsion of war. Monroe found no virtue in war's destruction. 'What is the fundamental, the essential and psycho-logical cause of war?' she asked, then answered, 'The feeling in men's hearts that it is beautiful' (*Poet's*, 341). Speaking against this perception of battles as beautiful, she shows the soaring planes 'swooping out of the sky', pointing 'down – down' to the ironic image of the living alongside the dead.

This movement forms a circular pattern of scale, beginning with a zoom inward to the woman's place confined on her porch, pulling out to a wide shot of the 'seas of war', then moving back in for a tight shot of the piled dead and repeating this pattern as it moves back out and zooms back in to the woman on the porch. At the heart of this movement are those dead, their bodies echoing a familiar image, an object found in many homes: a lifeless rag. This image links the dead to what sits on the periphery, in the separate stanzas which frame this poem, the speaker, the woman. One finds the connection of these two internal images in their place within the poem, their place of confinement, their minute-ness in contrast to the scale of the larger images of the poem, and their social importance. They echo one another in the structure of the poem as well as the stasis within the poem's action.

This relation of the dead to the distanced woman also represents the war between genders, a theme quite often explored by feminists of the period who saw the First World War and the philosophy of war as based on the same misogynistic principles. The image of the woman confined, minimalized, while the transparently phallic 'huge gun with its one blind eye' 'lunges and plunges' demarcates the division between male and female, aggressor and victim, warrior and peacemaker. This demarcation reflects the concerns about gender and the heightened tensions revolving around this topic at the time. 'War must be understood as a *gendering* activity,' write Margaret Higonnet et al. in *Behind the Lines: Gender and the Two World Wars*, 'one that ritually marks the gender of all members of a society, whether or not they are combatants' (4). In 'On the Porch', Monroe uses scale to categorize the feminine in the confined woman on the porch and the ignored heap of dead the soldiers march past. By linking the genders, Monroe calls into question the perceived unimport-ance of women within the male context of war.

Quite a few women at the time saw war as entirely masculine. As Monroe's contemporary, Christabel Pankhurst, described it in an editorial entitled 'The War': 'Had women been equal partners with men from the beginning, human civilization would have been wholly different from what it is. The whole march of humanity would have been to a point other than we have reached at this moment of horrible calamity' (301).

Like Pankhurst and the speaker in 'On the Porch', Monroe also felt separated from the creation of war. 'Poets have made more wars than kings,' she wrote in the September 1914 issue of *Poetry*, 'and war will not cease until they remove its glamour from the imaginations of men.'

Monroe requests for others to make this change, as if she is, like the woman on the porch, separated from this tradition. She puts forth in the introduction to her collected works, *Chosen Poems*, that she 'never joined forces with the many who believed in the spiritualizing influence of war, or thought that through such a holocaust war would meet its own doom' (ix). This statement is interesting to consider when one examines a poem of Monroe's which seems to support the United States' involvement in this battle. In her idealistic poem 'America' we a see a vision that includes an enlarged female, a woman greater than any notion of war, fear or horror yet a woman who is still a large part of the war. This woman is the country Monroe patriotically depicts as pure, proud and powerful.

> My country stood up tall to the height of the world –
> Straight and tall,
> From the blue Caribbean at her feet
> To her coronal of islands strung from the arctic sea. . . .
> My country,
> Beautiful and strong,
> Startled, slowly arising,
> Hearing at last the insult,
> Feeling the atrocious crimson mist in her eyes,
> My country stood up tall to the height of the world –

While this woman-country enlarges the scale of women, breaking free from the confinements of the speaker and the dead in 'On the Porch', she contradicts the editorial stance against war that Monroe often expressed, an opinion that she expressed in an editorial comment entitled 'What May War Do' in the June 1917 issue of *Poetry*:

> And thus we persuade ourselves that all is as it seems, that a scheme of things which, from the electron-fused atom to the remotest nebula of whirling stars, is flux and motion, vibration and vastness . . . , may become a social system complete and inexorable, a perfectly built mosaic of carefully mechanized human parts. And then comes War. War topples over the fixed and permanent things and breaks the immutable laws. It crashes through social systems and makes

chaos of the human mosaic, arranging a new one of its own and destroying that.

(142)

To Monroe, war's impact and its demise were all-encompassing, able to touch and demolish all of humanity. This look upon war as destructive does not seem to fit with the strong woman-country in Monroe's poem because she so adamantly expresses her hatred for war in her works of prose but so clearly writes about the war as a positive action in this poem.

One way to negotiate this contradiction is to look at it within the context of Monroe's state of mind about the future. 'Freed by the war, all but federated by its sacrificial agonies,' Monroe wrote in an editorial entitled 'The New Era', 'men and nations are just about to begin their militant march toward the common goal of a universal state organized for joy and beauty through mutual service and universal brotherhood' (195). This vision of a future filled with peace, this expanded vision of a world nation, fits quite nicely with the end of the poem where America is shown 'on her long march toward the far-off invisible goal'. Monroe was perhaps more able to cope with the First World War by looking forward, by looking past the vastness of war to the prospect of a 'far-off' peaceful world culture. Although not large within the scale of the time, this distant point was all she had to look toward.

Reading this poem within the context of scale, particularly the scale of gender and war, also illuminates some of its strengths. Unlike 'On the Porch', the focus in 'America' is on a fantastical creature, a personification of a nation. The woman-country is not a new one in metaphorical thought in regard to war. Propaganda for participation in the First World War often 'promoted a myth of British soldiers as pure young men who sacrificed their lives, innocently and willingly, to save their Mother-country and their womenfolk . . . ' (Tylee, 252). In depicting this country as a woman, Monroe demonstrates the impact of women on her country and on this male-centred war by creating a woman-country, an active participant in a 'society [where]', as Marcia Yadkin tells us, 'men have been the actual and potential perpetrators of war' (263). As greater than these many men, 'her millions of sons', woman(mother)-country America is shifting the scale of war by bringing a woman to the forefront and making men 'like flakes of snow to the storm'. While these men are the fighters in the battle, it is woman who is their strength, their homeland, their mother.

This mother image is one Monroe utilizes in many of her poems. One such poem is 'A Letter of Farewell'. The mother of a soldier serves as the audience of the poem, and right away we see the issue of scale. 'Mother, little Mother,' the poem opens, thus signifying the size of the mother in the scale of the issues the poem deals with. Each reference to the mother is preceded by the scaling down adjective 'little'. Mothers, wives and daughters served their purposes in this war. They 'came to characterize the Home Front', says Khan in her discussion of the war at home (69). As a cultural construct, the 'Little Mother' fits neatly into the scaled pattern of the time. Away from the action, the 'Little Mother' can do little but fret and imagine the horrors of war. As with the 'On the Porch', she is made powerless by what Tylee describes as her symbolic value: the home. 'Women themselves came to symbolize those values, and had to be protected and fought for on their behalf. A threat to the special position of women was a threat to the values they stood for' (12). This positioning of the mother as a vulnerable symbol of home life renders her powerless. It makes her a childlike figure rather than one of authority.[8] 'Little Mother', like Freud's vision of the mother, is a disappointment because she lacks what is required for active success. This fatal flaw causes her to shrink in cultural consciousness. In the consciousness of war, she is what ties men to the home front. She is a small anchor, submerged (perhaps even drowned) by the seas of oppression and connected only by the invisible umbilical cord of devotion to the battleship of war. The speaker in this poem is tied to his mother by this cord. His mother serves this function, but she also serves as his confessor. The image of her as an invisible yet (we assume) concerned presence takes the minimalizing image-scheme of scale one step further by causing her to disappear completely. The audience in this poem is less than Little. She is a valley, an absence of space, in which this soldier's confessions are echoed.

And what he confesses to this invisible entity of motherhood questions what the 'Little Mother' represents. For, what is most remarkable about this poem is that it simultaneously promotes and challenges gendered stereotypes in regard to war. Rather than telling of how he has killed to defend her, the soldier discloses that he does not want to kill again. He has spoken out against war, and he must now face his execution for this betrayal. '"Let the guns rot," I said, "and the cannon rust – / Look in your brother's eyes / And clasp his hand."' Since 'to be truly masculine is to be prepared to kill other men', the speaker in 'A Letter of Farewell' is feminized by his resistance to war (Tylee, 13). An enemy soldier, a man the speaker should be drawn to kill by his masculinity, shows him a kindness tainted with femininity. In this scene, almost homoerotic in nature, the enemy calls the speaker 'poor little one', using the adjective that had been maintained exclusively for the mother. The soldier becomes little because, like the mother, he is vulnerable.

The poem does not depict this feminization in a negative light, however. The soldier's feminization allows him to see the truth as Monroe sees it. He develops the same enthusiasm for the future Monroe expressed in the aforementioned 'A New Era'. The poem ends with just such a perspective:

> There will be a new nation –
> No one shall stop us from loving each other.
> So good-bye, little Mother.
> I don't mind dying for it – the nation.
> I see it.

By projecting her own beliefs onto the body of this boy awaiting execution, Monroe gives insight into her own psyche. The soldier's 'loathing [that] was a vomit in my heart' becomes Monroe's own feelings about war. However quietly, Monroe is standing up against war and is looking toward a brighter future.

Monroe's vision of the future and her complete faith in humanity's ability to become a world nation is well documented. In fact, Monroe died in Peru as an ambassador working toward this goal. Just as we saw this small point of hope in 'America', so too do we see Monroe look toward the future when, as she hopes in 'The New Internationalism', the world will see that 'the men of these nations will remain united at heart by the fierce ordeal through which they have passed together, and to a certain degree they will pass on their sense of comradeship in the stories they tell to their children and grandchildren' (146–7). Through the able and active character of the soldier, Monroe can assert the beliefs so much more easily dismissed if said through a woman character. Thus she legitimizes the opinions of a woman by reconstructing the voice of a man.

As Gillian Hanscombe and Virginia L. Smyers write in *Writing for Their Lives: The Modernist Women 1910–1940*, 'since a man's point of view has primacy and a woman's does not, it has traditionally passed unremarked that male writers have subsumed the female half of "human" experience and that they have done so without qualification' (5). This has happened with the writings on the First World War. It is only once we examine the work of 'the Other half' that we are able to see how widespread the effects of this war are on the general populace, and where better to search for clues to this quietly ignored version of history than in the writings of one of modernism's influential women, Harriet Monroe.

Notes

1. This position, of course, echoes that of many feminist scholars seeking to reclaim or rediscover women, minority, marginal and radical authors from their area of interest. For a more thorough examination of work being done on modernist women, see the *oeuvre* of Sandra Gilbert and Susan Gubar, particularly their three-volume series, *No Man's Land* (New Haven, CT: Yale University Press, 1988, 1989, 1994). See also, *The Gender of Modernism*, ed. Bonnie Kime Scott (Bloomington: Indiana University Press) and *Rereading Modernism: New Directions in Feminist Criticism*, ed. Lisa Rado (New York: Garland, 1994) among others.
2. My assertion about Harriet Monroe's influence on modernism can be documented by the numerous references to Monroe's *Poetry* magazine and its impact on American poetic modernism. While some critics choose to place responsibility on Ezra Pound, as touched upon below, most critics begin a discussion about American modernism with a discussion of Monroe's journal.
3. As 'employees', women found great strength in their new freedoms as working women. As 'Rosie the Riveter' in the Second World War was able to gain employment while maintaining her social acceptance, so too did women infiltrate the workforce as men went off to fight the Great War. In addition, many women took to the fields as nurses, Vera Brittain being one of the most well known of these 'employed' women. Still, women who were in the workforce or who were involved in the war more directly are marginalized in our historical construction of the battle. See Maurine Weiner Greenwald's *Women, War, and Work* (Ithaca, NY: Cornell University Press, 1990) for a more thorough discussion of the impact of the First World War on these women's lives.
4. As previously mentioned, there are also those critics who maintain that the glory of *Poetry* should go to Ezra Pound rather than Harriet Monroe. One such critic, Eric Homberger, writes: 'It was due less to Miss Monroe, however, than to the labour and good taste of her foreign editor, Ezra Pound' ('Chicago and New York: two versions of American modernism', in *Modernism: 1890–1930*, eds Malcolm Bradbury and James McFarlane. Sussex: Harvester, 1978, 153–4). How is it that the foreign editor can be so easily attributed with the generation of *American* poetry? The answer lies in Ezra Pound's position within the modernist tradition, within what Lisa Rado calls 'the boys club' (4). Had her foreign editor been a less-known woman writer, for example, I doubt such critics would look so fervently to other sources for the work Monroe did.
5. Again, the three volumes of *No Man's Land* argue this more thoroughly than my space here allows. An understanding of the impact of women's suffrage, the deconstruction of gender and the self on western culture, and an examination of contemporary critical responses to modernist women artists which perpetuated misogynous visions of their talent highlight some of the ways in which the new woman created a lot of anxiety for the new man.

6. As Monroe did not begin *Poetry* until her early fifties, this could be referring to any time before then. However, I am led to assume this refers to the time when she wrote 'The Columbian Ode' for Chicago's Columbian Exposition at the age of thirty-one.
7. This opinion also mirrors Harriet Monroe's poem 'The Difference' (*The Difference and Other Poems*. Chicago: Covici-McGee, 1924).
8. D. A. Boxwell's 'The (M)Other Battle of World War One: the maternal politics of pacifism in Rose Macaulay's *Non-Combatants and Others*' (*Tulsa Studies in Women's Literature*, 12 (1993): 85–101) addresses this more specifically.

Works cited

Cantor, Norman F. *Twentieth-Century Culture: Modernism to Deconstruction*. New York: Peter Lang, 1988.

Castro, Michael. *Interpreting the Indian: Twentieth-Century Poets and the Native American*. Albuquerque: University of New Mexico Press, 1983.

Chenault, Libby. *Battlelines: World War I Posters from the Bowman Gray Collection*. Chapel Hill: University of North Carolina Press, 1988.

Drake, William. *The First Wave: Women Poets in America 1915–1945*. New York: Macmillan – now Palgrave, 1987.

Ellis, Havelock. *The New Spirit*. Washington: National Home Library Foundation, 1935.

Gilbert, Sandra and Susan Gubar. *No Man's Land: The Place of the Woman Writer in the Twentieth Century. Volume One: The War of the Words*. London: Yale University Press, 1988.

Hanscombe, Gillian and Virginia L. Smyers. *Writing for Their Lives: The Modernist Women 1910–1940*. Boston: Northeastern University Press, 1987.

Higonnet, Margaret Randolph, Jane Jenson, Sonya Michel and Margaret Collins (eds), 'Introduction', in *Behind the Lines: Gender and the Two World Wars*. New Haven, CT: Yale University Press, 1987.

Hinz, Evelyn J. 'An Introduction to War and Literature: Ajax Versus Ulysses', *Mosaic*, 23.3 (1980): v–xii.

Khan, Nosheen. *Women's Poetry of the First World War*. Lexington: University of Kentucky Press, 1988.

Lakoff, George and Mark Turner. *More than Cool Reason: A Field Guide to Poetic Metaphor*. Chicago: University of Chicago Press, 1989.

Marcus, Jane. Afterward. *Not So Quiet . . . Stepdaughters of War*. By Helen Zenna Smith. New York: Feminist, 1989.

Monroe, Harriet. 'America', *Poetry*, 13 (1918): 133–5.

——. *Chosen Poems*. New York: Macmillan – now Palgrave, 1935.

——. *The Difference and Other Poems*. Chicago: Covici-McGee, 1924.

——. 'A Letter of Farewell', *Chosen Poems*. New York: Macmillan – now Palgrave, 1935.

——. 'The New Era', Editorial, *Poetry*, 9 (1917): 195–7.

——. 'The New Internationalism', *Poetry*, 13 (1918): 147–9.

——. 'On the Porch', *Chosen Poems*. New York: Macmillan – now Palgrave, 1935.

——. A Poet's Life: Seventy Years in a Changing World. New York: Macmillan – now Palgrave, 1938.

——. 'What May War Do', Editorial, Poetry, 6 (1917): 142–5.

Pankhurst, Christabel. 'The War', Suffragette, 7 August 1914: 301.

Rado, Lisa. 'Introduction', in Rereading Modernism: New Directions in Feminist Criticism, ed. Lisa Rado. New York: Garland, 1994.

Symons, Julian. Makers of the New: The Revolution in Literature, 1912–1939. New York: Random House, 1987.

Tietjens, Eunice. The World at My Shoulder. New York: Macmillan – now Palgrave, 1938.

Tylee, Claire M. The Great War and Women's Consciousness: Images of Militarism and Womanhood in Women's Writings, 1914–1964. Iowa City: University of Iowa Press, 1990.

Van Wienan, Mark. 'Women's ways in war: the poetry and politics of the Woman's Peace Party, 1915–1917', Modern Fiction Studies, 38.3 (1992): 687–714.

Yadkin, Marcia. 'Reflections on Woolf's Three Guineas', Women's Studies International Forum, 5 (1982): 263–9.

Part III
Nationality and Response

7
French Women Poets Respond to the Great War

Nancy Sloan Goldberg

Among the major western belligerents, France's literary response to the Great War is the least researched and analysed, and therefore the least understood.[1] The studies by Pierre Flottes, Léon Riegel and John Cruickshank, and the continuing work by Nicole Racine, while not comprehensive, nonetheless raised important issues that have remained unanswered in the recent outpouring of books and articles on the war era. Of the nearly two hundred new books on the Great War published in French in the last several years, only a few, including my own examination of anti-war poetry, are concerned exclusively with the study of imaginative writing. Investigation of Great War literature has fared better in Britain and the United States where scholars have made a considerable contribution to the field. These studies, from Paul Fussell's *The Great War and Modern Memory* to the most recent publications, have either focused exclusively on or privileged the writing of English-language authors.[2]

The large-scale project in recent years of scholars in all fields to retrieve and analyse the experience of women has brought needed attention to the neglected corpus of women's First World War narratives and poetry. The authoritative and noteworthy efforts by Catherine Reilly, Nosheen Khan, Claire Tylee and Sharon Oudit to present and examine British women's war writing have begun to narrow the conspicuous lacuna left by Fussell and others. These contemporary studies are in general thematic, historically oriented and include fiction and non-fiction writing. With the exception of Oudit's ideological analysis, these works are indifferent to the provocative theories on women and war that have stimulated a controversial debate among American scholars since the 1980s.

Briefly summarized, this discussion centres around the contention voiced in particular by feminist scholar Sara Ruddick among many others

(Salamone, Zanotti) that aggression and warfare are inherent in men's nature and that women are innate peacemakers. In her early writings, Ruddick based her theory on the work of sociologist Nancy Chodorow and educational psychologist Carol Gilligan to argue that the particular biological experiences of women cause them to develop a moral concept she calls 'preservation love'. The female connectedness to and responsibility for life which others term 'maternal thinking' become for Ruddick a preservative caring that resembles and is parallel to pacifism. Historian Joan W. Scott and social psychologist Anne Hunter are among numerous scholars who opposed this theory on the grounds that it assumes fixed and permanent meanings for human relationships that exclude cultural and/or social constructions. These critics indicate that such views of women are essentialist and determinist, and therefore defeat the purpose of feminist research by replicating arguments that have historically served to legitimize patriarchy and other unequal social systems (Scott, 1065). Some scholars accept neither the psychological nor the materialist position and instead adopt an orientation which assumes that gender constructions impart meaning in a variety of ways. They employ this methodology to interpret the interrelationship of war and the representation of gender:

> ...war must be understood as a *gendering* activity, one that ritually marks the gender of all members of society, whether or not they are combatants. The implications of war for women and men are, then, linked in symbolic as well as social and economic systems.
>
> (Higonnet et al., 4; italics in original)

Such a pluralist position suggests many provocative questions for the study of French women poets. While it is not within the scope of this essay to consider the general implications of the First World War for women in France, an examination of the literary response of four of the many established and celebrated women poets can begin to reveal the contemporary relationship of politics, social experience and creative activity.[3] How did each poet understand the war, and in what terms did she articulate that conception? What value systems operate in the poems, and how are these symbolized? What role do gender constructions play in the transmission of those codes? Do they lead to pacifism as Ruddick asserts ('Preservative Love', 249–51), and/or an understanding of power relationships in society as Scott implies (1067–8)? What were the psychological effects of the war on the poems' narrators? Did they discover a new sense of physical and emotional energy as Sandra

Gilbert and Susan Gubar submit in their influential study *No Man's Land* (2: 258–323)?

The four writers whose poems will illuminate these issues represent a variety of social groups, literary styles and attitudes toward the war. Anna de Noailles (1876–1933), a princess by birth and a countess by marriage, enjoyed world-wide fame for a personal lyricism which exalted love, nature and youth. In her more than twenty volumes of poetry and novels, Noailles celebrated her passionate attachment to the French countryside and the beauty she perceived in the world. Her social rank also allowed her access to her neighbour Clemenceau and other high government officials to whom she frequently offered her opinions on better management of the war (Brioche, 316–49). Cécile Périn (1877–1959), the popular author of some twenty volumes of poems from 1906 to 1956, was known as 'maternity's muse' for her eloquent and fervent celebration of mother–child relationships. Like Noailles, Périn supported the war. The traditional style and themes in her poetry underscore Périn's status as a recognized and accepted figure in the Parisian literary establishment. Conversely, Henriette Sauret (1890–1976), poet, journalist, biographer and short-story writer, began her long career in the heady environment of prewar avant-garde circles. After publishing two long collections of anti-war poetry, Sauret wrote mostly essays and stories which appeared in feminist newspapers in the 1920s and 1930s. Léonie Sourd was born in 1886 and in keeping with the activist tradition of French elementary school teachers, was a militant feminist, pacifist and syndicalist, as well as the long-time editor-in-chief of the periodical, *La Voix des femmes* [Voice of Women]. To conceal her identity from censors and school officials during the war, Sourd wrote articles and poems for the feminist pacifist press under the anagramic pseudonym Noélie Drous.

Despite differences in their attitudes toward the war, their world views, and poetic styles and sensibilities,[4] the theme of love dominates the works of these four poets. From the love of country in Noailles's poems, to that of mothers and spouses in the works of the other three poets, the concept of love and its power, rights and duties form the philosophical centre of the writing. Each poet's vision of love, however, is different and even antithetical to the others: love provides the motivation for combat as well as for opposition to the war, and it also justifies either the exercise or suppression of maternal rights and interests. For Noailles, the desire to fight and die to protect one's homeland is the highest form of love. Drous confers that designation on women who recognize the political power of their maternal love and join together to create a new civic order. Périn lauds those mothers who love their families enough to sacrifice them to the needs of the country, while Sauret considers women's resignation as proof of insufficient love. The goals of protection and preservation are integral to this multiple conception of love, yet love emerges as a possible path to pacifism, as Ruddick predicts, only in Drous's poems. In the works of the other poets, the manifestation of love and caring stimulates physical confrontation or compliance with war. Significantly, love causes the narrators in Sauret's and Drous's poems to meditate on women's role in warfare, leading to different levels of understanding of how gender constructions both represent and reinforce political authority. The effect of this realization is distinctly different in those two poets' works. Sauret's narrators are overwhelmed by the strength and presence of the war machine and react as helpless bystanders who can only look on in horror. Such a passive response is consistent with the historical situation of French women who possessed few civil rights and played almost no role in contemporary politics. For Drous's narrators, however, love is the justification and legal basis for mothers to use the power of the vote to change a governmental structure that feeds on warfare; their goal must be the creation of a new world founded on justice and reason.

The important place afforded in the poetry to women and mothers reflects more than the gender of the poets. Women's social roles had been increasingly politicized since the French Revolution, as the change from traditional authority to constitutional nationalism privileged the responsibility of the family in the instruction of national pride and obedience. Women became the official 'mother-teachers' and socializers of a new generation. While in the nineteenth century this recognition of civic obligation was in some ways an advance for women, it also isolated women from politics. By the end of that century, however, the figure of the 'Republican Mother' also became a justification for activism, social reform and the right of suffrage (Berkin and Lovett, 209–13). During the First World War, this view of the interdependence of women's biological, social and political roles continued, as both war supporters and dissidents used variations of the Republican Mother ideology to defend their viewpoint. Accordingly, mothers, female mythical figures and individual women, as we will see, occupy central places in the poetry of Périn, Sauret, and Drous. Noailles's poems are the exception, for her main focus is the mythopoeic death of soldiers, an experience, she states, even mothers cannot understand.

Noailles's view of soldiers, nonetheless, is similar to that of the other three poets, in that they are presented as young children or boys, bursting with energy and life like the buds of a tree. While the soldiers' resolve might be 'manly', their bodies are often small and frail, some-times undeveloped and childlike. Conceived thus as universal children, underscoring their filial relationship to the poet, the soldiers in the poems are praised or pitied, but never condemned or criticized. With the exception of Drous, the poets do not dwell on either the hope for victory or a determination of responsibility for the war. While Noailles curses the Kaiser, and Périn and Sauret note defects in the German char-acter, these judgements are rare. Drous, on the other hand, is vehement in her direct denunciation of glory-seeking generals and power-hungry politicians of both sides. Drous also denounces the historic role of religion and the church in warfare, while Sauret limits her criticism to the present conflict. Noailles and Périn consider the death and suffering of both soldiers and civilians to parallel that of Jesus, and their poems find that the experience of war teaches the Christian values of compas-sion and self-sacrifice.

The growing melancholy that would dominate Anna de Noailles's postwar works is present in her war-era volume, *Les Forces éternelles* [Eternal Strengths]. The unique focus of the collection's first part, *La Guerre* [The War], is the heroic and glorious death experienced by the young soldiers. Nearly every poem proclaims the deep power of the soldiers' love for France and their willingness to sacrifice themselves to preserve their country. For Noailles, their voluntary self-denial separates forever these dead and wounded soldiers from civilians, who, like she, cannot understand the thoughts of the combatants. This is not because the civilians did not witness the same physical reality of the battlefield, but rather because they cannot understand the transformation caused by that experience. The soldiers' love of France is so strong that it has conquered their fear of death and their regret at leaving life, thus allowing them to transcend reality in order to embrace History and the Universe. This apotheosis, Noailles acknowledges, is not always easily accepted by those left behind. Her narrators are troubled that the soldiers were too young to have experienced love before they died and that spring con-tinues to renew the earth, heedless of the blood, rather than water, that has irrigated the soil. The ultimate isolation inherent in each death further disturbs, but also fascinates the narrators, who try to understand the 'secret mystery' of death.

For Noailles, Verdun, where over 650 000 men were killed, is the 'greatest name in the world', for the land's wounds and the ever-present smell of blood will teach forever the 'unfathomable and holy power of the Homeland' (13–14). While Noailles admits that life is a 'noble goddess' and that people should not kill, her vision of the soldiers' self-sacrifice subverts these precepts to assume a transcendent meaning that denies the materiality of death:

> ... And yet, right now, I know that nothing equals
> The heroic abandon, supreme and without return;
> I know that honor is the pinnacle of love,
> And that a young death is a triumphant death.
>
> I know that they have attained the essential goal,
> That they have defeated the tomb and are not its victims,
> These boys raised up away from earthly fetters; ... [5]

Occasionally Noailles appears to hesitate before such extreme idealization of the soldiers' deaths. The few poems that begin with a lament for the soldiers' youth and the life experiences they would not have soon change to reiterate the volume's basic themes of sacrifice, redemption and spiritual renewal. In 'Entre les tombeaux et les astres' [Between the tombs and the stars], the dead soldiers, 'these radiant boys struck down at twenty' (72), reveal one unfulfilled desire in their otherwise peaceful existence. Though immortal, their souls floating endlessly around the sun, they regret not having experienced love. Noailles imagines a somewhat macabre wedding as women make their sole appearance in her war poems:

> ... Eyes always lifted, souls inhabiting space,
> The female nation, like a nation of birds,
> Will penetrate the noble skies where never are diminished
> The exploits bursting from your bones! ... [6]

Noailles often speaks collectively of the multitude of dead and wounded soldiers, who together personify the glory and honour of France. In several poems, however, a single dying youth becomes a kind of 'everyman', whose individual story is at the same time his own and the symbol of a shared fate. In 'Celui qui meurt' [The Dying One] Noailles reminds her readers that glorious armies such as those at Verdun, the Marne and the Somme were made up of individual men, who, like Christ, died alone, and bore their pain by themselves. In 'Le Soldat' [The Soldier], Noailles reiterates the theme of redemption through the sanctification of a naive and frivolous boy as the destiny of France:

You, frail body and heart, but in whom was emerging
Like the buds on the tree,
The reborn spring of the great French destiny,
Made of laughter and marble,
– Child who did not have, before the awful plague,
A soul preordained to a duty so lofty, – . . . [7]

The effect of the war on women and their families is a central theme
in Cécile Périn's *Les Captives* [The Captured Women]. With compassion,
Périn evokes the silent bravery of mothers and the heroic sacrifice of
their sons. Périn understands that war disrupts families and consequently a woman's sense of herself and her place in the universe. She
insists nonetheless that, while war is the antithesis of life and art, it is a
natural event that tests a woman's love and devotion to her family. For
Périn, the hope for fraternity is a fleeting dream of youth. Acceptance of
the inevitability of war and the universal suffering it brings is to learn
and understand the Christian values of caring and redemption through
sacrifice. While Périn mourns the death of so many young soldiers, she
does not dwell on their youth, but rather elevates them to the status of
leaders-in-death, whose example serves as a guide for all.

Although for Périn, war demands heroism of both men and women,
it is the mothers who figure most prominently in her poems. Their
sacrifice is great because they willingly give up their cherished husbands
and children for France, understanding that the soldiers now belong
only to 'la patrie', their homeland. In 'Les Mères' [The Mothers] Périn
praises the women's stoicism and silent consent:[8]

The mothers against their hearts have held their children close,
And then, opening their arms, said: 'Let be fulfilled,
France, because it must be, this first sacrifice . . . '
And watched them depart, saying nothing.

Too much pain knotted their throats. Silence
Alone was amply broad, amply pure, amply great
To contain their sorrow. And their eyes, simply,
Watched the vast road vanish.[9]

Périn shows that although war disrupts and destroys lives, the people
who experience it gain important insight and accomplish positive goals.
For Périn, a woman's obligation centres on the love and happiness of her
husband and family, and their absence is in a sense fortuitous, for it

affords women the opportunity to reflect on the performance of their responsibilities:

> ... Did we give all when it was possible
> To offer love like a bouquet?
> Of the days when happiness murmured, within reach
> And tender, what have we done? ... [10]

For Périn, separation from the family also teaches women compassion for others. Several of her poems advise women to turn their attention outside the family unit to consider the situation of other women just like them. The suffering that all women must endure takes many forms, but Périn counsels her readers to look carefully at passers-by, for 'the same light trembles under their eyelids, and their souls understand each other easily' (28). Périn here does not depart from her traditional view of women's obligation to love and care for her family, rather, her guidance reinforces that role by adding a transcendent dimension to the women's distress.

> There are expressions other than those of loved ones.
> There are, you know it well, other women who cry;
> There are, in the hideous poverty of dwelling places,
> Many abandoned children.
>
> Let us not press our heads in our hands in distress
> Where cruel regret deepens and sobs,
> Let pain create in us a more fraternal heart,
> Filled with boundless tenderness. [11]

Ascribing redemptive qualities to the women's suffering is additionally significant because it allows Périn to elevate their sacrifice to a spiritual level approaching that of the soldiers. This is a difficult metaphorical jump because Périn's more realistic depiction of women does not necessarily invite the reader to generalize about their situations. Conversely, Périn portrays soldiers in an almost allegorical style, withholding their real-life qualities so that only the transcendent value of their war experience remains. In general her view of them is *before* the battle: young and unscathed, full of enthusiasm, yearning for adventure and glory, waving gallantly at the train station with a rose in their caps. Périn, however, goes beyond simply defending the war effort by replicating a traditional image of departing soldiers. Her poems demonstrate the desired effect and correct response to such a portrayal:

> Your eighteen-year-old sons, your handsome boys, eager
> For adventure and glory, have left, singing.
> Their enthusiasm, noble and magnificent flame
> Blazed so purely that you said nothing,
>
> That the moans died on your timid lips,
> That before so much hope, nothing could be said,
> For these children of yesterday who became our guides
> Would have shamed us harshly for our cries.
>
> O youth of France, exalted and sublime,
> You go off on the road to death without having known life,
> And you soar toward the abyss or the heights
> Without wishing to acknowledge that you sacrifice yourself ... [12]

Henriette Sauret published two lengthy volumes of war-related poetry in 1918 and 1919, *Les Forces détournées* [Diverted Strengths] and *L'Amour à la Géhenne* [Love in Gehenna]. In these poems Sauret features the disastrous effect of war on women's lives through the destruction of their families. Her poems relate the long periods of separation and the helpless isolation of loving mothers and wives who suffer the torturous wait for news that is often sorrowful. The image of war in Sauret's poetry is somewhat disconnected from its human agents. Her narrators describe war as an all-consuming mythical beast served by science from whom they seek refuge through dreams or art. Though art is superior to science and all other forms of human achievement, the forces unleashed by knowledge have become uncontrollable and will lead humanity and nature to total destruction. For Sauret, war is an unmitigated evil: it does not bring salvation, glory or heightened experiences; it only accentuates what is already malevolent.

The most constant theme in Sauret's poems is the impact of the war on women. Whether presented individually or collectively, Sauret's wives and mothers exemplify traditional values of love and dedication to home and family. It is this devotion that Sauret praises but also demonstrates to be a cause of the women's suffering. Throughout both books, Sauret chides women for the submissive silence which aids and continues the destruction of their homes and loved ones. Sauret is not arguing against a traditional role for women as guardians of hearth and home; on the contrary, she is severely critical of women who, she feels, have failed in their duty to protect their loved ones by not speaking out against the war. The punishment women endure for this error is not only the torment of isolation, the endless waiting and constant fear, but also the knowledge of their own culpability. In 'Le Désespoir des femmes' [Women's Despair] and several similar poems, Sauret wavers between pity for abandoned and frightened women whose daily lives no longer have meaning and fierce condemnation of their failure to stop the war. The tender sympathy Sauret expresses for women who, with the departure of their husbands, have also lost the central purpose of their domestic role, is countered by a direct judgement of their inaction:

> ... Your men are in mass graves
> But you are at the jail's bottom
> And you carry on your shoulders
> The weight of boundless sin.
>
> How could you, o women, let this happen?
> O women, o women, it's you
> By your arms, your voices, your [protective] laps,
> Who were supposed to prevent the war! ...[13]

Sauret implies that women can affect change by influencing the men in their lives, even while admitting that women do not have any real power. Sauret speaks directly to her readers in many of the poems, attempting to explain how they are complicit in the war's destruction. In 'Elles' [Them, the women] Sauret seeks to undermine the traditional justification of war as protection of the family by underscoring the irony inherent in such an argument. With biting sarcasm Sauret jeers at women she calls 'baby makers', whose cooperation is bought by a medal or a compliment. Her forceful tone reveals no sympathy for the women who grieve for their lost sons and husbands and who, by believing that the war is fought for their benefit, are also forced to accept guilt for being the cause of their deaths:

> ... And that's it. They make your shackles out of ribbon.
> Who among you feels them? Ten thousand compliments
> Rain down every morning on your slavish heads.
> Misery! They are suppressing you, cheating you, lying to you! ...[14]

While Sauret condemns women for not stopping the war, she never suggests a specific course of action for doing so. Advocating a programme for change would necessitate an exact analysis of the war's causes and would imply that Sauret's readers had influence or power in the public sphere to alter governmental policy. Sauret does not address these issues in her poems, thus supporting the traditional, apolitical definition of women's place in society. Accordingly, she blames negative abstractions such as Hate or uncontrollable Science instead of generals or heads of state for leading humanity to destruction. War is evil, her poems state, and the immense sacrifice of life has no meaning. This reluctance on Sauret's part to attribute the war to the world's various leaders is further understood in conjunction with her portrayal of soldiers as victims. In several poems, including 'Aux jeunes morts' [To the Dead Youths], Sauret describes the soldiers as 'poor little ones', barely out of nappies, whose lives were destroyed for nothing. The child metaphor implies once again the responsibility of mothers in continuing the war. Thus Sauret avoids blaming the soldiers for their own deaths, a double victimization from which she refuses to spare the women. In 'Les Enfants de la guerre' [Children of War], a poem which demonstrates the negative effects of war on toddlers and young children, Sauret invokes as the ultimate act of futility the image of a pregnant mother who works in a munitions factory. Moreover, Sauret's negative portrait of the modern working woman further supports her acceptance of traditional female roles in society.

> ... Then there are the factory children,
> Here absurdity is overly meticulous,
> The woman whose work feeds the cannons,
> Is carrying a child in her bosom!
>
> Symbol of the modern hour!
> You who are taking form in the breath
> Of these terrible workshops,
> Should we be crying for you already? ... [15]

Using the pseudonym Noélie Drous, Léonie Sourd published her antiwar poems in such feminist pacifist periodicals as *L'Action féministe* [Feminist Action] and *La Lutte féministe* [Feminist Struggle]. In 1920 she collected this poetry, including that which had been previously censored, under the title *Sous la tempête* [In the Tempest]. In these poems Drous explains to her readers that war is the result of man's desire to kill, a primitive instinct rationalized throughout history by the masks of honour and glory. For her, war is simply a socially approved form of murder. She condemns not only government leaders, but also priests who urge their parishioners to fight and thereby subvert the peaceful message of the Gospels. She is bitterly critical of her readers, the mothers who do not heed the cries of their soldier-children. Nonetheless, Drous considers the greatest potential for world peace to be maternal love and mothers' universal objective to protect their children. This desire to preserve life grows out of the shared experience of pregnancy and childbirth and links women the world over to one another regardless of nationality or economic status. It is this connectedness that becomes for Drous, as it would some seventy years later for Sara Ruddick, a voice for justice and reason in government, powerful enough to neutralize man's instinct for violence. The many metaphors for human speech and the repetition of the word 'voix' [voice, vote] throughout the poems allude firmly to the possibility of women influencing public policy by 'voicing' their will through the vote. This defence of the right of women to vote, however, does not indicate that Drous has completely rejected women's traditional role in society. By recasting the birth process as both a moral and a political force, Drous enlarges a historical definition of maternity that women of that time were not willing or ready to discard. She subtly subverts the established image of Republican Motherhood, transforming its silence and submission in order to support and vindicate her double goal of peace and women's suffrage.[16]

In *Sous la tempête*, Drous speaks directly to mothers, explaining that they should not abdicate to society the supreme role they played in their child's early life. She describes maternity as a political energy long appropriated by men, and she urges women to take back that force and engage, once again, in the fight for life. Drous is generally sympathetic to her readers' grief at the loss of their sons, but she is nonetheless firm in her challenge to them to redefine their traditional role to save future lives. In 'Les Danaïdes', the classical story of the fifty daughters of Danaus doomed to spend eternity drawing water with a sieve, becomes a metaphor for women whose lives are occupied in a similar futile effort: successively giving birth, rearing children and finally losing them to war. Throughout her poetry Drous refers to many historical battles to illustrate that men are naturally disposed to warfare, and that they disguise their innate lust for blood behind a mask of honour and glory. Here she ridicules with sharp sarcasm the argument that war is a means to protect the home and family and labels it instead a pretext for men to retain all political power and to eliminate any possibility of mothers' influence. Drous is no less direct with women who, failing to recognize the deception, perpetuate warfare by teaching their daughters to accept without question men's penchant for war.

> ...But man, generous, spares your weakness,
> He has to carry off fine crops of prizes.
> Isolated from the guns his profound wisdom
> Commands you to spell out murder to your sons.
>
> And you, tied to the centuries-old yoke
> Walking obediently toward the loathsome goal
> You remain submissive to the thousand-year-old law
> And pass on that law as a sacred text....[17]

The metaphor of the Danaidae is one of several allusions to classical mythology in Drous's poetry. These images balance her steadfast condemnation of the church for its endorsement of the war and allow Drous to substitute values which pre-date male-centred Christianity and recall a historical period of female supremacy. For example, to encourage her readers' bravery, she advises them to pray to Themis, the mother-goddess, as the only force capable of forcing men's pride to recognize mothers' rights (9). In the last stanza of the long poem 'Aux Mères' [To the Mothers], the classical image of the Vestal underscores Drous's belief in women's suffrage as the means to make the potential moral power of maternal love a viable political force:

> ...Woman, your hour is sounding...tear off your shroud...
> Be confident in yourself...Then, if from his high throne
> Man wishes to apply the Law to himself alone,
> If he jeers at your mission, insults your faith,
> And even your reason, accusing it of utopianism,
> Then, cause to rise up, o crouching Vestal,
> From London to Madrid, from Vienna to Petrograd
> And from the Palais-Bourbon to the heart of the Reichstag,
> To cover forever the voice of retaliation,
> The supreme and searing cry of your entrails.[18]

From these centres of power, Drous imagines that the influence of mothers' superior sense of reason and equity might permeate all levels of society. Although it is clear that she would welcome newly re-educated men, 'enamored of serene Justice' (9) to her postwar world, Drous does not consider that the institution of the church could be rehabilitated.

Contrasting the truth she recognizes in Jesus's precepts with the distortion and misrepresentation of those principles by priests who support wars, she rejects all forms of Christianity in favour of a maternally-inspired belief in life and love. For Drous, however, the greatest obstacle to the creation of such a classless matriarchate are women themselves who 'chloroform their hearts with words, drums, fifes, and bells' (17) and remain insensitive to the reality around them. In 'Le Blocus' [The Blockade] Drous notes with sadness mothers' support of a policy that results in children's starvation, for she had considered women's previous isolation from politics as a guarantee of the purity of their reason and judgement.

> ... I thought that, uplifted by bitter suffering,
> We would see share, mother with mother,
> The bread of which the children dream in their cradles.
>
> I thought that woman, in spite of the barriers,
> Always outside the plots of Cain,
> Could hold out to woman an innocent hand.
> That similar torments and similar prayers,
> The same despair rising from the cemeteries
> That the weight of the same fate was bearing down on all my
>   sisters. . . . [19]

Drous's plan for creating world peace is the most radical of the responses of the four poets to the event of the Great War. Her analysis calls into question the forces that create war and establishes system-based changes to curtail and control political power. Drous's reaction, along with the idealization of patriotic death in Noailles's poems, Périn's praise of self-sacrifice and suffering, and Sauret's weak attempt at revolt and final resignation, each evoke the power, rights and duties of love. The startling differences in each poet's vision of the role of love in war, however, demonstrate the inherent variety in their reaction to the conflict. Valorization of maternal love can lead to pacifism, but also may justify and reinforce the reasons for warfare. Awareness of the role society plays in determining women's public and private lives does not in itself imply an understanding or even a meditation on power relationships. Nor is there any evidence in the poetry of these writers to support the contention that women drew psychosexual energy from their war experience. The variety of ways in which these four French women of letters articulated their encounter with war suggests a parallel spectrum of reaction in the general French population. This plurality of response correctly demands a reassessment of the unquestioned assumption by scholars that the French reaction to the war, embodied in the famous Union Sacrée, was monolithic and homogeneous.

Notes

1. This essay is part of a longer study devoted to the literary response of French women to the Great War. I would like to thank Jackie Eller, Harold Goldberg, Yasmeen Mohiuddin and Monica Wright for their helpful comments and suggestions.
2. The same is true even among the so-called 'international' studies. A notable exception is Tim Cross's insightful anthology, *The Lost Voices of World War I*, which, although limited to writers who died as a result of the hostilities, includes far more than the three French poets permitted in Jon Silkin's *The Penguin Book of First World War Poetry*. Elizabeth Marsland's otherwise illuminating *The Nation's Cause, French, English and German Poetry of the First World War*, cites relatively few French poets so that the resulting analysis is largely extrapolated from the German and British experience, leading to oversimplified and sometimes uninformed judgements regarding France. Similarly, Evelyn Cobley's important study of first-person narratives of front-line experience, *Representing War, Form and Ideology in First World War Narratives*, mentions few French writers.
3. Many of France's most acclaimed and distinguished female poets published collections of war poetry during or immediately after the conflict. Among them were Magali Boisnard, whose volume of 1917, *Le Chant des femmes, poemes de guerre et d'amour* was awarded a prize from the Académie Française, and Henriette Charasson, whose book *Attente, 1914–1917*, published in 1919, also earned honours from the French Academy. Marie-Louise Dromart received citations for bravery as well as recognition from the Académie Française for her poetry buried in her garden in the Ardennes during the war and printed in 1924 under the title *Bel Ete*. Amelie Murat's *Humblement, sur l' autel . . . 1914–1919*, appearing in 1919, was one of several works which brought the poet various literary prizes, as well as membership in the prestigious Légion d'Honneur. Among many other poets of note are Adrienne Blanc-Peridier (*Le Cantique de la Patrie, 1914–1917*, published in 1918), Marie-Louise Clement (*La Nouvelle Epopée, poèmes et récits de guerre*, 1916), Jeanne Perdriel-Vaissiere (*La Complainte des jeunes filles qui ne seront pas épousées, 1919*), and Hélène Picard (*Rameaux*, 1919).
4. Since the following essay is a thematic study of each poet's comprehension of the war and its impact, the formal qualities of the poems will not be examined. The translations of the quoted material are my own; the original text will appear in the accompanying note. I have retained the original spelling and punctuation of the poems without regard to present-day usage.
5.

> Et pourtant, à présent, je sais que rien n'égale
> L'héroïque abandon, suprême et sans retour;
> Je sais que l'honneur est le faîte de l'amour;
> Et que la jeune mort est la mort triomphale.

> Je sais qu'ils ont atteint le but essentiel,
> Qu'ils ont vaincu la tombe et n'en sont pas victimes,
> Ces garçons soulevés hors de l'étau charnel,...
>
> (53–4).

6.
> ... Les yeux toujours levés, l'âme habitant l'espace,
> Le peuple féminin, comme un peuple d'oiseaux,
> Fendra la noble nue où jamais ne s'effacent
> Les exploits jaillis de vos os!...
>
> (75)

7.
> ... Toi, corps et coeur chétifs, mais en qui se pressait,
> Comme aux bourgeons sur l'arbre,
> Le renaissant printemps du grand destin français,
> Fait de rire et de marbre,
> – Enfant qui n'avais pas, avant le dur fléau,
> L'âme prédestinée à un devoir si haut, –
>
> (9–10)

8. While Périn's view on the war is in general consistent, one of her poems contained in this volume, 'Les Femmes de tous les pays' [Women of All Countries], criticizes women for their silent acceptance of the war. Périn argues that since happiness for women resides in the family unit, women everywhere should have done more to preserve its integrity. The theme of this poem is not echoed elsewhere in the volume and in fact is directly contradicted by a number of Périn's other poems. Nonetheless, Romain Rolland included 'Les Femmes de tous les pays' in his 1920 anthology of French anti-war poetry. Rolland apparently, like all anthologists, chose the poems that best fit the overall purpose of his project, in this case to prove that support for the war had not been unanimous.

9.
> Les mères sur leur coeur ont serré leurs enfants,
> Et puis, ouvrant les bras, ont dit: « Que s'accomplisse,
> France, puisqu'il le faut, ce premier sacrifice... »
> Et les ont vu partir en se taisant.
>
> Trop de douleur nouait leur gorge. Le silence
> Seul était assez large, assez pur, assez grand
> Pour contenir leur peine. Et leurs yeux, simplement,
> Ont regardé s'enfuir la route immense.
>
> (18)

10.
> ... Avons-nous tout donné quand il était possible
> D'offrir l'amour comme un bouquet?
> Des jours où le bonheur chuchotait, accessible
> Et caressant, qu'avons-nous fait?...
>
> (25)

11.
> Il est d'autres regards que les regards aimés.
> Il est, tu le sais bien, d'autres femmes qui pleurent;
> Il est, dans la misère affreuse des demeures,
> Beaucoup d'enfants abandonnés.

N'appuyons pas nos fronts sur nos mains en détresse
Où le regret s'avive et sanglote, cruel;
Que la douleur nous fasse un coeur plus fraternel,
Empli d'une immense tendresse.

(63)

12.   Vos fils de dix-huit ans, vos beaux garçons, avides,
D'aventure et de gloire, en chantant sont partis.
L'enthousiasme en eux, flamme auguste et splendide,
Brillait si purement que vous n'avez rien dit,

Que les plaintes mouraient sur vos lèvres timides,
Que devant tant d'espoir on restait interdit,
Car ces enfants d'hier qui devenaient nos guides
Nous auraient rudement fait honte de nos cris.

O jeunesse de France, exaltée et sublime,
Tu t'en vas vers la mort sans avoir su la vie,
Et tu t'élances vers l'abîme ou vers les cimes,
Sans vouloir avouer que tu te sacrifices ...

(31)

13.   Vos hommes sont sur les charniers
Mais vous êtes au fond des geôles
Et vous portez sur vos épaules
Le poids de l'immense péché.

Comment avez-vous pu ô femmes, laisser faire?
O femmes, ô femmes, c'est vous,
Par vos bras, vos voix, vos genoux,
Qui deviez empêcher la guerre! ...

(*L'Amour à la Géhenne*, 173–4)

14.   ... Et voilà. On les fit en ruban, vos entraves.
Qui, d'entre vous, les sent? Dix mille compliments
Pleuvent chaque matin sur vos têtes d'esclaves.
Misère! on vous jugule, on vous pipe, on vous ment! ...

(*Les Forces détournées*, 101)

15.   ... Puis il y a ceux de l'usine,
Ici l'absurdité raffine,
La femme qui travaille à nourrir les canons,
Porte un enfant dans son giron!
Symbole de l'heure moderne!
Toi qui t'ébauches sous l'haleine
De ces terribles ateliers,
Faut-il pas déjà pleurer? ...

(*Les Forces détournées*, 90)

16. For excellent accounts of the French women's suffrage movement during the war, see both Bard and Hause. A more general summary is contained in Albistur and Armogathe, 2: 556–85.

17.   ... Mais l'homme, généreux, épargne ta faiblesse,
           Il lui faut, de lauriers, faire d'amples moissons.
           A l'écart des canons sa profonde sagesse
           T'ordonne d'épeler le meurtre à tes garçons.

           Et toi, liée au joug plusieurs fois séculaire,
           Marchant docilement vers le but exécré,
           Tu demeures soumise à la loi millénaire
           Et transmets cette loi comme un texte sacré....
                                                          (8)

18.   ... Femme, ton heure tinte ... Arrache ton suaire ...
           Sois confiante en toi ... Puis, du haut de sa chaire,
           Si l'homme, à lui tout seul, veut imposer la Loi,
           Raille ta mission, s'il insulte à ta foi,
           Jusques à ta raison, l'accuse d'utopie,
           Alors, fais s'élever, ô Vestale accroupie,
           De Londres à Madrid, de Vienne à Pétrograd
           Et du Palais-Bourbon et du sein du Reischtagd [*sic*],
           Pour couvrir à jamais la voix des représailles,
           Suprême et déchirant, le cri de tes entrailles!
                                                          (6)

19.   ... Je pensais que, grandis par la souffrance amère,
           Nous verrions partager, la mère avec la mère,
           Le pain que les petits rêvent en leurs berceaux.

           Je croyais que la femme, en dépit des barrières,
           Etrangère toujours aux complots de Caïn,
           Pouvait tendre à la femme une innocente main.
           Que semblables tourments et semblables prières,
           Qu'un même désespoir montant des cimetières
           Courbaient toutes mes soeurs sous le même destin....
                                                          (17)

Works cited

Albistur, Maïté and Daniel Armogathe. *Histoire du féminisme français*, 2 vols. Paris: Des femmes, 1977.

Bard, Christine. *Les Filles de Marianne. Histoire des féminismes 1914–1940*. Paris: Fayard, 1995.

Berkin, Carol and Clara Lovett (eds) *Women, War, and Revolution*. New York: Holmes & Meier, 1980.

Brioche, François. *Anna de Noailles, un mystère en pleine lumière*. Paris: Robert Laffont, 1989.

Chodorow, Nancy. *The Reproduction of Mothering: Psychoanalysis and the Sociology of Gender*. Berkeley, CA: University of California Press, 1978.

Cobley, Evelyn. *Representing War, Form and Ideology in First World War Narratives*. Toronto: University of Toronto Press, 1993.

Cross, Tim (ed.) *The Lost Voices of World War I*. Iowa City: Iowa University Press, 1988.

Cruickshank, John. *Variations on Catastrophe: Some French Responses to the Great War*. Oxford: Clarendon Press, 1982.

Drous, Noélie. *Sous la tempête*. Épone, France: Société d'édition et de librairie de l'avenir social, 1920.

Flottes, Pierre. *Histoire de la poésie politique et sociale en France de 1815 à 1939*. Paris: Pensée universelle, 1976.

Fussell, Paul. *The Great War and Modern Memory*. London: Oxford University Press, 1975.

Gilbert, Sandra and Susan Gubar. *No Man's Land*, 3 vols. New Haven, CT and London: Yale University Press, 1989.

Gilligan, Carol. *In a Different Voice*. Cambridge, MA: Harvard University Press, 1982.

Goldberg, Nancy Sloan. *En l'honneur de la juste parole: la poésie française contre la Grande Guerre*. New York: Lang, 1993.

Hause, Steven. 'More Minerva than Mars: the French women's rights campaign and the First World War', in Higonnet et al., 99–113.

——. *Women's Suffrage and Social Politics in the French Third Republic*. Princeton, NJ: Princeton University Press, 1984.

Higonnet, Margaret Randolph, Jane Jenson, Sonya Michel and Margaret Collins Weitz (eds) *Behind the Lines: Gender and the Two Wars*. New Haven, CT and London: Yale University Press, 1987.

Hunter, Anne (ed.) *On Peace, War, and Gender: A Challenge to Genetic Explanations*, Genes and Gender VI. New York: Feminist Press, 1991.

Khan, Nosheen. *Women's Poetry of the First World War*. Lexington: University Press of Kentucky, 1988.

McAllister, Pam (ed.) *Reweaving the Web of Life: Feminism and Nonviolence*. Philadelphia: New Society Publishers, 1982.

Marsland, Elizabeth. *The Nation's Cause, French, English and German Poetry of the First World War*. London: Routledge, 1991.

Noailles, Anna de. *Les Forces éternelles*. Paris: Fayard, 1920.

Ouditt, Sharon. *Fighting Forces, Writing Women*. London: Routledge, 1994.

Périn, Cécile. *Les Captives, poèmes 1914–1918*. Paris: Sansot, 1919.

Reilly, Catherine. *Scars Upon my Heart: Women's Poetry and Verse of the First World War*. London: Virago, 1981.

Riegel, Léon. *Guerre et Littérature: le bouleversement des consciences dans la littérature romanesque inspirée par la Grande Guerre*. Paris: Klincksieck, 1978.

Rolland, Romain (ed.) *Les Poètes contre la guerre*. Geneva: Sablier, 1920.

Ruddick, Sara. 'Maternal Thinking', in Treblicot, 213–30.

——. 'Preservation love and military destruction: some reflections on mothering and peace', in Treblicot, 231–62.

Salamone, Connie. 'The prevalence of natural law within women: women and animal rights,' in McAllister, 364–75.

Sauret, Henriette, *L'Amour à la Géhenne*. Paris: Société mutuelle d'édition, 1919.

——. *Les Forces détournées 1914–1917*. Paris: Librairie d'action d'art de la ghilde 'Les Forgerons', 1918.

Scott, Joan W. 'Gender: a useful category of historical analysis', *American Historical Review*, 91 (1986): 1053–75.

Silkin, Jon. *The Penguin Book of First World War Poetry*, 2nd edn. Middlesex, England: Penguin Books, 1981.

Treblicot, Joyce (ed.) *Mothering: Essays in Feminist Theory*. Totowa, NJ: Rowman & Allanheld, 1983.

Tylee, Claire. *The Great War and Women's Consciousness*. Iowa City: University of Iowa Press, 1990.

Zanotti, Barbara. 'Patriarchy: a state of war', in McAllister, 16–19.

8
Myrmidons to Insubordinates: Australian, New Zealand and Canadian Women's Fictional Responses to the Great War

Donna Coates

In her 1915 collection of essays titled *In Times Like These*, Canadian writer and activist Nellie McClung decries what she perceives to be a major problem in Canadian society – women's exclusion from war:

> War is a crime committed by men and, therefore, when enough people say it shall not be, it cannot be. This will not happen until women are allowed to say what they think of war. Up to the present time women have had nothing to say about war, except pay the price of war – this privilege has been theirs always.
>
> (15)

While I don't agree with McClung that the inclusion of women's voices in wartime will necessarily bring an end to war, I do lament that her words are still timely, for women's voices continue to be absent from war. Women have been robbed of the right to express themselves, for the war novels which have attained literary status have been written by men, and the study of war literature has, until recently, been an exclusive male domain.

In the three postcolonial cultures which interest me – Canada, Australia and New Zealand – the study of women's First World War writing has been completely neglected. Eric Thompson's 1981 essay, sweepingly titled 'Canadian Fiction and the Great War', purports to be comprehensive, but Thompson restricts his analysis to the experience of the Canadian fighting soldier, and omits entirely mention of the fine wartime novels by Nellie McClung (*The Next of Kin: Those Who Wait and Wonder*), Lucy

Maud Montgomery (*Rilla of Ingleside*), Francis Marion Beynon (*Aleta Dey*), Evah McKowan (*Janét of Kootenay: Life, Love, and Laughter in an Arcady of the West*), Gertrude Arnold (*Sister Anne! Sister Anne!!*) and Grace Blackburn (*The Man Child*). In his 1987 full-length study *Big-Noting: The Heroic Theme in Australian War Writing*, Robin Gerster mentions briefly fiction by Ethel Turner (*Brigid and the Cub, Captain Cub, The Cub*), Mary Grant Bruce (*From Billabong to London, Captain Jim, Jim and Wally*) and Angela Thirkell (*Trooper to the Southern Cross*), but disregards entirely works by Mabel Brookes (*Broken Idols, Old Desires, On the Knees of the Gods*), M[ollie] L. Skinner (*Letters of a V. A. D.* [under pseudonym R. L. Leake], *Tucker Sees India*), Annie Rixon (*The Scarlet Cape, Yesterday and Today*), Gladys Hain (*The Coo-ee Contingent*), Ray Phillips (*The White Feather*), M[ay] I. Howson (*Love's Sacrifice (Founded on Facts): A Book From the Trenches Depicting Undying Love*), Kathleen Watson (*Henriette Says!*), Katherine Pearson (*Hugh Royston*), Doris Manners-Sutton (*A Marked Soul*), Chrystal Stirling (*Soldiers Two*), Mary Marlowe (*The Women Who Wait*) and Linda Webb Burge (*Wings above the Storm*), most of which would have added valuable ammunition to his thesis.[1] In New Zealand, only Heather Roberts' *Where Did She Come From? New Zealand Women Novelists 1862–1987* acknowledges women's Great War writing; she discusses briefly works by Margaret Gibbons (*An Anzac's Bride*), Nelle M. Scanlan (*Tides of Youth*) and Jane Mander (*The Besieging City, The Strange Attraction*). The disappearance of women's fiction in Canada, Australia and New Zealand reinforces the deeply rooted belief that women, safe at home, never had any right to enter the discourse of war. The weaponless, critics have assumed, were wordless.

When I began to retrieve from obscurity Canadian, Australian and New Zealand women's Great War fiction, to unhide the hidden, I assumed that I would bring to light texts which contained similar patterns and themes for, at the outbreak of war, all three were small, sparsely populated postcolonial cultures eager to rush to the defence of Mother England during her time of need; all three countries had little martial experience and were vast distances from the field of battle. But comparative studies are useful for what they reveal; rather than similarities, I found primarily differences.

Australian women writers, I discovered, did not write their own novels, but had them written for them by the dominant ideology which permitted only one voice, a single interpretation of war which essentially glorified the Anzacs' participation in the hostilities. According to Gerster, Australian (male) war writers had a tendency to 'big-note', which he defines as 'the giving of extravagant praise to oneself or the exaggeration of one's own importance'; but while he further claims this proclivity is 'everywhere evident in First A. I. F. literature' (3), he refers almost exclusively to those writers who either participated directly in combat, gave orders from behind the lines or were male civilians who jumped on the Anzac adulation bandwagon. Women writers could not swap bayonets for pens, but they could sing the praises of the soldier, and did. In their texts, the figure of the Anzac looms large, his fighting prowess dominating to the extent that it 'kills' the woman's narrative altogether. Dutiful myrmidons, women writers took their orders from war correspondents like C. E. W. Bean and the poet C. J. Dennis, and were their mouthpieces or interlocutors, not tellers of their own stories. Furthermore, because women writers continuously laud the Anzacs' participation in war, their fiction is anachronistic and out of step with other literary traditions. That several of the most male-dominated texts appear as late as the 1940s indicates women writers' prolonged enthusiasm for the event, their slavish devotion to hegemonic tradition.

Whereas Gerster identifies these characteristics in Australian male writing as nonconformist, however, I suggest that when they appear in women's writing, they reflect a unique form of female powerlessness. In shoring up, not shattering, reigning ideologies, their texts differ significantly from those by British, American and Canadian writers which foreground strong women determined to make their part in war matter. In her study of American and British women's war writing, Sandra Gilbert argues that the Great War served to empower women psychologically, economically and sexually; throughout her essay, Gilbert employs words such as 'glee', 'exuberance' and 'triumph' to describe writers' enthusiastic response to war, which (alas only temporarily) liberated women from cloistered environments, confining clothing and tedious domestic chores.[2] Canadian writers demonstrate in their texts a less jubilant, more subdued response, but they do reveal women seizing war as an opportunity to loosen the patriarchal grip on their lives. And in both Canadian and New Zealand texts, heroines move out of the home and hearth and take up meaningful occupations which give them strength and confidence in their abilities. In Canada particularly, amid the chaos occasioned by war, writers insist that the time is ripe to restructure society, to create a 'new world order' which incorporates women's voices and values into the design.

But in Australia, women writers are obsessed with hero worship of the Anzac, not with societal reform or the liberation of women. Several women writers – Hain, Burge, Rixon – undergo paper sex changes and send a man off to war, thereby replicating the master narrative of the soldier in the trenches and nullifying their own voices as women, to whom they hand barely speaking parts and walk-on roles in their texts. Other writers – Stirling, Grant Bruce, Turner, Phillips, Brookes – play out a tug-of-war, a 'star wars' battle for centre stage between hero and shero, from which the Digger inevitably emerges victorious; writers deem *his* story more worthy of the telling. In allowing women's voices to evaporate, these women writers deny the legitimacy of a woman's story in war, and reaffirm the central importance of the soldier's story in Australian fiction.

In committing themselves to Anzac aggrandizement, women writers do not deploy their works as artillery to overcome marginalization. Instead, they uphold conventional pursuits for women: rarely do they argue that women's emancipation from marriage and motherhood is possible, or even desirable. Missing from the texts by Hain, Grant Bruce, Turner, Brookes, Burge, Phillips, Rixon, and Stirling is a candid confession of women's desire for power and control over their own lives; consistently, female characters remain male-identified as wives, daughters, sweethearts (rarely mothers – not only are these texts 'fathered', they are also 'de-mothered'). Moreover, these texts consistently display women suspended in holding patterns, waiting, in static and silent submission, for their loved ones to come home. While anticipating war's end (and hence a return to prewar existence), they cling to traditional pastimes: they knit, nurse, weep and wait. Some female characters engage in occasional volunteer wartime work, but halfheartedly; they view their tasks as diversionary, something to fill in the time or to relieve anxiety, but not as significant donations to the war effort. Moreover, women's volunteer tasks serve as opportunities for writers to give voice to the wounded, but never downhearted, Anzac. Other fictional characters concentrate on recruitment, on getting a man to the front, but their 'white-feather' activities are devoid of intellectual underpinnings. No women in these texts emerge from the private sphere to wear the pants, to step into men's shoes for paid employment or to take up 'brilliant careers'. Since marriage is the only profession open to women, it matters not if the soldier returns maimed, blind, armless or legless, for in this society, even a husband who cannot wear the pants is better than no husband at all. And because competition for a lifetime partner is stiff, women level much hostility at war brides; they regard one another as enemies, not allies, and routinely choose men as their confidants. None works collectively to overcome subordination, and any woman who shows signs of transgressing social codes is quickly punished and restored to her proper place as wife and homemaker. As well, Australian women writers create negative views of their sex, illustrating that they have internalized one of patriarchy's basic tenets – misogyny: several women refer to their sex as useless, others state that women are too emotional and irrational to hold public office.

Throughout their brief history, Australian women had been conditioned to think of themselves as the second sex, for they inhabited a patriarchal society which had since its inception as a penal colony either ignored them or treated them with indifference and even enmity. A surfeit of critics – Beryl Donaldson Langer, Anne Summers, Dorothy Jones, Miriam Dixson, Marilyn Lake, Susan Sheridan and Kay Schaffer – have documented Australian women's historically marginal status in their society. Langer contends that women's exclusion from Australian culture and identity became evident in the colonial period, but during the nationalist, myth-making 1890s their absence was explicitly confirmed. Prominent writers like Henry Lawson, Joseph Furphy, Banjo Paterson and Steele Rudd privileged the noble bushman's values of rugged manliness, anti-authoritarianism, ready initiative in a hostile environment and irreverence; at the same time, these writers viewed women as agents of restriction and restraint, as inhibitors of male pleasure, and dismissed them as overly concerned with manners and fashion (Langer, 78). Summers writes that male writers of the period were anxious to transpose what they deemed positive male characteristics into a living legend, and they succeeded (36–7). And in this society, charges Dorothy Jones, where men mythologize themselves and exclude women, the latter's only defence against isolation is to try to fit themselves into the myth, to be 'myth-fits' ('Mapping', 74). (Jones derives this clever term from Thea Astley, who coined it in *An Item From the Late News*.) Some writers, like Barbara Baynton and Miles Franklin, became adept at camouflage: they chose the bush as their setting and depicted, in bush vernacular, typical egalitarian values. In accommodating their writing to the bush, writes Sheridan, they earned approbation from such patriarchal figures as Henry Lawson and A. G. Stephens, editor of the influential and 'offensively masculine' *Bulletin* magazine, who praised them for 'transcending their female qualities and preoccupations' and contributing to 'this masculine construction of "the Bush"' (54). But Summers argues that, in writing within male tradition, 'myth-fits' inevitably suffer: their situation becomes 'precarious and almost inevitably dishonest, for by conforming to men's ideals, they are denying something in themselves' (40). They cannot write about the bush as if they are men: rather, they are forced to 'draw a wide canvas and to write about whole settlements and communities', or to write about individual women as if they are somehow 'separated from the norm' (37). Women writers dared not create strong females who might rival the bushman, nor dared they hazard writing honestly about what life in the bush looked like from their more familiar vantage point of the kitchen or child's bedroom (37–8). Women were trapped in a catch-22: if they failed to write about the bush and male experience, they found their work dismissed for being outside the range of serious subjects; if they examined subjects like marriage, pregnancy, sexual hypocrisy, their fictions were deemed not relevant to national literature (Langer, 78). Sheridan argues that the novels by the 1890s writers Ada Cambridge, Mrs Campbell Praed and 'Tasma' (Jessie Couveur) were published in accessible forms, widely circulated and garnered a large readership (51), but because women wrote about social life in the cities and the relations between the sexes, they were discredited for writing inferior novels (53). Jones concurs, finding that women authors who did not extol the virtues of mateship and the bush but chose instead to draw their matter from urban and domestic life found their worked 'criticized as lightweight, and even un-Australian' ('Canon', 72). Even though these 'women's books' were acclaimed on publication (Sheridan, 51), they nonetheless fell rapidly out of sight, whereas those which upheld nationalist masculine values formed the traditional canon (Jones, 'Canon', 73).

The advent of the First World War compounded this already problematic situation for women writers, because the myth of the noble bushman, on the wane by the beginning of the twentieth century, did not die out as Australian society became increasingly urban, but zoomed like a boomerang from bush to battlefield and became entrenched as the myth of the Anzac soldier or the Anzac legend. Writing against the bush myth had always been difficult for Australian women writers, but writing against this revised, more potent myth was even more intimidating. In the brave new Digger figure's reincarnation, he picked up some stellar characteristics while retaining the old. He was newly handsome, cosmopolitan, well read, suave, charming to women, as well as a ferocious foe. Several critics – Lake, Summers, Schaffer – have observed the progression from noble bushman into Anzac, but none has considered the negative impact this mythical figure had on women's wartime literature. This larger-than-life warrior demanded attention – and got it, for in spite of the many obstacles in their path, many female 'recruits' attempted the pen. Women writers sublimated their own needs and desires, absented themselves from the war narrative, took the battlefront as their focus, and backed the Diggers' attack. In writing about men at war, they would have felt they were tackling serious subject material. But they lost the literary war, for their writing, which meticulously followed the dictates of the dominant ideology, was overlooked. Unlike women writers of the bush, who received praise for adopting the standards and preoccupations that patriarchal society defined for them, women wartime writers were completely ignored. Gerster's omission is proof of that neglect.

Women suffered more than indifference, however, for in 'big-noting' the Anzac, they failed to take up issues considered of special interest to women, such as pacifism or temperance. No female characters discuss conscription, a curious omission since women were intensely involved in the heated debates that proved so divisive on the home front.[3] None challenges the makers of war; none questions how war affects women's lives; none interrogates why men go to war. Ideological discussions on war are brief and sketchy, and take place primarily between soldiers. Whatever male writers said about Australian men at war, women writers mimicked; they did not determine their own views of war, or try to come to terms with what it meant to them as women. Thus their novels are, for the most part, a working out in fiction of a male assessment of Australian soldiers – these men who displayed extreme valour and courage against overwhelming odds and achieved 'nationhood' for Australia.[4]

In making Anzacs superheroes, tenacious and indefatigable good 'mates' and savage fighters, Australian women writers were repeating the master narrative, retelling Bean's official story. But their worship of the Anzac estranged women from their own experiences, for they could not reflect them while mimicking a man's view. Women writers, forced to celebrate an event they could not attend, were unable to use their writing to record their frustration at being handed passive and trivial roles on the homefront; unable to be the stars of their own home front wars, they could only shoot blanks at patriarchy. In foregrounding male adventure, disseminating values they did not help formulate, they produced inauthentic art, and wrote dangerous and distorted views of war. And in allowing their narratives to be completely usurped, they fell prey to what Mark Schorer terms women's ultimate anonymity, to be 'storyless' (cited in Heilbrun, 12). In succumbing to what Sharon O'Brien terms 'combat envy' (188), Australian women writers facilitated their own domination, and left no path for future women (writers) to follow.

That so many Australian women writers meticulously replicate the narratives of the dominant patriarchal discourse is singular, and for this reason I would argue that their writing is of unique literary interest. In making this claim, I differ from Bassett, who contends that '[p]oetry and verse, personal narratives, and popular novels written by Australian women about the Great War are generally of much greater historical interest than literary significance' (223). But no other sources inform readers of the extent to which women were oppressed in Australia during the war. Historians like Michael McKernan document that Australian women failed to hunt out paying jobs; social historians like Patsy Adam-Smith apprise the fervour with which women threw themselves into volunteer work. Only women fiction writers, especially those who efface their own stories, confirm how insignificant the dominant culture considered women to be.

In New Zealand and Canada, by contrast, women writers do not have to adhere to a single myth, a prescribed set of values, or act as magnifying mirrors to bolster male ego and fighting prowess. Their soldiers, primarily located on the margins of these stories, most often go to war reluctantly and return, as soon as possible, to the farms and factories of peace. Both Canadian and New Zealand texts feature sensitive young men who do not wish to fight, but enlist out of a deep sense of duty and loyalty, a dilemma these women writers, particularly Montgomery and Scanlan, explore with compassion. In both countries as well, soldiers may suffer from shell shock, an affliction unheard of in Australia except as it affects the Tommy, whom writers like Mabel Brookes routinely portray as weak and puny. In her texts, she implies that a form of 'tommy rot' has set in, for the English soldier is a product of a dismal climate and a social class which tolerates indolence and dissipation; hence he is no match for the stalwart Anzac, who never exhibits any deficiencies whatsoever. In Canada and New Zealand, while men are 'good' at combat, women writers staunchly resist the notion of either individual or collective heroism. Significantly, the most praiseworthy act a soldier performs in a Canadian novel is a literary feat; in Montgomery's *Rilla of Ingleside*, a young soldier writes a poem, a classic from its first printing, thereby distinguishing himself and his country with the point of a pen, not the tip of a bayonet. And unlike Australian texts, where the Aussie never admits defeat, is never downhearted but finds being at war 'a wonderful life',[5] Canadian and New Zealand soldiers send letters home from the trenches acknowledging that they're fighting under inhumane conditions and testifying that any notions they might have held about the honour and glory of war have quickly evaporated.

While the representation of soldiers is similar in New Zealand and Canada, the depiction of women varies significantly. It's difficult to generalize about New Zealand women's wartime fictions, however, because there are only a handful of texts to consider, none of which takes the war exclusively as its focus.[6] Heather Roberts speculates that the large-scale devastation of human life – of the 100 000 New Zealand men who went to war, 16 000 died and 45 000 were wounded, so that well over half suffered physically in combat – meant that 'the war was too painful an experience for novelists to feel confident writing about' (39). This argument is unconvincing, though, for many women novelists in Australia and Canada also suffered keenly, yet many took up the war-time pen. Murray further posits that women saw war as being outside their experience; here, she may be correct, since few novels concentrate exclusively on the war years.[7] The only one which does, Margaret Gibbons's *An Anzac's Bride*, is set in England during the war. It features a 'stalwart' Anzac who has survived the 'hellfire' of Gallipoli. He meets a talented young violinist in England whom he marries before going to fight, this time in Flanders Fields; but on their honeymoon, the New Zealand soldier falsely accuses his innocent English bride of infidelity and then cruelly deserts her. Since she's a penniless orphan charged with the care of her crippled sister and preyed upon by a deranged man, it could be argued that she endures as much physical pain and anguish as her Anzac husband, even though he fights at the Somme, is taken prisoner of war and suffers the loss of an eye. While the heroine is 'plucky' and the Anzac eventually redeems himself, the storyline is melodramatic and implausible, the war merely a shadowy backdrop for the action.

Popular fiction writer Scanlan's *Tides of Youth*, the second volume of her popular *Pencarrow* series, provides a brief account of how New Zealand women 'occupied' their time when their sons and lovers sailed away to war. The text features a lawyer who readily takes on 'the work of three men' (245), and a mother who raises several children at the same time as she singlehandedly runs a large-scale farming operation; both women also carry out extensive fundraising and organizing duties. Their engagement in such exhausting undertakings helps keep them sane when their personal lives are collapsing, yet at the same time assures them they are making worthwhile contributions to the war effort. Scanlon also offers a fascinating glimpse into the workings of the Military Appeal Board, giving her readers some idea of the process by which men could evade conscription. But as Terry Sturm argues, although the first three volumes of the *Pencarrow* series are 'remarkably skilled in their manipulation of local conflict, exploiting it to the full but knowing when and how to absorb it into the novel's powerful general illusion of a universal drama of civilization and progress', the books lack 'conscious engagement with ideas in the novels' (509), and topics such as 'politics, economics, race relations . . . barely touch the novels in their own terms, but simply provide occasions for the unfolding of a drama whose true centre lies in the power relations of the domestic life of the family' (510). To that list, Sturm might have added war, for while Scanlan gives a brief account of New Zealand's participation in the First World War, she does not provide any serious discussion of the issues arising out of the war, or women's place in it.

Similarly, although Jane Mander reputedly draws upon her own experiences working for the Red Cross in New York in *The Besieging City*, her central character, Chris Mayne, comes from Australia, has lived for long periods in England, is a recent graduate of Columbia University and a freelance writer and budding novelist. Chris declares that she longs to do useful wartime work and quickly finds a job at the Red Cross, but she expresses disdain for her duties, which she considers appropriate for wealthy women only. She confesses that she wants to gain from her war work 'something more than the satisfaction of "doing her bit" and enough money to pay for her rent and food' (36); yet what she really seeks is a lover, 'somebody she could care greatly about' (36). As a result, she tells us almost nothing about how the war affects her and other New Yorkers, and since peace is declared one-third of the way through the text, Mander quickly drops the subject altogether. Even though the critic Dorothea Turner describes the novel, surprisingly, as an 'immense ode to wartime and immediate postwar New York' (87), she makes no further mention of the war again in her analysis of the text, perhaps because the subject is 'missing'. The war does intrude at the end of Mander's *The Strange Attraction*: her protagonist, the feisty journalist Valerie Carr, wants to be 'in' war so badly that she abandons her dying husband (he has inoperable cancer and, withholding the true reason, dismisses her from their partnership) and rushes off to 'enlist' in Auckland. Mander seems reluctant to consider what role her somewhat cavalier (s)hero might play in war, for she ends the novel at this point.

In Canadian texts, by contrast, no similar reticence exists. Rather, one of the common threads which runs through these fictions is women writers' awareness that their voices and values are marginalized in wartime. McClung points directly to this omission in *The Next of Kin* by having one of her characters complain that her husband has enlisted without first consulting her; the man's response is telling: 'The country's business concerns men, not women. . . . Men are concerned with the big things of life' (177). Women, in his opinion, are 'missing' from the subject of war. To be sure, at the outbreak of war, many women in these fictions feel that they have no role to play in wartime; with few historical or literary predecessors to tell them how to 'occupy' themselves in wartime, they are characters without texts. The occasional women written into war literature provide unsatisfactory role models: Penelope weaves and re-weaves; Desdemona is merely a 'captive' audience to her soldier's tale of fortune. Not surprisingly, then, Montgomery's youthful Rilla expresses bitter resentment at her lover's repudiation of her when the Empire calls, especially since she believes she has nothing (except tears) to substitute in his place: 'Women . . . just had to sit and cry at home' (35). To her, war signifies absence and rejection.

Rilla's observation about gendered activities in wartime is astute; a man can respond to a 'roll call' whereas a woman has to devise her own 'role' without benefit of manuals or reference books which prescribe her duties. But once a man decides to enlist, the rest is easy: the military attends to his physical needs and dictates his movements thereafter. Moreover, a recruit knows (or thinks he knows), what going to war entails.[8] Nancy Huston contends that the enlisted man can conjure up centuries of illustrious models from history which 'reinforce his conviction to fight and justify his acts' (272). Correspondingly, several recruits in Canadian women's novels envision their participation in war based on the accounts of war they have read. Blackburn's inductee in *The Man Child* enlists because he has assimilated tales of 'honour and glory' (234). One of Montgomery's conscripts, a medical man in training, is enticed to war because he has ingested the heroic actions of a doctor on the battlefront during the Balkan War (25). In going to war, draftees may be hoping to satisfy what Nancy K. Miller, drawing upon Freud's theories on dreams and wish fulfilment, terms 'egoistic and ambitious wishes' (346). In master narratives, the hero knows that he will be exposed to danger, undergo perilous adventure but eventually emerge triumphant. Because history and literature are written by winners, and war narratives are 'heroic' not 'enemic' tales (Huston, 273), he feels invincible: 'Nothing can happen to me' (Miller, 346). Should the young man not survive the conflict, he dies a hero 'in action', making a sacrifice in the service of his country, making *his*tory. In answering the call to arms, he cannot lose; he faces what might be termed a positive catch-22. But war absents women, renders them unimportant in the face of mighty concepts and the male anguish of battles. And at the time of the Great War, love and marriage are women's prime destinies, so adolescents like Rilla can have only 'erotic wishes' (Miller, 364). When her sweetheart vanishes, the message to Rilla is clear: 'Nothing can happen to me' (Miller, 346). Rilla suffers from 'combat envy' (192), but not for long.

Anything can, and does, happen to Canadian women in the wartime climate, for the absence of men brings about positive results. In fact, it could be argued that Canadian writers are war profiteers, seizing the chaos occasioned by war to vanquish women's subordinate status. In their texts, they insist upon bringing an end to the image of women as care-givers and nurturers, and forcefully reiterate that women deserve a place in society alongside men, not as their subalterns. Writers express their anger that women have been denied access to public and political realms, caution that they can no longer afford to be onlookers in a man's world, and beseech their characters to make their presence felt during the war. With women's voices and values part of a 'new world order', they argue, Canada will be a better place for all.

Although it sounds callous, in *The Next of Kin* and other texts, there is a feeling of jubilation in the air, a sensation akin to the cliché, 'While the cat's away, the mice will play.' One of McClung's characters captures this statement, stating,

> 'I was like the mouse who timidly tiptoed out to the saucer of brandy, and, taking a sip, went more boldly back, then came again with considerable swagger; and at last took a good drink and then strutted up and down saying, "Bring on your old black cat!"'
>
> (191)

Prior to the war, this woman was docile and submissive, obedient to her autocratic husband's every command. Thanks to the war, she learns to defy his dictates, and to stick up for what she believes in and what she knows is right. But that McClung, a well-known supporter of the women's temperance movement, should depict a woman drinking brandy is remarkable. After a tiny sip, her character gains courage; she's back for more. Both drink and power ('swagger') are addictive. McClung thus urges women not to be dutiful myrmidons, but to be insubordinate, to 'fight the good fight' against the patriarchal structures that imprison them. *The Next of Kin* issues a warning to men: look out, it says, for the battle between the sexes is just beginning, and women are determined to win.

Throughout their texts, Canadian women writers emphasize that women are intelligent beings who have been prevented from developing their talents and mental faculties to the full, and stress that it is a foolish society which denies women's unique ways of knowing. In order to sharpen women's defences, writers entreat their female characters to develop their intellectual might. One of the oft-repeated words in these texts is 'think'. The novels admonish women to eschew simplistic thinking, to recognize that most issues are complex, and to reject the notion that only men can lay claim to authority. McClung, for example, refers to the war as a 'great teacher' (99), and in part what she means is that, without so many men around telling women what to think, they can learn to reason for themselves. Several novels deconstruct the notion of authority by refusing to tell readers what conclusions to draw, or what opinions about war to hold. Montgomery, for instance, explores the war from a variety of points of view, but leaves readers free to find their own answers.[9] And while historians assume that Beynon's fiction (like her journalism) argues in favour of pacifism, I suggest that, like Montgomery, she refuses to orchestrate her readers' opinions.[10] Beynon simply counsels her characters to ensure they are in possession of all the facts, for only then can they reach sound conclusions and make the best decisions. While she encourages her characters to read, she also recommends they trust to their basic instincts, for personal experience, she advises, is also a worthy basis from which to govern one's behaviour. Blackburn has a similar 'message': like Beynon, she abhors the suppression of any voices or experiences, especially women's.

It is misleading, though, to imply that all women speak with 'uniform' voices, or hold similar ideological positions about the waging of war, for McClung (unlike the others) takes a pro-war stance and encourages men to fight.[11] While McClung's truculence cannot be denied, I believe that her major concern in *The Next of Kin* is to bring about long-lasting social change, which she envisions will occur once women become actively involved in Canadian society. For example, through her narrator, she urges members of her community to work together to counteract childhood poverty and death from disease, and to bring about an end to 'extravagance' and 'general shiftlessness' (95). The narrator pushes for prohibition, much-needed legislation in times like those, for when alcohol was cheaper than milk men drank to excess, depriving their families often of ready cash, and battering their wives as well (40). Identifying a number of social ills, McClung's text throws down the gauntlet to Canadians, challenging them to restructure their society so that it includes women's worth and experience. With so many men overseas holding up the pillars of Empire, McClung's narrator urges that the time is ripe to take advantage of their absence. Once liberated from their homes, women can take up residences at important houses like the House of Commons and the House of Lords. Both institutions (which hitherto have denied women access to important positions) will benefit from women's independent thinking. She advises women to seize the day for

reform, to ensure that on the day of reckoning – war's end – there will
be more to show for it than bloodshed and waste. In *The Next of Kin*,
McClung sends her narrator on the warpath, exhorting women to disrupt
and destabilize the patriarchal structures which imprison them.

One of the tactics Canadian women writers employ in order to
emphasize that women are not men's inferiors is to show women 'in
action', functioning in the workplace as effectively as any man. In
Canadian novels, many women 'enlist' in the public sphere, wearing
the pants in the absence of men on the home front. Specifically, novels
like McKowan's stress that women can succeed at any occupation they
choose: anything a man can do a women can do even better. McKowan's
protagonist, who hates being trapped inside a house, has several times
challenged the circumscribed nature of women's place in society. She
has been a teacher, a reporter and homesteader in Ontario, Manitoba
and Saskatchewan respectively. Moving 'farther west', she arrives in
British Columbia in 1917, where she intends to 'do a man's work' as a
mixed farmer (21). Initially, she faces harsh criticism: the men doubt
her ability to farm at all (29); the women ridicule her for wearing riding
breeches and leggings (20); and the members of the rural community
assume that Janet has come to the region because she has 'matrimonial
designs' (39).

But before long, Janet wins the respect of the community because she
survives so well on her own. With the war raging, and the plumbers,
plasterers and stonemasons all away fighting Germans, Janet proves
that she is far from defenceless. She 'plumbs' from a book, lays her own
dynamite, and handily erects her house and outer buildings by herself.
To her correspondent, Nan (the novel takes an epistolary style), she
expresses her jubilant victory: 'Every man, I felt sure, expected me to end
by calling in his superior masculine aid – and how I would have loved
to have done so – but I felt it was up to me to demonstrate my theories
of feminine independence, then and there' (48). In quick time, Janet
establishes herself as a superb market gardener, fruit farmer and stock
raiser, and thus serves as a role model for younger women in the community, who testify that they have gained inspiration from witnessing
her struggle. As a result of Janet's influence, these 'new women' wear
pants and ride motorbikes (155). Janet's agricultural ventures burgeon
to the extent that she eventually needs a partner; of course, she joins
forces with another capable woman.

In making the claim that women can be effective co-workers in the
labour force, Canadian women writers also address the place of women
within the institution of marriage. McKowan's Janet, for instance, is not

against marriage per se, but she wants union with a partner on her own terms, as her non-traditional engagement attests. Janet herself proposes marriage to that rarest of creatures – a nurturing man – who has proven that he is attracted to, and not threatened by, an energetic, efficient woman. A British officer (significantly non-Canadian?) wounded at the Marne, he cheerfully goes along with Janet's plans. She furnishes a car, plans to drive it on their honeymoon, and quite rightly rejoices in the fact that her intended never once objects to her arrangements. 'That should auger well for our future together,' she writes Nan (277). Indeed.

In *The Man Child*, Blackburn also underscores the importance of work, and illustrates that a woman can live happily even after the death of her husband. Her central character Emma Winchester is distraught when she learns that she has insufficient funds to support herself and her newborn child. Only temporarily stymied, Emma takes in sewing and gives piano lessons, and thus raises her son without relying on others. Through dint of hard work, frugality and resourcefulness, she manages to provide her son with a university education. Shortly after being widowed, Emma receives a proposal from a man she admires greatly; she declines the offer, even though marriage would make her life considerably easier. In suggesting that women can be self-sufficient and independent workers in the public sphere, in arguing that women can be fulfilled without husbands, Canadian women writers were rewriting the conventional marriage plot. Signalling their dissatisfaction with the general destiny of women, writers like Blackburn and McKowan were utilizing the home front in their books as a radical site for social change.

Another of the writers' main objectives was to document women's responses to war, a task McClung takes up with gusto. In *The Next of Kin*, she sends her unnamed narrator to speak at a Red Cross function in a windswept northern Alberta town; the meeting quickly turns into a type of home front military engagement. Before beginning her lecture, the narrator discerns that '[t]here was a distinct air of preparedness about everything' (5), and subsequently comments that the women have gathered to discuss 'the affairs of the state' (6). After her talk, as the women air their views, one asks the narrator to accept a 'commission' (14), to be the women's historian and to record for posterity what Canadian women feel and say about the First World War. A written record, the woman argues, will remind women of their emotional response to the First World War: 'We will forget this when it is all over and we will go back to our old pursuits and there will be nothing – I mean no record of how we felt' (13). She wants the chronicle in order to prove to future generations that women opposed the war, fearing not the question, 'What did you do in the war, Mommy?' but the more serious charge, 'What did you do *about* the war?' The narrator agrees to write what might be termed 'counter' stories of women at war, tales not destined to make their way into 'official' historical accounts or heroic novels. Similarly, Montgomery's Rilla keeps a diary of the war years, which her father observes 'should be a very interesting thing to hand down to one's children' (177). Like McClung, Montgomery was emphasizing the need for women to preserve their responses to war by writing them down.

Additionally, prior to writing *The Next of Kin* (1917), McClung had declared herself vociferously opposed to women's omission from the subject of war. *In Times Like These* expresses her frustration with traditional, male-dominated accounts of history and literature which honour purely economic movements, political decisions, dates and pivotal battles: 'Invasions, conquests, battles, sieges make up the subject-matter of our histories' (14). Ever optimistic, McClung expresses her hope that the future will bring an end to one-sided representations of history and literature:

> Some day . . . there will be new histories written, and they will tell the story of the years from the standpoint of the people, and the hero will not be any red-handed assassin who goes through peaceful country places leaving behind him dead men looking sightlessly up to the sky. The hero [*sic*] will be the man or woman who knows and loves and serves.
>
> (16)

Never one to complain without proposing an alternative or positing a solution, McClung herself takes up the task of 'talking back', as bell hooks puts it, to the 'official', male-dominated histories and stories of war which traditionally exclude women's voices and experiences. In 1917, she publishes *The Next of Kin*, a collection of woman-centred stories which radically reverse the notion of who speaks with authority in war; she displaces the voices of soldiers, of fathers, brothers, sons, renders them almost 'missing' by putting their stories on the margins. Further, McClung refuses to write a conventionally plotted novel, her text calling for a redefinition of what constitutes a war story: *The Next of Kin* is a series of short stories, a chorus of women's voices, McClung's testament to her belief that 'counter' stories of ordinary citizens and their experiences (especially women's) are worthy of the telling. In her text, she gives voice to mothers, wives, urban women, rural women, young women, middle-aged women; those who encourage men to go to war, those who prevent them; those who cope well with adversity, those who do not. And, as if to underscore the multiplicity of women's stories, at one point in her fiction, McClung situates her narrator at a train station, where she watches troops depart for war. What strikes the narrator is that 'men in uniform look much the same' (193) (thereby implying that soldiers' stories are 'uniform'), whereas the people waving goodbye *at* the station – Ukranian women; heavily veiled women; sad-faced mothers; tired, untidy women; brave little girls and boys; babies; chattering young people; brides of the day – are *'from* every station in life' (emphasis added, 193). *All*, she intimates, have stories to tell, and in *The Next of Kin*, she tells a range of them.

Montgomery, too, challenges the traditional concept that a war story is monolithically comprised of a hero in the trenches; she rewrites the term 'total war' by arguing that war is a castastrophic event which affects every living creature. Like McClung, she does not allow men's voices to drown out women's, or men's deeds and experiences to efface them. Montgomery permits only those men who would naturally remain on the home front – the middle-aged or elderly, pacifists or ministers – to speak, and then only briefly. *Rilla of Ingleside* tenders a kaleidoscopic view of war; the text gives voice to a wide cross-section of the inhabitants of a small Canadian wartime community which commonly includes cats, dogs, babies and children, and imbues them with an extraordinary intelligence and perspicacity not customarily afforded such creatures. Her text, then, assures us that there are no innocent people or creatures in wartime; the assumption that those removed from the field of battle are unaffected by war is groundless.

Several of the texts also exhort women to make their views public, never an easy task for women conditioned by patriarchy into silence, but especially difficult in an intensely male-dominated period like war. As bell hooks maintains, 'within feminist circles, silence is often seen as the sexist "right speech of womanhood" – the sign of woman's sub-mission to patriarchal authority' (6). Silent women do not question author-ity or raise subjects deemed inappropriate to their sex. Women who dare to ask uncomfortable questions about who makes decisions in their society are considered abrasive, out of line. In speaking out, they are 'unwomanly' or 'unladylike', and run the risk of being considered fools should they turn loquacious. In *The Next of Kin*, McClung's narrator is rudely reminded of this danger marked 'For Women Only' when she arrives at a town to give a speech. The station agent who greets her declares with certainty that she will not gather a large crowd, although a few will turn out to hear her out of 'idle curiosity' (2). Making no apologies to

Dr Johnson, he says, 'it *is* great to hear a woman speak in public . . . even if she does not do it very well. It's sorto' like seeing a pony walking on its hind legs; it's clever even if it's not natural' (2). McClung's narrator, confident in her role as public speaker, is nonplussed, but the agent's remarks echo the kinds of prejudices women are up against should they choose to speak in public. Those who air their views are violating the expectation of female silence: like children, women are meant to be seen but not heard.

Both *The Next of Kin* and *Rilla of Ingleside* provide role models for their readers, demonstrating by example that several women hold such strong convictions about the war that they cannot be silenced: in each text, middle-aged women who have never spoken in public before rise to their feet spontaneously and, without the advantage of prepared texts, make electrifying speeches which achieve their aims. These characters are neither placating audiences nor seeking male approval, but speaking against popular opinion (McClung, 16; Montgomery, 223). Montgomery's housekeeper initially feels guilty about her 'unbecoming conduct' and 'unladylike behaviour' (223) and does not take pride in her success, even though her speech results in a record sale of bonds. Soon after, though, she throws off her apron, dons overalls and takes to the fields to help in the war effort, a signal of her growing emancipation from confined women's work, her ability to take on a man's job. As bell hooks says:

> Moving from silence into speech is for the oppressed, the colonized, the exploited, and those who stand and struggle side by side a gesture of defiance that heals, that makes new life and new growth possible. It is that act of speech, of 'talking back,' that is no mere gesture of empty words, that is the expression of our movement from object to subject – the liberated voice.
>
> (9)

Coming to speech is for the women in these texts a liberating moment from which there will be no back-sliding; as one of McClung's characters says after making her first public speech, 'I know I will never be scared again' (16). Thus both Montgomery and McClung use their texts as social and political tools to show women that speaking out is not difficult. Both texts urge women to recognize that patriarchy deliberately silences women, conditions them to believe that they are too irrational to speak in public.

The wartime texts by Beynon and Blackburn focus specifically on the need to include all voices, to suppress none. Beynon uses her central character to urge those who would be silenced to speak against their oppression, stressing in *Aleta Dey* (1919) that any woman who dares speak against the dominant culture's wartime ideologies must be fearless. In documenting the difficulties a woman faces in finding her public voice, Beynon's Aleta reflects a woman's quandary in any era, but the wartime climate is more intimidating and exacerbates her character's dilemma. At the outset, Beynon illustrates the conditions which force women into passive submission to authority, and then establishes the types of barriers a woman encounters should she wish to speak her piece in wartime.

The authority figures in Beynon's text (teachers, preachers, fathers) think exclusively in black/white, right/wrong terms; unable to rationalize their positions intellectually, they demand utter obedience from their charges, and either verbally humiliate or physically beat transgressors like Aleta into silence. As a result of the severe punishment she suffers at the hands of patriarchal figures, especially her violent father, Aleta's confidence in her ability to think and speak is shaken; even as a mature journalist who knows how to use words, she stills her own voice and allows others' to hold sway. Uncomfortable in her silence, often seething inwardly at others' irrationality, especially during the war, she remains deaf and dumb, a 'coward' who adopts a 'wait and see' attitude towards life.

To date, articles on Beynon have centred primarily on the anti-war views which she expressed while a journalist for the *Grain Growers' Guide*, but several of these non-violent arguments also surface in *Aleta Dey*. As the war years grind on, Aleta becomes increasingly disturbed by the reactions of her fellow countrywomen/men to war. She identifies their wartime ideologies as unimaginative, selfish and bloodthirsty; she is horrified by their open declarations of hatred for the German people, angered that they fail to recognize the prevalence of both propaganda and war profiteering, and discouraged that prewar suffragists and pacifists have suddenly turned litigious (207–13). It is not Aleta's abhorrence of these vengeful positions, however, which brings her the courage to voice her views, but the government's suppression of her right to speak against them which catapults her into 'action'. As she says, 'I might have muddled along to the end had not the government begun to forbid us to discuss the war at all, except favourably' (216). Her telephone tapped, warned by the government censor not to oppose conscription, Aleta finds her 'courage'. Defiant, she takes to the streets, distributing pamphlets demanding that freedom of speech and of the press be preserved (217). This act of resistance challenges the dominant culture, and Aleta is thrown into jail. While incarcerated, she continues to wrestle with her cowardice. Although she cannot be certain that her pacifist views are infallible, she comes to the decision that she must 'serve' humanity in the only way she knows: she must denounce violence publicly and speak her pacifist opinions forthrightly (222). Uppermost is her belief that it is wrong to silence *any* voices.

At the end of the novel, Aleta forgoes meeting her beloved McNair, a soldier returning from combat, in order to make a public address against the war. Knowing she runs the risk of being jailed again, she willingly takes it, for 'the whole point of the meeting is that it is to be addressed by one who has been in jail and who refuses to be silenced' (227). Her 'fearless' deed proves her undoing, however, for her behaviour poses serious threats to the wielders of oppressive power. While exercising her freedom to speak, a soldier who is going overseas to fight for freedom (and to protect women), knocks Aleta off the public podium and the blow eventually kills her. Hundreds of people with pacifist leanings, too 'cowardly' to declare themselves openly, throng to Aleta's funeral. Here, Beynon uses her text didactically to address those who did not go along with the government's wartime injunctions, but who either lacked the courage to speak their piece or on other grounds were reluctant to voice their objections. Joan Byles sets out one of the justifications many women had for remaining silent:

> [Women] had a deep sense of loyalty to their men and were acutely aware of their sufferings and sacrifices. Not for the world would they say anything which would seem to undervalue their men, or suggest that they were offered for a wrong or mistaken cause. So that, in backing their men in the war in which they were actually fighting, many women seemed to be backing warfare itself, although most probably they abhorred it. They were caught in the classic situation of women when their men are away at war.
>
> (476)

Beynon's heroine has a loved one in the trenches, so she is also caught in the 'classic' situation. Nonetheless, she urges her comrades not in arms to speak with her: a lone voice can be suppressed; many cannot. Through Aleta, Beynon encourages Canadians to be fearless, and together, fight censorship and suppression.[12]

Similarly, given the time at which *The Man Child* was published (1930), it is another bold or 'fearless' fiction which questions the omission of women's voices, specifically by unveiling the secrecy surrounding one of women's most common experiences, childbirth. The text queries why we know so little about a woman's battlefield, the birthbed, and why records of suffering describe only men's pain. Blackburn's text focuses on a woman's view of the creation of life: it uncovers the range of a woman's emotional and physical responses to her pregnancy; it demonstrates the strength of the familial bond which develops between mother and child, and it exposes the sacrifices and hardships a mother willingly endures to raise a child. In focusing on life, not death, the text calls for a revision of patriotic ideals in order to emphasize the sacredness of human life, not its destruction. Blackburn's Emma also criticizes a man-made society. She objects that men brandish all the power, whereas women are told that giving birth 'suffices'. She laments that men perceive women to be children, lacking in 'inventive faculty or analytical thought' (150). It is foolish, she insists, to overlook women's wisdom. Throughout *The Man Child*, Blackburn presents Emma as both inventive and analytical. For example, railing against a society which allows men to make 'life hideous and death vile' (266), she devises a plan reminiscent of Aristophanes' *Lysistrata*, but without chastity as a weapon. Her thoughtful proposal emphasizes to what extent the war machine depends on women's efforts, and not just as producers of cannon fodder. Emma advocates that women should not cooperate with the war effort: they should refuse to nurse, knit or work in munitions factories. If they 'struck' (212), the war couldn't last more than a month. In her argument, the military meets the maternal. If women reveal the secrets of motherhood, the rhetoric of maternity will help foster a belief in the sacredness of life; if women refuse to aid the military cause that depends on it, they will hinder the makers of war.

Blackburn's notice of the power of collective action points to another of the strategies that Canadian women writers utilize: their recognition that battles can only be won through strength in numbers. To that end, one of the most distinguishing and forward-looking features of McClung's text is her belief that 'women are women's best friends' (86). In emphasizing that women must be one another's allies, not enemies, she anticipates Virginia Woolf, who laments in *A Room of One's Own* that literature rarely depicts women's friendships (86). Ahead of her time, McClung advocates sisterly solidarity; her gathering together of women, particularly in the Foreword to *The Next of Kin*, resembles an early consciousness-raising group where women come together and openly share their feelings with one another about the war. The atmosphere is non-combative, the terrain a supportive 'all-woman's land'. Women take their conversational turn in these groups and hear one another out in a non-competitive atmosphere; there are no men present to ridicule women's thoughts or demean their ideas. Through such groups, women can empower themselves; they can formulate strategies and develop tactics against male domination, and by engaging in 'team-play' (19) make a difference. Australian critic Rita Felski's depictions of female friendships in contemporary novels echo McClung's visions of what women working together can achieve. When women befriend one another, writes Felski, they can 'overcome the negative value which women have been conditioned to place upon their sex; recognizing other women serves a symbolic function as an affirmation of self, of gendered identity' (138).

> Such identification provides a means of access into society by linking the protagonist to a broader social group and thus rendering explicit the political basis of private experience.... [I]t also functions as a barrier against, and a refuge from, the worst effects of a potentially threatening social order by opening up a space for nonexploitative relationships grounded in common goals and interests.
>
> (139)

Group solidarity 'inspires activism and resistance rather than private resignation, and makes it possible to project a visionary hope of future change' (139).

These are all arguments McClung's narrator makes in *The Next of Kin*. She emphasizes that because patriarchy encourages competition among women, they wage civil war among themselves, dissipating their energies and diminishing the powers they can harness if they regard their sex favourably. One of the reasons McClung's narrator travels to rural townships giving speeches is to help break down women's isolation; when they come together to hear what the speaker has to say, they recognize that they share common concerns. Without opportunities to air their views collectively, they acquiesce to submission. But working together, pooling their energies and resources, they can make political change work to their advantage. Optimistically, the narrator says, 'Discussions are raging in women's societies and wherever women meet together, and out of it something will come. Men are always quite willing to be guided by women when their schemes are sound and sane' (101). In *The Next of Kin*, McClung's narrator asserts that female solidarity, which helps bring about women's emancipation, will result in the creation of a better society for children and men, too. McClung writes women's recent victories into her text, thereby instilling confidence in others that they can be winners at social change, but she also recognizes the dangers of complacency. Writing in 1917, one year after prairie women received the vote, McClung recognized that women's 'worst troubles' were not over, for a 'second Hindenburg line' had been set up to prevent them from entering the field of politics, and seemed harder to 'pierce' than the first (*Next*, 232). But the narrator seems undaunted, almost eager to take up the challenge.[13]

Ultimately, Canadian women's novels are, in subtle ways, pleas for peace, instructions on how to avoid war. Although women writers cannot fight war itself, they can expose war mentality: they point to the dangers of propaganda, and make their characters cognizant of the hype generated by war. They warn them to be wary of slogans that 'get' men to enlist, and encourage them to see through patriotic fervour, to recognize that soldiers will find neither glory nor glamour in the trenches. One of the strengths of these novels lies in their promotion of non-violent ways of solving problems. Writers encourage their characters to be tolerant of others' beliefs, and to solve disagreements by exploring differences of opinion through mediation. Montgomery depicts her characters making compromises, occasionally swallowing large slices of humble pie, but always more anxious to foster a harmonious environment than to exact small victories or take revenge over minor matters.

In addition, one of the most effective strategies Canadian women employ is humour (sorely missing in the texts by Australian and New Zealand writers), pervasive in the novels by McClung, Montgomery and McKowan. Montgomery's description of a decidedly unromantic war wedding, which features a flat-faced, commonplace bride and a groom who sobs uncontrollably throughout the ceremony, is a howler, as are McClung's not-so-subtle digs at men who postulate that only they are capable of running the world. By utilizing wit, Canadian writers dispel the myth that women (especially feminists) have no sense of humour. Further, their use of humour makes the subject of war accessible, and thus an appropriate vehicle for social reform.

At liberty to criticize their society, it is obvious that Canadian women write from a more powerful place within their literary tradition than do New Zealand or Australian writers, but what accounts for the difference? Langer argues that the lack of a clearly defined Canadian identity has benefited women writers. Because Canadians continue to search for an identity but so far have never found one, they have never completely (or even partially) come to terms with what a Canadian is. Canadians know only what we are not – not 'British', not 'American' – and since there is no one approved type, as there is in Australia, Canadian women have not been automatically excluded from the realm of the typical (Langer, 79). Furthermore, Langer argues, Canada's history of polyethnicity, with the presence of the French as well as large numbers of other Europeans, precludes a monolithic notion of what a Canadian is. (At the outbreak of war, inhabitants of New Zealand and Australia were overwhelmingly British in origin.) Because Canada is a mosaic, there are more 'gaps' in the structure of patriarchy through which women can more easily find their place in culture (Langer, 80). (As we are quickly realizing, however, the 'gaps' do not allow minority groups cultural space.) In *The Lovely Treachery of Words*, Robert Kroetsch discusses 'meta-narratives' which define nationhood through stories, and he suggests that, unlike Americans, who have many meta-narratives that tell them who they are, 'Canadians cannot agree on what our meta-narrative is' (21). Unlike Australians, or at least Australian *men*, who can pinpoint their getting of nationhood to the dawn landing at Anzac Cove on 25 April 1915, Canadians cannot decide for all the world when we became a nation (Kroetsch, 27). Kroetsch labels Canada a 'post-modern country', a polyphonic place which refuses privilege to a restricted cluster of meta-narratives. We survive, he declares, by 'working with a low level of self-definition and national definition. We insist on staying multiple' (26). Unlike Australians, who claim their heroes as noble bushmen-cum-Diggers, Canadians are uncertain who their heroes are, but they are certainly not soldiers or farmers. Lacking a clearly defined national myth, then, Canadian women have not had to be 'myth-fits'. They have been free to shape their own cultural space.

It is precisely the restraining environment in Australia and New Zealand which I argue needs literary investigation. For the past several decades, a number of feminist critics have documented women's exclusion from the national myth-making in Australia, but they have paid insufficient attention to the force of the Anzac legend, which is even more debilitating, I would argue, than the bush mythology. The war proved a more difficult discourse for women to write themselves into, in part because, added to the bushmen's already sterling traits were the Diggers' laudable qualities of courage, valour, duty and self-sacrifice. Moreover, the Anzac handed Australian (men) nationhood, not merely a unique personality. And unlike the bush myth, which has continued to wane through the decades, the Anzac legend keeps coming back, reinforcing itself every 25 April, as anyone who has ever visited Australia on that day can attest. An exploration of women's literature is crucial to an understanding of women's place in Australian society, for it demonstrates, as no other writing in the tradition does, the extent to which women's voices can be decimated by a forceful dominant ideology. And although a number of contemporary writers like Olga Masters, Joan Dugdale and Gwen Kelly in Australia, and Elizabeth Knox in New Zealand, are writing back to the Great War, perhaps out of the desire to furnish missing links with the past, the stories they tell are very different than those written during the actual historical period. I would argue that we need both: we must fill in the gaps of women's experiences during the Great War by examining works emerging during that period, for only then can we comprehend how a potent myth can silence a woman, estrange her from her own story. In order to deflect these powerful myths and to gauge the force of their power, we need to know where they come from.

In Canada, our understanding of the writing of the past facilitates the passing on of a vigorous and healthy tradition. Critics have done the heritage a disservice by ignoring Great War women writers, whose contributions to a vital legacy have not been marked. In assessing why Canadian women have such a strong place in our literary tradition, critics have looked to our grandmothers, or great-grandmothers like Catherine Parr Traill or Susanna Moodie, not the women writers who, in this century, in modern memory, were showing women how to write themselves into an intensely male-dominated discourse, and at the same time, teaching women how to secure powerful positions in their society. In the current agenda to expand or dissolve the boundaries which exclude women writers, critics have argued for the admittance of marginalized women's genres like memoirs, diaries and autobiographies. To that list, I would add women's Great War writing. Not only will such a rereading have implications for how we read the fiction women produced in subsequent wars, it will inform us how Canadian women writers managed to gain small victories during a turbulent historical period. Conversely, an analysis of Australian and New Zealand women's wartime writing will provide clues to how women lost the literary war and the battle of the sexes. Forewarned is forearmed.

Notes

1. Jan Bassett (223–33) identifies some common themes and issues, but she omits from her discussion a number of women who wrote about the war; she also overlooks entirely the dominating presence of the Anzacs. For an analysis of their central role, see Donna Coates, 'The Digger on the Lofty Pedestal: Australian Women's Fictions of the Great War' (1–22), from which sections of this chapter are excerpted.

2. Gilbert's essay should be read in light of the critics who argue that her thesis is biased and her use of examples cavalier. See Jane Marcus (49–81) and Claire M. Tylee (199–210). My own research reveals that Gilbert disregards the Australian writer Mary Marlowe's *The Women Who Wait* and Helen Zenna Smith's *Not So Quiet... Stepdaughters of War*, both of which were published in England, presumably because they do not fit her thesis.
3. See Pat Gowland (216–33), Darryn Kruse and Charles Sowerwine (42–58) and Carmel Shute (7–23).
4. Several women wrote exceptional texts. Lesbia Harford wrote *The Invaluable Mystery* in the early 1920s, but the novel, which features an urban woman who overcomes patriarchal oppression, failed to find a publisher until it was discovered by researchers in the Australian National Archives (Canberra) in 1981. For an analysis of this text, see Donna Coates, 'Lesbia Harford's Home-front Warrior and Women's World War One Writing' (19–28). Similarly, Mollie L. Skinner's *Letters of a V. A. D.*, published under the pseudonym R. E. Leake, focuses on a nurse who prefers nursing to marriage, and in her line of duty, praises Anzacs and Tommies equally. Although I hesitate to introduce biographical material, I need to mention that Skinner remarks in her auto-biography, *The Fifth Sparrow*, that because she was living in India, she did not hear of the outbreak of war until April 1915. Thus she would have missed the exemplary reports on the Anzacs' fighting prowess emanating from overseas by Bean and other war correspondents such as Ellis Ashmead-Bartlett and John Masefield. Without male views of war to mimic, Skinner was free to devise her own impressions of the conflict. Perhaps for the same reason, Skinner's *Tucker Sees India* is also singular: it features an atypical Anzac who does not wish to fight. For an analysis of these two exceptional texts, see Donna Coates, 'Guns 'n' Roses: Mollie Skinner's Intrepid Great War Fictions', *Southerly* (March 1999), forthcoming.
5. See in particular Ray Phillips, *The White Feather*.
6. I am not considering Katherine Mansfield's five wartime stories here, primarily because three are set in Europe, and the other two – 'Prelude' and 'At the Bay', do not address the war specifically. For an analysis of Mansfield's wartime stories, see Constance Brown (329–45).
7. Robin Hyde draws upon her journalist background to tell the story of Doug-las Stark ('Starkie'), tracing his life from his childhood and adolescence in poverty and crime, through his experiences as hero and rebel in the First World War (*Passport to Hell*), to his life as an itinerant labourer in the boom of the 1920s and as one of the unemployed in the early 1930s (*Nor the Years Condemn*). In Canada, too, Nellie McClung, also a journalist, recounts a soldier's story in *Three Times and Out: A Canadian Soldier's Experiences in Germany*. McClung differs from Hyde, however, in that she also writes about Canadian women on the home front, whereas Hyde does not.
8. In *The Great War and Modern Memory*, Paul Fussell writes that 'every war is ironic because every war is worse than expected' (7). The Great War, however, was more ironic than any before or since: eight million people were destroyed because two persons, the Archduke Ferdinand and his Consort, were shot (8). Based on their knowledge of previous wars, enlisted men could not have foreseen what an inhuman(e) slaughter this war would be.

9. I disagree in part with Alan R. Young's claim that 'ideologically all ... [Montgomery's] voices concur' (110), including the voices of mothers and fathers with sons at the front. Young does not take into account that their reactions to their sons' enlistment differ sharply.

10. See Ramsay Cook (187–208) and Barbara Roberts (48–65).

11. In her story 'Men and Money: A Story With a Purpose', McClung leaves no doubt that she believes all able-bodied men should enlist. For the reasons why McClung, a pacifist prior to the war, did such an about-face, see R. R. Warne, 'Nellie McClung and Peace' (35–47).

12. No doubt Beynon was speaking from the heart, for as Anne Hicks notes in her Introduction to *Aleta Dey*, Beynon was forced to resign as women's editor of *The Grain Growers' Guide* in 1917 due to her public opposition to male conscription; Hicks speculates that the tapping of Aleta's telephone is probably biographical fact (xiii). Roberts writes, too, that Beynon may have even feared physical attack, for at anti-war rallies, several activists had been beaten up and right-wing vigilantes staged brutal riots all over the west from 1917 to 1920. According to Roberts, Beynon moved to New York in 1917, writing *Aleta Dey* while in exile (52).

13. Aside from urging their characters to document their feelings about war and to voice their opinions publicly, Canadian women writers also utilize militaristic language as a strategy for overcoming oppression. See Donna Coates, 'The Best Soldiers of All: Unsung Heroines in Canadian Women's Great War Fictions' (66–99). Sections of this chapter are excerpted from that publication.

Works cited

Adam-Smith, Patsy. *Australian Women at War*. Melbourne: Nelson, 1984.

Arnold, Gertrude. *Sister Anne! Sister Anne!!* Toronto: McClelland & Stewart, 1919.

Astley, Thea. *An Item From the Late News*. Ringwood, Victoria: Penguin, 1984.

Basset, Jan. '"Preserving the White Race": Some Australian Women's Literary Responses to the Great War', *Australian Literary Studies*, 12 (1985): 223–33.

Bean, C. E. W. (ed.) *The Anzac Book: Written and Illustrated in Gallipoli by the Men of Anzac*. Melbourne: Cassell, 1916.

——. *The Official History. The Story of Anzac: From the Outbreak of War to the End of the First Phase of the Gallipoli Campaign, May 4 1915*, Vol. 1, 1921. Sydney: Angus & Robertson, 1934.

Beynon, Francis Marion. *Aleta Dey*, 1919. London: Virago, 1988.

Blackburn, Grace. *The Man Child*. Ottawa: Graphic, 1930.

Brookes, Mabel. *Broken Idols*. Melbourne: Melville & Mullen, 1917.

——. *Old Desires*. Melbourne: Australasian Authors' Agency, 1922.

——. *On the Knees of the Gods*. Melbourne: Melville & Mullen, 1918.

Brown, Constance. 'Dissection and Nostalgia: Katherine Mansfield's Response to World War One', *The Centennial Review*, 23 (1979): 329–45.

Bruce, Mary Grant. *From Billabong to London*. Melbourne: Ward, 1915.

——. *Captain Jim*. Melbourne: Ward, 1919.

——. *Jim and Wally*. Melbourne: Ward, 1916.

Burge, Linda Webb. *Wings above the Storm*. Melbourne: National, 1944.

Byles, Joan. 'Women's Experience of World War One: Suffragists, Pacifists, and Poets', *Women's Studies International Forum*, 8 (1985): 473–87.

Coates, Donna. 'The Digger on the Lofty Pedestal: Australian Women's Fictions of the Great War', *Australian and New Zealand Studies in Canada*, 10 (December 1993): 1–22.

——. 'Lesbia Harford's Homefront Warrior and Women's World War One Writing', *Australia Literary Studies*, 17.1 (1995): 19–28.

——. 'The Best Soldiers of All: Unsung Heroines in Canadian Women's Great War Fictions', *Canadian Literature*, 151 (Winter 1996): 66–99.

——. 'Guns 'n' Roses: Mollie Skinner's Intrepid Great War Fictions', *Southerly* (March 1999), forthcoming.

Cook, Ramsay. 'Francis Marion Beynon and the Crisis of Christian Reformism', in *The West and the Nation: Essays in Honour of W. L. Morton*, eds Carl Berger and Ramsay Cook. Toronto: McClelland & Stewart, 1976, 187–208.

Dennis, C. J. *The Moods of Ginger Mick*. Sydney: Angus & Robertson, 1916.

Dixson, Miriam. *The Real Matilda*, 1974. Ringwood, Victoria: Penguin, 1984.

Felski, Rita. *Beyond Feminist Aesthetics: Feminist Literature and Social Change*. Cambridge, MA: Harvard University Press, 1989.

Fussell, Paul. *The Great War and Modern Memory*. New York: Oxford University Press, 1975.

Gerster, Robin. *Big-Noting: The Heroic Theme in Australian War Writing*. Melbourne: Melbourne University Press, 1988.

Gibbons, Margaret. *An Anzac's Bride*. London: Herbert Jenkins, 1918.

Gilbert, Sandra. 'Soldier's Heart: Literary Men, Literary Women and the Great War', in *Behind the Lines: Gender and the Two Wars*, eds Margaret Higgonet et al. New Haven, CT: Yale University Press, 1987, 197–226.

Gowland, Pat. 'The Women's Peace Army', in *Women, Class and History: Feminist Perspectives on Australia 1788–1978*, ed. Elizabeth Windshuttle. Melbourne: Fontana, 1980, 216–33.

Hain, Gladys. *The Coo-ee Contingent*. London: Cassell, 1917.

Harford, Lesbia. *The Invaluable Mystery*. Ringwood, Victoria: Penguin, 1987.

Heilbrun, Carolyn. *Writing a Woman's Life*. New York: Ballantine, 1988.

Hicks, Anne. 'Introduction', *Aleta Dey*, by Francis Marion Beynon, 1919. London: Virago, 1988, v–xv.

hooks, bell [Gloria Watkins]. *Talking Back: Thinking Feminist, Talking Black*. Toronto: Between the Lines, 1988.

Howson, I. M[ay]. *Love's Sacrifice (Founded on Facts): A Book From the Trenches Depicting Undying Love*. Melbourne: Imperial, 1917.

Huston, Nancy. 'Tales of War and Tears of Women', *Women's Studies International Forum*, 5 (1982): 271–82.

Hyde, Robin. *Nor the Years Condemn*, 1938. Auckland: Auckland University Press, 1986.

——. *Passport to Hell*, 1936. Auckland: New Women's Press, 1986.

Jones, Dorothy. 'Canon to the Right of Us, Canon to the Left of Us', *New Literature Review*, 17 (1989): 69–79.

——. 'Mapping and Mythmaking: Women Writers and the Australian Legend', *Ariel*, 17.4 (1986): 63–86.

Kroetsch, Robert. *The Lovely Treachery of Words: Essays Selected and New*. Toronto: Oxford University Press, 1989.

Kruse, Darryn and Charles Sowerwine. 'Feminism and Pacifism: "Women's Sphere" in Peace and War', *Australian Women: New Feminist Perspectives*, eds Norma Grieve and Alisa Burns. Melbourne: Oxford University Press, 1986, 42–58.

Lake, Marilyn. 'The Politics of Respectability: Identifying the Masculinist Context', *Historical Studies*, 22 (1986): 116–31.

Langer, Beryl Donaldson. 'Women and Literary Production: Canada and Australia', *Australian and Canadian Studies: An Interdisciplinary Social Science Review*, 2 (1984): 70–83.

Leake, R. E. [M[ollie] L. Skinner]. *Letters of a V. A. D.* London: Melrose, 1918.

McClung, Nellie. *In Times Like These*, 1915. Toronto: University of Toronto Press, 1972.

——. 'Men and Money: A Story With a Purpose', *Maclean's Magazine*, November 1919: 15–17, 99–100.

——. *The Next of Kin: Those Who Wait and Wonder*. Toronto: Thomas Allen, 1917.

——. *Three Times and Out: A Canadian Boy's Experiences in Germany*. Toronto: Thomas Allen, 1918.

McKernan, Michael. *The Australian People and the Great War*. Melbourne: Nelson, 1980.

McKowan, Evah. *Janet of Kootenay: Life, Love, and Laughter in an Arcady of the West*. Toronto: McClelland & Stewart, 1919.

Mander, Jane. *The Besieging City*. London: Hutchison, 1926.

——. *The Strange Attraction*. London: John Lane, 1923.

Manners-Sutton, Doris [C. Gentile]. *A Marked Soul*. Melbourne: McCubbin, 1923.

Marcus, Jane. 'The Asylums of Antaeus: Women, War, and Madness – Is There a Feminist Fetishism?', in *The Difference Within: Feminism and Radical Theory*, eds Elizabeth Meese and Alice Parker. Philadelphia: John Benjamins, 1988, 49–81.

Marlowe, Mary. *That Fragile Hour: An Autobiography*. Sydney: Angus & Robertson, 1990.

——. *The Women Who Wait*. London: Simpkin, 1918.

Miller, Nancy K. 'Emphasis Added: Plots and Plausibilities in Women's Fictions', in *The New Feminist Criticism*, ed. Elaine Showalter. New York: Pantheon, 1985, 339–60.

Montgomery, L. M. *Rilla of Ingleside*, 1920. Toronto: Seal, 1982.

O'Brien, Sharon. 'Combat Envy and Survivor Guilt: Willa Cather's "Manly Battle Yarn"', in Helen M. Cooper, Adrienne Auslander Munich and Susan Merrill Squier (eds), *Arms and the Woman: War, Gender and Literary Representation*. Chapel Hill: University of North Carolina Press, 1989, 184–204.

Pearson, Katherine. *Hugh Royston*. Sydney: Cornstalk, 1924.

Phillips, Ray. *The White Feather*. Melbourne: Melville & Mullen, 1917.

Rixon, Annie [Mrs Richard de Clare Studdert]. *The Scarlet Cape*. Sydney: Criterion, 1939.

——. *Yesterday and Today*. Sydney: Criterion, 1940.

Roberts, Barbara. 'Women Against War, 1914–1918: Francis Marion Beynon and Laura Hughes', in *Up and Doing: Canadian Women and Peace*, eds Janice Williamson and Deborah Gorham. Toronto: Women's Press, 1989, 48–65.

Roberts, Heather. *Where Did She Come From? New Zealand Women Novelists 1962–1987*. Wellington: Allen, 1989.

Scanlan, M. Nelle. *Tides of Youth*. London: Jarrolds, 1933.

Schaffer, Kay. *Women and the Bush: Forces of Desire in the Australian Cultural Tradition.* Sydney: Cambridge University Press, 1988.

Sheridan, Susan. '"Temper Romantic: Bias Offensively Feminist"': Australian Women Writers and Literary Nationalism', in *A Double Colonization: Colonial and Post-Colonial Women's Writing*, eds Kirsten Holst Petersen and Anna Rutherford. Aarhuis: Dangeroo Press, 1986, 49–58.

Shute, Carmel. '"Blood Votes" and the "Bestial Boche"': A Case Study in Propaganda', *Hecate* 1.2 (1975): 7–23.

Skinner, M[ollie] L. *Tucker Sees India.* London: Martin, 1937.

——. *The Fifth Sparrow.* Sydney: Sydney University Press, 1972.

Smith, Helen Zenna [Evadne Price]. *Not So Quiet... Stepdaughters of War*, 1930. London: Virago, 1988.

Stirling, Chrystal. *Soldiers Two.* Sydney: Bookstall, 1918.

Sturm, Terry. 'Popular Fiction', in *The Oxford History of New Zealand Literature in English*, ed. Terry Sturm. Auckland: Oxford University Press, 1991, 493–541.

Summers, Anne. *Damned Whores and God's Police: The Colonization of Women in Australia* Ringwood, Victoria: Penguin, 1975.

Thirkell, Angela [Leslie Parker]. *Trooper to the Southern Cross*, 1934. London: Virago, 1985.

Thompson, Eric. 'Canadian Fiction and the Great War', *Canadian Literature*, 91 (Winter 1981): 81–96.

Turner, Dorothea. *Jane Mander.* New York: Twayne, 1972.

Turner, Ethel. *Brigid and the Cub.* London: Ward, 1919.

——. *Captain Cub.* London: Ward, 1917.

——. *The Cub.* London: Ward, 1915.

Tylee, Claire M. '"Maleness Run Riot" – The Great War and Women's Resistance to Militarism', *Women's Studies International Forum*, 11 (1988): 199–210.

Warne, R. R. 'Nellie McClung and Peace', in *Up and Doing: Canadian Women and Peace*. Toronto: Women's Press, 1989, 35–47.

Watson, Kathleen. *Henriette Says!* Melbourne: Alexander McCubbin, 1921.

Woolf, Virginia. *A Room of One's Own*, 1929. New York: Harcourt, 1957.

Young, Alan. 'L. M. Montgomery's *Rilla of Ingleside* (1920): Romance and the Experience of War', in *Myth and Milieu: Atlantic Literature and Culture 1918–1939*, ed. Gwendolyn Davis. Fredericton: Acadiensis Press, 1993, 95–122.

9

'Dear, Tender-Hearted, Uncomprehending America': Dorothy Canfield Fisher's and Edith Wharton's Fictional Responses to the First World War

Mary R. Ryder

In her sketch 'A Honeymoon...Vive L'Amerique', first published in August of 1918, Dorothy Canfield Fisher describes the generosity of a middle-aged American couple who, prior to America's entry into the Great War, spend their honeymoon helping war-torn France:

> Then I knew of what they had reminded me. They had reminded me of America, they *were* America incarnate, one side of her, the dear, tender-hearted, uncomprehending America which did not need to understand the dark old secrets of hate and misery in order to stretch out her generous hand and ease her too happy heart by the making of many gifts.
>
> (*Home Fires*, 241)

If not an accurate portrait of the First World War generation, Canfield's account of Americans' unbridled generosity, coupled with a kind of cultural ignorance, was, at least, an effective one for rallying American philanthropic and political responses to the plight of western Europe in the late years of the War. This story, collected with ten other vignettes and titled *Home Fires in France*, was not alone, however, in jarring American sensibilities and complacencies, arousing both indignation and guilt, and accomplishing active participation in the war effort. In the same year, Edith Wharton who, like Canfield, was living in France and working actively in relief, published a novella *The Marne* in which she too extolled the potential of Americans to aid in repulsing the German menace. Skilfully using the same propaganda techniques as Canfield, Wharton tells the story of a tender-hearted and uncomprehending American boy who, disillusioned by the attitudes of his leisured class, commits his heart and person to 'the cause'.

While throughout the war both amateur and professional writers flooded publishing houses and magazines with manuscripts on the romance and atrocities of the conflict, what singled out Wharton and Canfield was their ability to write compelling stories which promoted American virtues while chastising American shortcomings. Whether their reading audience was simply too unsophisticated to take offence at the portraits of themselves or was eager finally to see themselves explained in print, both *Home Fires in France* and *The Marne* were read eagerly by Americans. The texts have lapsed almost into obscurity today but deserve a resurrection and re-examination as astute psychological profiles of Americans as they wrestled with committing themselves to 'the war to end all war'.

Although these texts are now to some degree literary curiosities and intriguing historical artefacts, their importance as part of the genre of women's writing on war should not be overlooked. As two of the leading women writers of their day, Canfield and Wharton knew their reputations could serve them well as propagandists for American participation in the First World War, but, more importantly, they knew Americans. In these stories of France, Canfield and Wharton seized the opportunity to confront Americans with their essential selves, not always without bitterness on the writers' parts, and to celebrate that brief moment in American life before 'the world broke in two' (Cather, v), the last historical moment in which Americans believed themselves capable of saving the world.

Upon its publication in September 1918, Canfield's *Home Fires in France* was met with enthusiastic reviews. Critics consistently praised it for its accuracy, truthfulness and authenticity. While Canfield's purpose in releasing the stories in book form was to raise money for her war funds, the realism of her accounts could not be denied. By 1922, breaking a personal rift of some twenty years, Willa Cather would appeal to Canfield to read the war scenes of *One of Ours* and to give advice on their accuracy. Canfield received similar recognition from Edith Wharton, who sent one of her recent books with the flyleaf inscribed 'To Dorothy Canfield Fisher with an appreciation of the complete honesty of her stories about war time France' (Yates, 134). *Home Fires in France*, indeed, 'touched hearts, stirred consciences' (Yates, 134), including that of

Canfield's mother. Canfield wrote to her mother, 'I'm glad to know you wept over it, for I wept over some of these stories, and went to bed *sick* after working over them. It would be a pity if I hadn't communicated some of that emotion' (qtd in Washington, 160).

One would rightly assume that graphic descriptions of Belgian victims of the German invasion were largely responsible for Canfield's 'sickness'. Still, the emotionally wrenching aspect of the pieces for Canfield involved efforts to explain France and America to each other and 'to reconcile their differences' (Washington, 160). To achieve this end, Canfield's principal characters in nearly half of the stories are Americans. She focuses on those qualities of Americanness which 'most puzzle the French' (Washington, 160–1) and, perhaps, most puzzled Americans themselves. These stories project a cultural theory designed to pacify readers' animosities and guilt without criticizing the values they hold most dear. The Great War becomes, then, the backdrop against which an 'interplay between cultural forms and self-definition' takes place (Higonnet et al., 3).

In the opening story 'Notes From a French Village in the War Zone', American doughboys, for the first time, confront the past as a 'smartingly real phenomenon, full, scaringly full of real people', entirely like themselves (2). War ceases to be merely a cultural form through which governments fall and land boundaries shift. Young soldiers from Virginia, Ohio, California and Connecticut all express amazement at 'the age of the place' and the 'thousand years of really social community life' which their American rural villages lack (1, 5). In specifying their diverse states of origin, Canfield makes her story that of every American and universalizes the importance of the soldiers' enlightenment. They look upon the walled gardens of ordinary French villagers with genuine admiration but then reconstruct their ideas 'with racial rapidity': 'But for the Lord's sake, how ever do they get the money to pay for building those miles of huge stone walls? It must cost every family a fortune!' (7). The 'inevitable American challenge' is couched in both monetary and social terms, but rather than criticizing this response, Canfield writes that she always rejoices to hear 'the brave new note from the New World' (7). The reader smiles quietly with Canfield (who narrates this piece) at the 'fresh candor of [these] invading barbarians' who simultaneously reject the privacy of a walled garden and admit that there '*must* be something kind o' nice about the quiet of it' (9). With slowly developing insight, the New World youth begin to accept other cultural forms – a communal *boulangerie* and *lavoir*, a voluntary division of labour rather than competition and rivalry, and even the community bath tub (17).

Canfield shows that Americans, rather than being foolish in their cultural naivety, can be open and receptive to otherness without relaxing their self-confidence. She admires the young soldiers' plans to 'keep all the good ways of doing [things] we've got already, and then add all the French ones too' (17). Such readiness to see another people as just that – no better and no worse than themselves – is the Americans' greatest trait. Canfield's purpose is clear; the supposed cultural superiority which Americans harboured and which, in part, delayed their entry into the war was a misconception. The story ends with a lengthy description of the villagers watching with pride their troops' departure, caring for tired and wounded men, and honouring their war dead. The story of the French village of Crouy thus becomes the story of any small town in America, and like the American boys, the reader 'is brought to a halt, a long, scrutinizing inspection, and much profitable meditation' (20).

Canfield once advised a young reader,

> Don't feel you can teach or give to others everything . . . and guard yourself from the Prussian idea that Providence has given your country any monopoly of what is desirable and virtuous. If you look down, even in your heart of hearts, on people, no amount of technical doing them good will prevent your doing them harm.
>
> (quoted in Yates, 134)

Herein was Canfield's principal concern in her stories about Americans. With typical self-assuredness, they approached even postwar France with the desire to 'help' by foisting American ideas of progress and profit upon a culture unlike their own. But, Canfield does not chide Americans for thinking they alone can rescue bleeding France; rather, she reveals their potential for altering their preconceived ideas, including their ideas of progress.

'A Fair Exchange', first published in September 1918, examines closely the profit-motive which is typically American, but Canfield neither satirizes nor condemns her protagonist, Randolph Hale, President of the Illinois Association of Druggists. With characteristic American curiosity, he studies the antique waiting room of Monsieur Portier and wonders that in France there is 'Never anything new!' (86). Hale's sincere desire 'to help make up to France for the way she's been having the rough end of all this war' (86) is accompanied by a naive idea that American business acumen can solve all France's economic problems. Once again, however, an American confronts cultural forms which he cannot comprehend and which force him into redefinition of self. Hale admits that he would be a poor one for mending personal lives, for reconstructing villages or caring for refugees. But, he is an American, and Americans know how to make money '*for* France' (87). Unable to convince a local druggist to let his American company mass produce and market a remarkable but ancient formula for a cold cream, Hale is amazed, confused and incredulous of the way the French people 'stay put' (91) and would prefer to 'sit quietly and watch the stars come out' (103) than to make millions. His reaction to the Frenchman's polite but insistent refusal of a business proposition is, at first, an accusation of cultural laziness, a commercial backwardness that, he argues, 'gave the Boches their strangle-hold on French commerce before the war' (104). In contrast, the pharmacist Monsieur Requine sees Americans as 'a circle of frenzied worshipers around a fiery Moloch, into whose maw they cast everything that makes life sweet and livable, leisure, love, affection, appreciation of things rare and fine' (105).

Yet, in spite of the confrontation, a reconciliatory tone dominates at the story's close. Requine thinks perhaps his son should have travelled a year in America to study American business, and Hale, after a harried evening of figuring transportation costs, admits 'Maybe we *do* hit it up a little fast' (110). Canfield writes that he had never before truly believed the adage that 'it takes all kinds of people to make a world' (110); he had always believed it only took Americans. In this story, Canfield appeals to readers to re-evaluate what America has to offer France and to accept that France has much to offer in return.

In the third of her 'American stories' – 'A Little Kansas Leaven' – Canfield addresses the subject of young Americans learning to empathize and thereby discovering the 'power for active heroism lying dormant in the human spirit' (Washington, 161). This piece, more than others of the collection, has the flavour of a propagandistic war poster. Ellen Boardman, descendant of Puritans, revolutionists and anti-slavers, rejects the pacifist sermons she hears from the pulpit in Marshallton, Kansas; takes a leave of absence from her steady but unfulfilling work as a stenographer; and withdraws all her savings to embark for France and *do* something. Undeterred by her friends' objections that the French are all immoral and that her contribution would mean nothing in light of the 'millions and millions of dollars being poured out' by the United States (146), Ellen persists quietly in believing that participation in the war is a personal, not just a national, duty. Affected by the utter simplicity of her convictions, the embarrassed minister winces and begins speaking out for war relief while the mocking reporter finds reason to enlist in an ambulance corps.

While most of the story describes Ellen's successful reorganization of a fumbling relief effort set up in Paris by wealthy American socialites, Canfield nearly canonizes her protagonist. With saint-like devotion, Ellen spends every evening at the Gare de l'Est, helping soldiers and their loved ones in any way she can, from holding a baby to providing a lunch with the money she saves from eating only an apple for dinner. Canfield writes, 'She sat there, armed with nothing but her immense ignorance, her immense sympathy' (160). Her stammered apology for cultural ignorance – 'I am sorry that I cannot understand French. I am an American' (160) – is always met with surprise and 'extremely articulate Gallic gratitude' (160). What Canfield takes to task in her story is not the naive and empathetic Ellen, but those who disapprove of 'those foolish American volunteers ... ignorant, awkward, provincial boors, for the most part, knowing nothing of all the exquisite old traditions of France' (166). Canfield lambastes such sentiments, applauding instead the Americans, like Ellen, who respond empathetically to a human tragedy. The leaven in the whole lump is the individual American, whose capacity for feeling and doing makes a hero of the ordinary citizen. Upon returning to Kansas, Ellen relates very simply what she has seen, and 'Marshallton looked aghast and for the first time believed that what it saw was real, that such things were happening to real men and women like themselves' (170).

This, then, was Canfield's purpose in writing *Home Fires in France* – to show that 'war is an experience of people and hence deserving of human sympathy and understanding' (Washington, 161). But, Canfield extends her sympathy and understanding to Americans as well. They did not always know what to do; they did not have a cultural history upon which to draw in order to know themselves. National feelings of inadequacy and guilt were, perhaps, appeased by 'throwing money' at the problem, but Canfield was convinced that Americans could do more. *Home Fires in France* is a call to reassess the American self and to act.

'A Honeymoon ... Vive L'Amerique!', one of the most touching of the stories, shows Americans doing more. Mr and Mrs Robert Hall arrive in Paris like 'two Olympian guests' (228), fairly glutted with money and eager to help. Their riches, coupled with their honesty and good faith, make them easy targets for 'every cosmopolitan mondaine who now felt about her own pet "war-work" the same competitive pride she had had ... for her collection of pet dogs, or Egyptian rings' (241). Ready 'to laugh at the unsophistication of the barbarians' (245) and confident that they can be duped, the worldly and elitist Duchesse de Sazarat-Begonine, for example, underestimates these simple Americans. The

Halls reject her plea for money for her Home for One-armed and Tubercular Soldiers and instead subsidize fully the poor widow Marguerite who cares for wretched slum children in her own two little rooms. As Canfield saw them, Americans had the power to discriminate between the just cause and the self-serving one and would readily throw aside 'a sound business basis' (255) when human concerns took precedence. Regardless of what they perceive as an impracticality of Europeans about money matters, the Halls 'like to put money right in the fists of the people who need it, and then go away and leave them to spend it the way they want to' (236). Like Ellen Boardman, they are embarrassed by their government not doing anything and consequently address the European crisis in the only way they know how. Seeing crisis situations with an 'inimitable, straight, clear gaze' (254), they are 'like super-people', Canfield writes, like 'the last inhabitants of the world before the war, the only happy human beings left' (258).

Home Fires in France is thus as much about America as about France, and, as William Lyon Phelps predicted, made a 'powerful impression on America' (qtd in Washington, 160). With almost overt propagandistic techniques, Canfield appealed to readers' nationalism and pride, roused their sense of guilt, and heralded Americans' simple virtues. One can, indeed, imagine 'new life [coming] into dismal hearts' of women as they sat sewing or rolling bandages while listening to the book being read aloud (Yates, 134). The same might be said of the initial reception of Edith Wharton's *The Marne*, a novella published in December 1918 after America had declared war on Germany. Early reviewers raved about the stylistic beauty of the book and praised it as 'the best description we have yet seen of the attitude of certain classes of Americans toward the war' ('Mrs. Wharton's Story', 7: 1). Like Canfield's collection, *The Marne* was a 'French-American book' (Washington, 161), extolling the virtues of the Gallic culture and arguing for an American appreciation and even adoption of some of those virtues. Wharton's publisher Rutger B. Jewett considered *The Marne* 'the most poignant story of the war' which he had read (qtd in Lewis, 422) and issued Wharton a $4000 advance against the royalties (Benstock, 346). By the spring of 1919, however, sales had dropped off, as had the patriotic fervour of the previous summer when the American armies had curtailed the last major German offensive.

One might speculate that sales were also affected by the 'stinging frankness' that one reviewer thought would 'no doubt antagonize many a complacent reader' (Cooper, 2033). Just as Canfield had done in her vignettes, though, Wharton focused on Americans' ability to change their viewpoints, to move from condescension and self-righteousness to understanding and appreciation of a culture different from their own. Wharton does not, however, expatriate herself from these 'well-meaning, ignorant folk' ('New Novels', 642); they are, after all, her countrymen. Rather, *The Marne* applauds America's belated but enthusiastic entry into the War, as she 'tore the gag of neutrality from her lips' and as Americans found themselves 'not only happier but more sensible than when a perpetually thwarted indignation had had to expend itself in vague philanthropy' (Wharton, 45). *The Marne* becomes, then, a document – admittedly a propagandistic one – of American character, with all its simplicity, self-consciousness and potential.

Wharton's story, unlike her postwar novel *A Son at the Front* (1923), is a simple one. Troy Belknap, the son of wealthy New Yorkers, spends his youth in France and, under the influence of his French tutor, becomes a Francophile. When the War breaks out, his family, after some delay, returns to the United States where Troy is mocked by schoolmates for his fanatic commitment to the cause and where he is shamed by the callousness, self-righteousness and boredom with the war which his fellow Americans exhibit. Convinced that 'There had never been anything worth while in the world that had not had to be died for' (44), Troy sails to France on his eighteenth birthday to serve in an ambulance corps. Returning to the scene of his tutor's death, Troy abandons his disabled vehicle, takes up a rifle and joins the American troops at the second battle of the Marne. Inexperienced and merely imitating what the other men do (119), Troy is wounded when he tries to rescue a fallen compatriot. He is saved from death by the ghost of his tutor and awakens to find himself heralded as a hero in an event 'in which he had played an unconscious part' (125).

While the story-line smacks of sentimentality and a 'strong sense of cinema' (Clough, 6) and varies little from scores of other serialized tales of the war, what distinguishes Wharton's work is the realistic backdrop of Americans and their gradual change of attitude over the three years which the novel's action covers. David Clough rightly assumes that the novella is 'basically emotional propaganda for American intervention to save civilisation from the barbarian Hun' (2), but the novel also provides an insightful study of what it was to be American at that time. Wharton's strongest criticism focuses on the 'frivolous nature of American socialites' (Joslin and Price, 10), both at home and abroad. The Belknaps are 'dreadfully upset' by the first attacks on France solely because they 'could get no money, no seats in the trains, no assurance that the Swiss frontier would not be closed before they could cross the border' (10).

The war is simply a terrible inconvenience for them, and their tendency is 'to regard the war as a mere background to their personal grievances' (15). Once assured of passage out of the country, the Belknaps feel sorry for the French and 'subscribe to all the budding war charities' (11). Such a response irritates and humiliates Troy, who resents the American idea that giving money in generous amounts absolves one of responsibility while appeasing one's conscience. Wharton's descriptions of the expatriate Americans are some of the most effective and certainly the most scathing in the book. She, along with Troy, is repulsed by 'the indignant chorus of compatriots stranded in Paris, and obscurely convinced that France ought to have seen them safely home before turning her attention to the invader'. After all, they had 'really spent enough money in Europe for some consideration' (17–18).

Until her safe return to New York, Mrs Belknap and others of her set offer assistance to 'their beloved city' (22), pour tea occasionally at fashionable hospitals and take convalescent officers on drives in the country. Their 'unawareness of the meaning of war' (32) follows them to their home turf where they play at charity ('New Novels', 642), request that their gifts be acknowledged, and compete with one another in telling the best first-hand tales of woe. These passages, as R. W. B. Lewis has noted, are the best of the novella, evoking Wharton's 'contempt for the imperturbable blindness of Americans back home during the war and the self-inflation of those who had glimpsed the devastated areas through the windows of a chauffeur-driven car' (422). The prevailing national sentiment that war is terrible but that this is not 'our war' (37) was a true reflection of American complacency.

Troy, like his creator, is outraged by America's neglect of moral responsibility, and the shame he feels is typical of adolescence, as Lev Raphael has pointed out (157). But, that shame is also typical of an adolescent nation which, after the attack on the *Lusitania* and the subsequent declaration of war, responded with a defensive posture, not admitting as moral error its previous reluctance to be involved but defending that reluctance on the basis of moral superiority. The few, like Sophy Wicks, who had always professed boredom with the war and were 'too self-conscious to renounce [that stance]' (46) fare much better under Wharton's pen than those who suddenly take up the cause in an effort to enlighten poor, backward France. Like Canfield's Americans, Wharton's set out for Europe 'full of the importance of America's mission': 'This was Liberty's chance to Enlighten the World . . . ' (58–9). They would teach France efficiency and domestic science; purify her morally; and teach Frenchmen to respect women, to love their children, and to love the outdoor life (59–61). Troy is ashamed of such condescending attitudes and 'desperately needs to prove that he is brave, important, strong' (Raphael, 155).

So, one might suspect, did many young American soldiers have the same need. Their mission, like Troy's, became 'an adolescent's daydream ... given the weight of a national myth', a myth which is 'curiously and typically American' (Clough, 5). Wharton describes the troops as virtuous and noble knights, 'out on their real business at last', pouring forth 'from the reservoirs of the new world to replenish the wasted veins of the old' (79). They have honest and innocent faces and 'an air of simple daylight friendliness' (92) as they gather in the cellar of a YMCA hut. Like Canfield's doughboys in 'Notes', they speak in American slang and are jolly among themselves, but they lack the verisimilitude that Wharton sought. They are flat figures and too much the 'Boy Scouts out on a field trip ... giving their lives as a sort of good deed for the day, with the merit badge of "Glory" for their reward' (Cooperman, 42). While this chivalric portrait of Americanness undoubtedly appealed to contemporary readers, it makes the novel 'now an almost total embarrassment to read', as Peter Buitenhuis remarks (497).

Still, in *The Marne*, Wharton chronicles a change in Americans' attitudes that commends them as a compassionate people, capable of redefining self and reaching new understandings of cultural forms. Hinda Warlick, a Midwestern girl whose limited knowledge of France is a confused idea of Joan of Arc being guillotined with Marie Antoinette (60), becomes, along with Troy, Wharton's representative of the 'dear, tender-hearted, uncomprehending America' who comes to appreciate both France and the righteousness of her struggle. Speaking to the American troops in France, Miss Warlick confesses to her previous cultural blindness and wrong-headed belief in France's inferiority. 'I've got to know the country they're dying for – ' she remarks, 'and I understand why they mean to go on and on dying ... I know France now – and she's worth it!' (97–9). As reviewers noted, the 'well-meaning, ignorant' Americans are converted ('New Novels', 642); they 'learn their lesson in proper humility' (Cooper, 2033) and earn the respect of Wharton and her readers.

Although *The Marne* could rightfully be considered 'the most naive and sentimental fiction that [Wharton] ever wrote' (Buitenhuis, 497) or 'old-fashioned, even reactionary' (Lauer, 88), this slim volume offers 'very interesting, and at times very curious, light ... on contemporary American attitudes to the war' (Clough, 1). In this aspect *The Marne* is a 'better' novel than Wharton's postwar work *A Son at the Front* (1923).

While the latter novel shares with *The Marne* realistic details of the war, couched in the jingoism and patriotic fervour of the period, it is far less successful in tracing the growth of a national consciousness and the shift from isolationism to global participation. John Campton's story is that of the expatriate artist who rediscovers his muse through the death of his son in the war and painfully comes to accept that the old values and old order are gone. (In this aspect *A Son at the Front* bears closer resemblance thematically to *The Age of Innocence* than to Wharton's other war pieces.) Wharton focuses on the self-centredness of Campton, not as a representative of his native land but as an artist whose detachment is threatened by the passions aroused by war. As in *The Marne*, France serves as the idea of civilization, and it is the younger generation – George Campton and his fighting compatriots – who sense that 'all they had believed in and been guided by would perish' should France fall (*Son*, 366). The elder Campton feels this sentiment 'but dully, through a fog' (366) until after his son's death when he, too, kneels before 'the altar of conviction' (397).

While Wharton's melodramatic language and action appear in this novel, too, giving the reader the same 'feeling of taking an old enlistment poster out of an attic trunk' (Auchincloss, 27), the poster message is not the same as that of *The Marne*. The central figure of John Campton does not represent 'a typical American consciousness' coming into 'an awareness of responsibilities – from personal to the national and finally to the international', as Peter Buitenhuis claims (503). Campton is far from typical, and the shadowy images that float about him are not of trenches and barbed wire, sacrifice and honour. His crisis of consciousness is intensely personal and exudes more of the author's concern about an artist's response to war than about the general populace's.

Troy Belknap, on the other hand, is every American's idealized 'son at the front'. Simple and naive, he is nonetheless the poster boy who brings into reality the potential heroism, self-sacrifice and compassion of a nation. With sometimes rash action and romanticized vision, Troy defines the best of what Americans think themselves to be. The power of *The Marne* lies in Wharton's skill at characterizing such an idealist and 'deliberately exploit[ing] American foibles' (Clough, 7) to reveal the American capacity for personal growth and self-understanding.

The Marne is propaganda, but like Canfield's *Home Fires in France*, it explores the transformation of the American character during the Great War as Americans developed new 'cultural repertoires of meaning' (Leed, ix) and enlarged their sympathies without destroying their simplicity. Both these works thus deserve a place in the expanding canon of war literature, not as idle curiosities from the pens of two of the era's most popular writers but as legitimate studies of national attitudes, cultural awakening and redefinition of the American self.

Acknowledgements

All excerpts from the works by Edith Wharton are reprinted by permission of the Estate of Edith Wharton and the Watkins / Loomis Agency.

Works cited

Auchincloss, Louis. *Edith Wharton*, University of Minnesota Pamphlets on American Writers 12. Minneapolis: University of Minnesota Press, 1961.
Benstock, Shari. *No Gifts From Chance: A Biography of Edith Wharton*. New York: Scribner's, 1994.
Buitenhuis, Peter. 'Edith Wharton and The First World War', *American Quarterly*, 18 (1966): 493–505.
Canfield, Dorothy. *Home Fires in France*. New York: Henry Holt, 1918.
Cather, Willa. *Not Under Forty*. New York: Knopf, 1936.
Clough, David. 'Edith Wharton's War Novels: A Reappraisal', *Twentieth Century Literature*, 19 (1973): 1–14.
Cooper, Frederic Taber. 'A Clear-cut Gem of War Fiction', review of *The Marne* by Edith Wharton, *Publisher's Weekly*, 28 December 1918: 2033.
Cooperman, Stanley. *World War I and the American Novel*. Baltimore, MD: Johns Hopkins Press, 1967.
Higonnet, Margaret Randolph et al. (eds) 'Introduction', in *Behind the Lines: Gender and the Two World Wars*. New Haven, CT: Yale University Press, 1987, 1–17.
Joslin, Katherine and Alan Price (eds) 'Introduction', in *Wretched Exotic: Essays on Edith Wharton in Europe*. New York: Peter Lang, 1993, 1–16.
Lauer, Kristin Olson. 'Can France Survive This Defender? Contemporary American Reaction to Wharton's Expatriation', in *Wretched Exotic: Essays on Edith Wharton in Europe*, eds Katherine Joslin and Alan Price. New York: Peter Lang, 1993, 77–95.
Leed, Eric J. *No Man's Land: Combat and Identity in World War I*. London: Cambridge University Press, 1979.
Lewis, R. W. B. *Edith Wharton: A Biography*. New York: Harper & Row, 1975.
'Mrs. Wharton's Story of the Marne: Remarkable Romance of the War, Picturing Certain American Types in France', review of *The Marne* by Edith Wharton, *New York Times*, 8 December 1918, sec. 7: 1.
'New Novels: *The Marne*', review of *The Marne* by Edith Wharton, *Times Literary Supplement* (London), 19 December 1918: 642.
Raphael, Lev. *Edith Wharton's Prisoners of Shame*. New York: St. Martin's Press – now Palgrave, 1991.
Washington, Ida. W. *Dorothy Canfield Fisher: A Biography*. Shelburne, VT: New England Press, 1982.

Wharton, Edith. *The Marne*. New York: Appleton, 1918.
——. *A Son at the Front*. New York: Scribner's, 1923.
Yates, Elizabeth. *The Lady from Vermont: Dorothy Canfield Fisher's Life and World*. Brattleboro, VT: Stephen Greene Press, 1971.

Part IV
Modernists at War

10
Fatal Symbiosis: Modernism and the First World War

Milton A. Cohen

In 1909, Ezra Pound, standing on a chair in a London café and assuming the persona of the troubador poet and warrior, Bertrans de Born, declaimed the following lines from his new poem, 'Sestina: Altaforte':

> Damn it all! all this our South stinks peace....
> There's no sound like to sword's swords opposing,
> No cry like the battle's rejoicing
> When our elbows and swords drip the crimson....
> Hell grant soon we hear again the swords clash!
> Hell blot black for alway the thought 'Peace'!

That same year, in Paris, the Italian Futurists declared in their 'Foundation Manifesto' on the front page of *Le Figaro*: 'We will glorify war – the world's only hygiene – militarism, patriotism, the destructive gesture of freedom-bringers.... Except in struggle, there is no more beauty. No work without an aggressive character can be a masterpiece. Poetry must be conceived as a violent attack on unknown forces....' (Marinetti, 41–2).

Ominous images of war and apocalypse marked the Expressionist poems published in the Berlin avant-garde journals *Die Aktion* and *Der Sturm* beginning about 1911. By 1912–13, motifs of cannons and marching soldiers, exploding shells and burning cities proliferated in modernist painting, regardless of whether the canvas was painted in London or Berlin, Paris or Prague. And in the same month as the assassination of Archduke Franz Ferdinand, the British composer Gustav Holst completed the first of his pieces for *The Planets*: 'Mars, the Bringer of War'.

As anticipations of the First World War, these images of war have been typically treated either as instances of artistic naivety (in glorifying a horror that artists could scarcely imagine) or as artistic prescience in sensing the blood that was already 'in the air'. Yet such clichés miss the complexity of modernism's relation to the First World War. For beyond merely anticipating or even welcoming a new war, avant-garde artists across Europe drew upon war in its multiple meanings – war as metaphor and as actuality, war as language, as visual images, as models of both organizing and destructive power, and, most of all, war as focused energy. The modernists' relation to war, however, proved symbiotic: as they drew energy from these *constructions* of war, their own energies, in turn, were quickly sucked into the real war's immeasurably larger vortex – with profound consequences for the arts.

Modernist artists had been at war long before they were mobilized in August 1914. Their primary enemies were the forces of artistic reaction: the hostile press, the conservative academies, the reactionary critics, the smug, self-satisfied bourgeoisie. Of course, this battle was hardly new in the 1910s, evolving through a series of skirmishes and scandals throughout the nineteenth century. By the early 1910s, however, as modernist innovation intensified, so did its struggle against reaction, and increasingly, modernists turned to war and violence for the vocabulary to depict it. Franz Marc, for example, writes in *The Blaue Reiter Almanac* of 1912:

In this time of great struggle for a new art, we fight like disorganized 'savages' against the old established power. The battle seems to be unequal, but spiritual matters are never decided by numbers, only by the power of ideas. The dreaded weapons of the 'savages' are their new ideas. New ideas kill better than steel and destroy what was thought to be indestructible.

('The Savages of Germany', 61)

The German Expressionists were especially prone to aggressive language because they saw themselves in a *Kulturkampf* against Wilhelminian stagnation. Berlin poet Ernst Blass recalls: 'What I was engaged in ... was a literary movement, a war on the gigantic philistine of those days. ... a spirited battle against the soullessness, the deadness, laziness, and meanness of the philistine world. ... *We were definitely the opposition*' (Cross, 5). Fire-eaters such as Ezra Pound pushed war metaphors still further to energize this call to arms in January 1914:

The artist has at last been aroused to the fact that the war between him and the world is a war without truce. That his only remedy is slaughter. ... He must live by craft and violence. His gods are violent gods. . . . [The new] sculpture with its general combat, its emotional condemnation, gives us our strongest satisfaction . . . The artist has been at peace with his oppressors for long enough. . . . We turn back, we artists, to the powers of the air, to the djinn who were our allies aforetime, to the spirits of our ancestors. It is by them that we have ruled and shall rule. . . . And the public will do well to resent these 'new' kinds of art.

('The New Sculpture', 67–8)

At times, modernists borrowed the rhetoric of imperialist generals and politicians. Apollinaire spoke of 'annexing' new domains for poetry and called for artists to 'marshall their forces' so as to confront the hostile public 'with a solid [and united] front' (quoted in Gibson, 191). Kandinsky described how his *Blaue Reiter Almanac* would advance with 'a left . . . and right wing' (quoted in Lankheit, 14). As if in response, the *Mercure de France* referred to the riot produced at the 1913 premiere of the Ballets Russes' *Le Sacre du Printemps* as having the gravity of an international border incident (*Le Figaro*, 1).

The very extremity of this language shows how thoroughly it belonged to a realm where 'slaughter' was entirely metaphorical. In his memoir of the period, Wyndham Lewis (who, with Pound, led the Vorticist group) recalls the safety of these mock-battles: 'the months immediately preceding the declarations of war were full of sound and fury, and . . . all the artists and men of letters had gone into action before the bank-clerks were clapped into Khaki. . . . Life was one big bloodless brawl, prior to the Great Bloodletting' (Lewis, 35–6).

Note that these quotations typically come from artists in groups and movements: the Blaue Reiter of Munich, the poets of Berlin's *Die Aktion*, the Italian Futurists, Pound's and Lewis's Vorticists in London. Such groups emboldened like-minded artists in their art, their ideas and their behaviour. Organized and led by dynamos and mavericks such as Ezra Pound, Wyndham Lewis, Filippo Marinetti, Herwarth Walden, David Burliuk and Wassily Kandinsky, such groups were aggressive by their very nature. They declared war through belligerent manifestos of their aesthetics (one was aptly named 'A Slap in the Face of Public Taste'); and they joined battle through collective exhibitions, publications, concerts and multimedia 'evenings' that frequently ended in a shouted row or a fist-fight. Here, modernist combat left the metaphorical realm to become actual – a planned and realized brawl. The most famous of these mêlées, the riot that greeted the Paris premiere of Stravinsky's *Le Sacre du Printemps*, has recently been shown to have been not just the spontaneous reaction of a hostile audience, but a *two-sided* battle largely anticipated and eagerly joined by young Stravinsky partisans (Eksteins, 10–42).

In their struggle for recognition, modernist groups fought each other almost as much as the hostile public. Artists like Pound, Kandinsky and Larionov often split off from their own groups, which now seemed too conservative, to form newer, more radical groups, prompting internecine warfare. Fledgling groups like the English Vorticists fought to maintain their identity and keep from being swallowed by more imperialistic groups like the Italian Futurists. As Wyndham Lewis, the Vorticists' co-leader, described these manoeuvres: '*Putsches* took place every month or so. Marinetti for instance . . . brought off a Futurist *Putsch* about this time. . . . I counter-putsched.' And as Lewis also observed, these bloodless battles, reported at length in the press, provided the public with much entertainment and became a kind of performance art:

As *chef de bande* of the Vorticists I cut a figure in London. . . . I might have been at the head of a social revolution, instead of merely being the prophet of a new fashion in art.

Really all this organized disturbance was Art behaving as if it were Politics. . . .

The Press in 1914 had no Cinema, no Radio, . . . so the painter could really become a 'star'. . . . 'Kill John Bull with Art!' I shouted. And John and Mrs. Bull leapt for joy, in a cynical convulsion. For they felt as safe as houses. So did I.

(Lewis, 35–6)

As Lewis suggests, the modernist battles of 1910–14 not only played at war, but also uncannily prefigured the real violence to come. Immersed as they were in their own battles, artists, writers and composers were not oblivious to the European political situation that had grown increasingly threatening since the unresolved Agadir Crisis of 1911. Parisian artists would have noted the torchlight military parades that resumed in 1912 after a twenty-year hiatus; German modernists would immediately feel the war tax imposed in 1913 to pay for a newly expanded army. Artists everywhere would read of the European war scares brought on by the Balkan Wars of 1912–13; and several artists fulfilled their military obligations in these years. The most visible modernist of the time, the Italian Futurists' leader, Filippo Marinetti, made the connection between art and politics explicit by using his war experience as a journalist covering the Balkan Wars and Italy's Libya campaign to justify the modernity of his telegraphic free-form poetics that he called 'Parole in libertà'.[1]

Responses to both of these stimuli – international tensions and avant-garde struggle – can be seen in modernist paintings of these years. In 1913 Jacques Villon paints a semi-abstract image of *Marching Soldiers* in Paris, while across the Channel, Wyndham Lewis does a series of prewar abstractions with martial motifs and titles such as *Plan of War* and *Slow Attack* in 1914. In Bavaria, Franz Marc dresses a horseman in a German officer's blue tunic and spiked headgear in his 1913 *St. Julian, the Hospitaler* and entitles another painting *Wolves: Balkan War*. At the same time, his Blaue Reiter associate, Wassily Kandinsky, shows cannons obliterating hints of buildings and hills in his semi-abstract *Improvisation No. 30: Cannons*. Kandinsky subtitles his next *Improvisation* 'Naval battle'.

Several middle-European painters envisioned apocalyptic scenes of cities or woods being blown apart. And although these images point to a larger cultural destruction, war is typically the solvent. At least three of Ludwig Meidner's apocalyptic pictures of 1911–13 – *Shelling of a City* (1913), *Horrors of War* (1911) and *Apocalyptic Landscape* (1913) – trace their destructions specifically to war. Franz Marc's *Animal Destinies* is even more disturbing: jagged blood-red diagonals rip apart a forest while animals cower, bellow and die as they are sucked into the maelstrom. Such violence shocked even its creator when he saw a postcard reproduction of this painting two years later while he was at the front: 'I was startled and astonished by its immediate effect on me. I saw it as an utterly strange work, a premonition of war that had something shocking about it. It is a curious picture, as if created in a trance.'[2] Curious, too, was the ambivalent mood of these middle-European painters; for if their images were violent, often apocalyptic, their mood in these prewar years was essentially optimistic and expectant. Almost to a person, they adopted Nietzsche's view that such destruction necessarily preceded a greater creation and felt that their canvases were really the 'signal fires' (as Marc put it) for the pathfinders of a more spiritual epoch to come ('Two Pictures', 13).

It is not surprising, therefore, that modernists across Europe greeted the mobilizations of August 1914 with the same naive enthusiasm as did most other citizens of the belligerent nations. The War, Marc predicted in an article written at the front, would provide the 'purifying fire' to clean out European decay and leave a 'refined and hardened culture' ('In War's Purifying Fire', 161–5). Some modernists, like Apollinaire and Léger, even found new sources of creative inspiration in the life of the artilleryman and foot soldier. But like the tiger in the limerick, this war could not be ridden without consequences; indeed, *it* was the rider.

The war disrupted virtually everyone's life: artists put aside brushes and pens to volunteer or follow their mobilization orders; émigrés like Kandinsky suddenly found themselves living in an 'enemy' country and hurriedly returned 'home' or sought safe haven in a neutral country, as did more than a few nationals avoiding the war. Groups that had been the lifeblood of prewar modernism disbanded, never to reform, their members in uniform, exiled, dead. Modernist journals folded: *Les Soirées de Paris*, *The Blaue Reiter Almanac*, eventually *BLAST*, *Lacerba*, *Pan* and many others.[3] The mock-wars artists had been fighting now seemed childish beside the real thing, and the public no longer cared. Modernist concerts, poetry readings and exhibitions were seldom held in the belligerent countries and failed to arouse much controversy when they were.

Artists out of uniform found it difficult to work in a war milieu. Picasso and Matisse each wrestled with guilt over being safe while their friends (and sons in Matisse's case) risked death. Expatriates like Juan Gris, who had thrived in the cosmopolitanism of prewar modernism, were stunned by the bloodthirsty xenophobia that now prevailed in Paris and Berlin. Ernst Ludwig Kirchner was doubly a victim. The war he served in, which gave him such harrowing fears of mutilation and castration seen in his *Self-Portrait as a Soldier* and which ultimately caused him a complete mental breakdown, now threatened to rob him of creative purpose as a civilian. As he wrote to a friend: 'The pressure of the war and the increasingly prevailing superficiality weigh more heavily than everything else. One feels that crisis is in the air. . . . Turgidly one vacillates, whether to work, where any work is surely to no purpose.'[4] Perhaps the Cubist painter, Albert Gleizes, summarized these conditions best: 'The present conflict throws into anarchy all the intellectual paths of the pre-war period, and the reasons are simple: the leaders are in the army and the generation of thirty-year-olds is sparse. . . . The past is finished' (Shapiro, 152).

More completely 'finished' than Gleizes could have realized in 1915. The war's physical toll was immense: it killed or severely maimed scores of artists, including some of the very best; it drove numerous others to physical or nervous breakdowns and weakened still others to make them vulnerable to the 1918–19 influenza epidemic or to pneumonia (see Appendix).

The war also killed the modernists' prewar mood of buoyant optimism about the future and about the war's role in bringing it about. Two years into the war, Franz Marc's expectancy about the war as a cultural scourge had turned to leaden despair. He wrote to the widow of his close friend, the painter August Macke, that the War was 'the cruelest catch of men to which we have abandoned ourselves'. And in a letter to his wife – one of his last before he too was 'caught' – he reflected: 'It is terrible to think of; and all for *nothing*, for a misunderstanding....' (Partsch, 91). Oskar Kokoschka painted the trauma of his multiple woundings and loss of idealism into a 1915 self-portrait, *The Knight Errant*. Amid an apocalyptic setting of darkness, flood, devastation and the angel of death, the artist lies in rigor-mortis-like stiffness, one arm awkwardly extended. Though his tunic is contemporary, his leg irons make him appear a knight, overweighted with armour, who has fallen from his charger and cannot right himself. The grotesque inadequacy of a chivalric conception of this war could not be clearer.

Finally, modernism itself became a war casualty: it survived, but profoundly changed. As Kenneth Silver has documented in *Esprit de Corps*, the war provided the perfect opportunity for conservative opponents of modernism to counter-attack. In a wartime climate of extreme nationalism and xenophobia, modernism's international character, elitism and abstract experimentation proved easy targets. Conservative French critics branded it the epitome of prewar decadence, something insidiously foreign and debilitating: Cubism was now spelled with the Germanic 'K'. The critics' call for a return to the 'classical' French values of balance, restraint and order attracted even such dedicated prewar modernists as Apollinaire, Picasso and Cocteau. In all of the belligerent countries except perhaps Russia, modernism was now attacked as decadent and subversive, and most modernists pulled in their horns. The London *Times* called the Second Exhibition of the London Group 'Junkerism in Art' and 'Prussian in spirit'. In Prague, Arnold Schoenberg withdrew his relatively tame *Chamber Symphony* from a 1916 performance because 'he did not want to excite aesthetic controversy now that the national emergency took priority over everything else' (Moldenhauer, 215). In England a year later, Pound and Eliot began prescribing 'rhyme and regular strophes' to counteract the excesses of free verse,[5] and by 1918, perhaps responding to Picasso's return to figurative portraiture, Apollinaire's poetry adopted 'classic rhyme' in contrast to his brashly pictorial *Calligrammes*.[6]

Counterpoised to this conservative shift was modernism's most radical movement of the war years, Dadaism. Yet Dada's nihilism itself was a product of the war; its brittle laughter that proclaimed nothing, least of all art, was worth saving was far removed from prewar modernism's high ambitions and optimistic battles for cultural rejuvenation. Indeed, between Dada's nihilism and conservative neoclassicism, and in a Europe so utterly ravaged by the war that 'cultural rejuvenation' itself was a Dada joke, there seemed little room and less reason for the prewar modernist programme to continue. It had become a casualty of the war that it had so confidently anticipated and emulated.

Appendix: Modernist Casualties of the First World War*

> How much is lost for all of us; it is like a murder. . . .
> Franz Marc, on learning of August Macke's death

Killed in action

Kurt Adler, German poet (1892–1916)
Peter Baum, German novelist and poet (1869–1916)
Rudolf Börsch, German writer (1895–1915)
Hans Ehrenbaum-Degele, German poet (1889–1915)
Gerrit Engelke, German poet and writer (1890–1918)
Walter Ferl, German writer (1892–1915)
Eugen Fischer, German writer (1891–1915)
Georg Hecht, German poet (1885–1915)
Paul Heller, Austrian writer (?–1916)
Hugo Hinz, German poet (1894–1914?)
Robert Jentzsch, German poet (1890–1918)
Alfred Lichtenstein, German poet and novelist (1889–1914)
Ernst Wilhelm Lotz, German poet (1890–1914)
August Macke, German painter (1887–1914)
Franz Marc, German painter (1880–1916)
Albert Michel, German writer and poet (1895–1915)
Wilhelm Morgner, German painter (1891–1917)
Franz Nölken, German painter (?–1918)
Walter Rosam, German painter (1883–1916)
Wilhelm Runge, German poet (1894–1918)
Gustav Sack, German poet and novelist (1885–1916)
Reinhard Johannes Sorge, German poet and playwright (1892–1916)
Ernst Stadler, German poet (1883–1914)
Hermann Stenner, German painter (1891–1914)
August Stramm, German poet and dramatist (1874–1915)
Kurt Striepe, German writer (?–1917)
Albert Weisgerber, German painter (1878–1915)
Robert Zellermayer, German writer (?–1917)

Giosué Borsi, Italian poet (1888–1915)
Nino Oxilia, Italian film director, playwright and poet (1888–1918)
Antonio Sant'Elia, Italian architect (1888–1916)

Alain-Fournier, French novelist (1886–1914)
Robert Besnard, French painter (1881–1914)
Henri Doucet, French artist (1883–1915)
René Dupuy (pseud. Dalize), French poet (1879–1917)

Henri Gaudier-Brzeska, French sculptor (1891–1915)
Léo Latil, French poet (1890–1915)
Olivier-Hourcade, French poet (1892–1914)
Charles Péguy, French poet (1873–1914)
Ernest Psichari, French writer (1883–1914)
Roger Vincent, French writer (1886–1915)

George Butterworth, English composer (1885–1916)
T. E. Hulme, English poet and theorist (1883–1917)
H. H. Munro ('Saki'), English short-story writer (1870–1916)
Wilfred Owen, English poet (1893–1918)
Isaac Rosenberg, English poet and painter (1890–1918)
Edward Thomas, English poet and writer (1878–1917)

Georges Antoine, Belgian composer (1892–1918)
Valadimir Burliuk, Russian painter (1886–1917)
Franz Janowitz, Bohemian poet (1892–1917)
Aladár Rado, Hungarian composer (1882–1914)

Died from war wounds or war-related causes

Guillaume Apollinaire, French poet and journalist (1880–1918; died of pneumonia, severely weakened by head wound and trepanning)
Umberto Boccioni, Italian painter (1882–1916; died from fall from his horse)
Hans Bolz, German painter (1887–1918; died of exhaustion)
Rupert Brooke, English poet (1887–1915; died of uremic poisoning while en route to Dardenelles)
Raymond Duchamp-Villon, French painter and sculptor (1876–1918; died of typhoid contracted in trenches)
Roger de la Fresnaye, French painter (1885–1925; died of pneumonia, severely weakened by lung haemorrhages in war)
Enrique Granados, Spanish composer (1867–1916; drowned after torpedo attack on English ship)
Franz Henseler, German painter (1883–1918; died of exhaustion and insanity)
Alfred Heymel, German poet and publisher (1878–1914; died of illness contracted at front)
Hans Leybold, German poet (1894–1914; suicide at the front)
Wilhelm Lehmbruck, German sculptor (1881–1919; suicide from depression partly caused by his war work as hospital orderly and self-exile to Switzerland)
Alexandre Mercereau, French writer, closely connected with French painters and poets (1884–d?; severely wounded, never fully recovered)
Otto Mueller (1874–1930; died of lung disease caused by two lung haemorrhages in war)
Georg Trakl, Austrian poet (1887–1914; drug overdose (accident or suicide unknown) while in military hospital)

Died from influenza epidemic, 1918–1919

Gustav Klimpt, Austrian painter (1862–1918)
Bohumil Kubišta, Czech painter (1884–1918)
Tadeusz Nalepinski, Polish poet, novelist, and playwright (1885–1918)

Morton Schamburg, American painter (1882–1918)
Egon Schiele, Austrian painter (1890–1918)

Severely wounded

George Braque, French painter (head wound, trepanned)
Blaise Cendrars, French poet (arm amputated)
Otto Dix, German painter (wounded three times)
Othon Friesz, French painter
Ernest Hemingway, American novelist (badly wounded in leg)
Oskar Kokoschka, Austrian painter (shot in head, bayonetted in lung)
Franticek Kupka, Czech painter (awarded Legion of Honour by French)
Mikhail Larionov, Russian painter (concussion)
Fernand Léger, French painter (gassed)
F. T. Marinetti, Italian poet
Luigi Russolo, Italian painter and composer (head wound)
Josef Sudek, Czech photographer (arm amputated)
Laurence Stallings, American playwright
Jacob Steinhardt, German poet
Georgy Yakulov, Russian painter

Suffered nervous or physical breakdown during or just after war

Max Beckmann, German painter
Alban Berg, Austrian composer (physical breakdown)
Oskar Graf, German novelist (psychological breakdown)
Ivor Gurney, English composer (complete mental breakdown)
Erich Heckel, German painter (painting impaired for a time after war)
David Jones, English poet and artist (mental breakdown)
Ernst Ludwig Kirchner, German painter ('complete physical and mental breakdown')
Oskar Kokoschka (shell shock)
Karl Schmidt-Rottluff, German painter (painting impaired for a few years after war)
Arnold Schoenberg, Austrian composer (physical breakdown)
Georg Trakl, German poet (after treating casualties as medic)

Foreign national returning to native country

Natan Altman, Russian graphic designer (from Paris)
Zhenia Bogoslavskaya, Russian artist (from Paris)
Marc Chagall, Russian painter (from Paris)
Giorgio De Chirico, Italian painter (from Paris)
Natalia Gontcharova, Russian painter (from Paris)
Wassily Kandinsky, Russian painter (from Bavaria after stays in Switzerland and Sweden)
El Lissitzky, Russian painter (from Darmstadt)
Max Pechstein, German painter (from Palau Islands)
Elie Nadelman, American sculptor (from Paris)

Liubov Popova, Russian painter (from Paris)
Ivan Puni, Russian artist (from Paris)
Nadezhda Udaltsova, Russian painter (from Paris)

Foreign national moving to neutral country

Alexei Von Jawlensky, Russian painter (Switzerland from Munich)
Daniel-Henry Kahnweiler, German art dealer (Switzerland from Paris)
Marie Laurencin, French painter married to a German (Spain from Paris)
Wilhelm Uhde, German art dealer (Switzerland? from Paris)
Marianne Werefkina, Russian painter (Switzerland from Germany)

Citizen moving to neutral country

Alexander Archipenko, Russian painter and sculptor (Switzerland)
Hugo Ball, German writer (Switzerland)
Robert and Sonia Delaunay, French painters (Spain and Portugal)
Marcel Duchamp, French painter (USA)
Albert Gleizes, French painter (USA)
Richard Huelsenbeck, German writer (Switzerland)
Ernst Ludwig Kirchner, German painter (Switzerland)
Else Lasker-Schüler, German poet (Switzerland)
Wilhelm Lehmbruck, German sculptor (Switzerland)
Gabriele Münter, German painter (Switzerland, Sweden, Denmark)
Max Oppenheimer, Austrian painter (Switzerland)
Julius Pascin, Bulgarian painter (London, USA)
Francis Picabia, French painter (USA and Spain)
Hans Richter, German painter and filmmaker (Switzerland)
Romain Rolland, French novelist (Switzerland)
Christian Schad, German painter (Switzerland)
Igor Stravinsky, Russian composer (Switzerland)
Tristan Tzara, Romanian poet (Switzerland)
Edgar Varese, French composer (USA)

Imprisoned during war

e. e. cummings, American poet and painter (briefly imprisoned by French, 1917)
Lyonel Feininger, German-American painter (interned by Germans, 1917–18)
Otto Gutfreund, Czech sculptor (interned three years by French Foreign Legion for insubordination)
Karl Hofer, German painter (interned as enemy alien in France until 1917)
Max Pechstein, German painter (interned in New Guinea)
Jacques Riviere, French writer, p.o.w. of Germans
Heinrich Vogeler, German painter (incarcerated by Germans)

---

* 'Modernist' here is determined by an artist's work, by inclusion in modernist journals or by affiliation with modernist groups.

Notes

1. See 'Destruction of Syntax – Imagination without Strings – Words-in-Freedom 1913'; rpt. in *Futurist Manifestos (The Documents of 20th-Century Art)*, ed. with introduction Umbro Apollonio, trans. Robert Brain, R. W. Flint and Caroline Tisdall (New York: Viking Press, 1973): 95–106.
2. Letter to Bernhard Koehler, March 1915; quoted in Frederick Levine, *The Apocalyptic Vision: The Art of Franz Marc as German Expressionism* (New York: Harper & Row, 1979): 77.
3. Of 16 German Expressionist journals extant in August 1914, only five survived the first year of the war and all underwent rigorous censorship; the literary circles surrounding these journals likewise disbanded or suffered drastically altered memberships (Roy F. Allen, *Literary Life in German Expressionism and the Berlin Circles*, Ann Arbor, MI: UMI Research Press, 1983: 33–4). The same held true for Paris: 'General mobilization ... meant suspension of almost all publications' (Kenneth Cornell, *The Post-Symbolist Period: French Poetic Currents, 1900–1920*, New Haven, CT: Yale University Press, 1958: 134).
4. Pound, Ezra. 'Harold Monro', in *Ezra Pound: Polite Essays* (Plainview, NY: Books for Libraries, 1966): 14.
5. Apollinaire wrote to Picasso: 'What I am doing now will accord better with your present preoccupations. I am trying to renovate the poetic tone, but in the classic rhyme' (4 September 1918; qtd. in Kenneth Silver, *Esprit de Corps*).

Works cited

Allen, Roy F. *Literary Life in German Expressionism and the Berlin Circles.* Ann Arbor, MI: UMI Research Press, 1983.

Cornell, Kenneth. *The Post-Symbolist Period: French Poetic Currents, 1900–1920.* New Haven, CT: Yale University Press, 1958.

Cross, Tim. *The Lost Voices of World War I: An International Anthology of Writers, Poets and Playwrights.* Iowa City: University of Iowa Press, 1988.

Eksteins, Modris. *Rites of Spring: The Great War and the Birth of the Modern Age.* London: Bantam, 1989.

Le Figaro, 2 June 1913: 1.

Gibson, Robert. *Modern French Poets on Poetry.* Cambridge: Cambridge University Press, 1961.

Lankheit, Klaus. 'Introduction', *The Blaue Reiter Almanac*, ed. Klaus Lankheit. New York: Da Capo, 1974.

Levine, Frederick. *The Apocalyptic Vision: The Art of Franz Marc as German Expressionism.* New York: Harper & Row, 1979.

Lewis, Wyndham. *Blasting and Bombadiering*, 1937. London: J. Chalders, 1982.

Marc, Franz. 'In War's Purifying Face', *Voices of German Expressionism*, ed. Victor H. Miesel. Englewood Cliffs, NJ: Prentice-Hall, 1970: 161–5.

——. 'The Savages of Germany', *The Blaue Reiter Almanac*, eds Wassily Kandinsky and Franz Marc. Munich: 1912; Documentary Edition, ed. Klaus Lankheit. New York: Da Capo, 1974: 61.

——. 'Two Pictures', *The Blaue Reiter Almanac*, eds Wassily Kandinsky and Franz Marc. Munich: 1912; Documentary Edition, ed. Klaus Lankheit. New York: Da Capo, 1974: 69.

Marinetti, F. T. 'Destruction of Syntax – Imagination without Strings – Words-in-Freedom 1913', *Futurist Manifestos (The Documents of 20th-Century Art)*, ed. Umbro Appollonio. New York: Viking, 1973.

——. 'The Foundation and Manifesto of Futurism', *Marinetti: Selected Writings*, ed. R. W. Flint. New York: Farrar, Straus & Giroux, 1971: 41–2.

Moldenhauer, Hans and Rosaleen. *Anton Webern: A Chronicle of His Life and Work*. New York: Knopf, 1979.

Partsch, Susanna. *Franz Marc: 1880–1916*. Cologne: Benedikt Taschen, 1991.

Pound, Ezra. 'Harold Monro', *Ezra Pound: Polite Essays*. Plainview, NY: Books for Libraries, 1966.

——. 'The New Sculpture', *Ezra Pound and the Visual Arts*, ed. Harriet Zinnes. New York: New Directions, 1980.

Shapiro, Theda. *Painters and Politics: The European Avant-Garde and Society*. New York: Elsevier, 1976.

Silver, Kenneth. *Esprit de Corps: The Art of the Parisian Avant-Garde and the First World War, 1914–1925*. Princeton, NJ: Princeton University Press, 1989.

11
Artistry and Primitivism in *The Enormous Room*
William Blazek

The literature produced from prison experience is often grim in tone and centred on naturalistic description, psychological analysis or polemical argument. Bunyan, Dostoevsky and Dickens all spent some time in prison and wrote works relevant to my concerns here, but it would be misleading to draw close comparisons with e. e. cummings' experience as a detainee in the First World War or with the book which he saw published in 1922, *The Enormous Room*.[1] For one thing, cummings seems to have enjoyed being in La Ferté-Macé, and, for another, *The Enormous Room* is a mischievously funny text. It sustains a rich verbal inventiveness, and displays both the naive optimism of the author's youth and a concerted exposition of his ideas about modern art. A close reading of the book reveals a particular dimension – involving primitivism expressed in terms of childhood and play – which yields insights into the artistic methods and principles of postwar American modernism.

cummings' modernism is demonstrated in his book as great technical invention aspiring to child-like simplicity. The challenge faced by the modern, sophisticated artist, he believed, was to return to an uncultured state of perception in order to create art that was fresh, and superior to the worn-out creations of the past or the sterile designs of the commercially oriented present. cummings' defiant behaviour during his months as a volunteer with the Norton-Harjes Ambulance Corps reflected his artistic evolution away from conventional forms and ideas. Peter Buitenhuis has identified what he sees as the most important lesson that cummings learned during the war: 'The prison was his exposure to the primitive, just as Tahiti was to Gauguin'[2] (Buitenhuis, 21). cummings' book supports the contemporary idea that primitive cultures had retained the basic, atavistic sources of artistic creativity and that a study of tribal or folk artefacts could help the sophisticated modern artist to apply untutored expression and natural vitality to imaginative works. It also follows a trend among white authors of the 1920s to create idealized black characters to suit the writers' thematic designs. Jean Le Nègre in *The Enormous Room* is sentimentalized by cummings, transformed from his real-life model at La Ferté-Macé. William Slater Brown, the young American who was interned with cummings and helped in the creation of the book, thought that all of the characters in *The Enormous Room* were accurately drawn from the reality of the detention camp – all except Jean Le Nègre, who was not the jolly free-spirit of the book and was the only person in the camp who stole things from them.

Jean Le Nègre and some other primitives in *The Enormous Room* are equally savages motivated by vital life-forces and innocents free from guilt and moral constraints. From both standpoints they are present to shock conventional sensibilities and serve the author's intention to oppose the manners of America's genteel society and, more specifically in the context of his war experience, to thumb his nose at the pretensions and prejudices he found in the would-be gentlemen of section 21 of the volunteer ambulance corps. In cummings' terms, the most unlikely creatures in *The Enormous Room* are true gentlemen, noble individuals who are genuinely (to use his most generous laudation) 'alive'. Furthermore, the narrative is underpinned by assumptions about the artist's role in shaping cultural ideals, whether in accord with contemporary society or in opposition to it. cummings celebrates both individuals and the artist in *The Enormous Room*, which can be seen as his personal artistic manifesto.

From the moment they find each other together in The Enormous Room of the book's title, the characters B and C express an innocent amazement and incongruous optimism in their surroundings. The Enormous Room is the hall where detainees spend their days and nights. The newcomers are fascinated by their fellow inmates: 'There's a man here who is a friend of Vanderbilt and knew Cezanne,' B tells C. 'There are people here who speak English,Russian,Arabian. There are the finest people here!' (*ER*, 45–6). In a later passage C declares, '"By God. . . . this is the finest place I've ever been in my life." "It's the finest place in the world," said B's voice' (*ER*, 80).

The 'God-sent miracle' of their 'escape from Vingt-et-Un' (*ER*, 62) places them in a world of divine eccentricity. The situation lends itself to exaggeration: C shares 'the most cordial salutation . . . that I have ever exchanged with a human being . . . ' (*ER*, 23); one of the 'Delectable Mountains' met in The Enormous Room has 'perhaps the handsomest face that I have ever seen' (*ER*, 73); the women there 'possessed the most terrible vitality and bravery of any human being, women or men,whom it has been my extraordinary luck to encounter,or ever will be(I am absolutely sure)in this world' (*ER*, 112); a woman and her children are 'the most beautiful people we had ever seen,or would ever be likely to see' (*ER*, 160); Jean Le Nègre has 'the whitest teeth on the earth' (*ER*, 197), and so on throughout the narrative. The broad strokes of these descriptions owe something to cummings' interest in Cubism, especially its use of wide, flat spaces adapted from African tribal models. Another source for cummings was Bunyan's *The Pilgrim's Progress*, which develops its allegory through a medley of character types, suitably heightened in description for allegoric and dramatic effect. Like Bunyan's pilgrim, C encounters divine beings on his way to salvation: a cherub carries his baggage for him, The Divine Man gives him food and drink, 'divine people' watch his progress, and he achieves a kind of revelation through The Delectable Mountains. Religious allusions like Dantean spirals move up and down (Satan's minion is there, too, in the Directeur of the camp), within a child's view of Providence. The most common-place introductions become miraculous visitations.[2]

C's invigorated perceptions and his attunement to the whole of creation allow him to encounter not only unusual people but also animate objects. In a jail cell on the way to the concentration camp, he looks curiously inside a can placed in a corner: 'At the bottom reposefully lay a new human turd' (*ER*, 17). That night the turd (named 'Ça Pue'), and the silhouette of a creature outside his window, along with *la lune*, share his company. Animated substances add to the population of an absurd world, a place where otherwise ordinary people following unmemorable lives are thrown into extraordinary circumstances – modern lunatics awaiting their prescribed fates.

To say that C makes the most of his surroundings would be an unjust comment on a narrative overflowing with exuberance. To less lively imaginations the meals at the internment camp may seem unpalatable, but not to the effervescent narrator:

> I . . . addressed myself to La Soupe. I found her luke-warm, completely flavorless. I examined the hunk of bread. It was almost bluish in colour; in taste moldy, slightly sour. 'If you crumb some into the soup,' remarked B, . . . 'they both taste better.' I tried the experiment. It was a complete success. . . . Between gulps I smelled the bread furtively. It smelled rather like an old attic in which kites and other toys are gradually forgotten in a gentle darkness.

> (*ER*, 68)

La Soupe (the gendered noun allows the object to be metamorphosed by the artist's imagination) is treated in the language of seduction: indifferent to C's first advances, but when he entices her into some experimentation she is transformed. The simile at the end of the passage introduces a pervading image in *The Enormous Room* and goes beyond simply emphasizing the poor quality of the bread (although there may be a religious allusion to transubstantiation). Like toys left to gather dust in an attic, the internees of *The Enormous Room*, on the top floor of the building, are forgotten, left to fade away, victims of bureaucratic red tape and ministerial indifference. Once, like kites, they may have soared in the free air, but in the stagnant atmosphere of prison they lie limp and useless.

The imagery of toys continues throughout the remaining narrative, but one must backtrack to find that C popped up into B's presence like a jack-in-the-box (*ER*, 46). The chapter called 'A Group of Portraits' presents a collection 'like a vast grey box in which are laid helter-skelter a great many toys' (*ER*, 82). Each one of the playthings has its own individual mechanism, each displays a unique gift of animation and captures the attention of the reader. The jack-in-the-box narrator constantly surprises with the originality of his description and the incisiveness of his observation. He has a huge playground to entertain him, The Enormous Room strewn with mattresses, like the padded floor of a playpen.

On the other hand, a playpen has bars to confine children. One of the infant-like inhabitants of The Enormous Room, the tiny Machine-Fixer, snuggles up to B and C for consolation. The Machine-Fixer cannot repair his own damaged spirit, so he turns to them, the ambulance drivers who should have carried wounded soldiers and did repair vehicles, 'much as a very minute helpless child comes to a very large and omnipotent one' (*ER*, 99). This 'terrible doll' poses a threat to the authority that imprisoned him, though, for he and his kind are indomitable. Thus, 'when Governments are found dead there is always a little doll on top of them' (*ER*, 103). Played with by *la gouvernement française*, the doll-like characters are also sometimes merely amusements for C. Figures like Monsieur Malvy, who collects butterflies, and The Bear, a cuddly teddy bear of a man, pass through the story to be stacked on a heap of temporary diversions.

Emphasizing the child-like vulnerability of the inhabitants of The Enormous Room, the narrative paves the way for Jean Le Nègre's introduction by describing the antics of The Wanderer's boy, The Imp. A genuine child in the company of bearded men, the 'irrepressible creature' looks like a raggedy doll, with 'lolling buttons of eyes sewed on gold flesh'. The Imp likes to climb trees. 'You will fall,' warns one of the men; and a guard threatens to shoot the lad: '"Let him climb" his father said quietly. "I have climbed trees.I have fallen out of trees. I am alive."' After The Imp's inevitable fall, the father comforts his son: 'Don't be sad my little son,everybody falls out of trees,they're made for that by God' (*ER*, 162). The suggestion is that both men and boys can make mistakes, but in the adult world the penalties are more severe than a bump on the head, and not everyone who falls in society will be picked up again. The simplicity of the parable is reminiscent of cummings' later works such as *The Christmas Tree* (1928) and his 'morality play' *Santa Claus* (*CP*, 192).

Many of the internees are particularly mindful of the restrictions against physical contact with women. The mixture of females in the camp, respectable women and *putains*, includes four 'incorrigibles'. Among them is Renee, standing out on account of her costume, 'immaculate in tightfitting satin' and thereby seeming 'to have somehow escaped from a doll's house overnight' (*ER*, 119). Presented with chances during the day to gesture or speak to the women, the male inmates are punished when caught doing so. The camp director lures them with the promise of free will and the temptation to communicate before exercising his quasi-divine authority. A poem written by cummings while detained in La Ferté-Macé, the 'Song' beginning 'Doll's boy's asleep', further underscores the distance between contact and desire experienced by the inmates in the story of *The Enormous Room* (*ER*, 15). The piece hints, too, at the poet's continued thoughts in La Ferté-Macé of the 'doll' he met in Paris during his first weeks in France, and it suggests the emotional content of the autobiographical element in *The Enormous Room*.

If the house of *Le Directeur* is filled with men who must confine their masculine impulses, the character Jean Le Nègre contains a sensual energy unrestrained. For cummings, Jean was a largely fictive creation. To C, Jean is the finest of the people in La Ferté-Macé. Though Jean's self-image is battered by the scorn of other inmates and he is bruised by injustice, his 'inexhaustible imagination' and vitality soon return. As a model for the primitive man, Jean is natural and uninhibited, free from conventions.[3] He is illiterate, but like The Zulu he communicates through unspeakable expression, 'the homogeneously tactile' (*ER*, 174). Free as a child in his self-absorbed play, he is called 'Jean L'Enfant'. The narrator asks the 'Boy, Kid, Nigger with the strutting muscles–take me up into your mind,' where the wisdom of the child is preserved. 'Take me up(carefully;as if I were a toy)and play carefully with me,once or twice before I and you go suddenly limp and foolish' (*ER*, 214). Carried by the sensual – and overtly sexual – power of this man-child, C touches a life-force of creativity, rejuvenation and essential goodness.

In contrast to the relaxed authority of The Wanderer and the expressiveness of Jean, the military authorities wield tremendous powers of repression. Their rules are petty, their codes of behaviour dishonourable. Both the *Chef de Section Vingt-et-Un* and the *Directeur* offer rewards for 'proper' behaviour and appearance. B and C had been denied *permission* (leave) by the head of the section because of their misconduct and non-conformity. In a dialectic transcription that anticipates the phonetic utterances of such poems by cummings as 'YgUDuh,' Mr A delivers

> The daily lecture:'I doughno what's th'matter with you fellers. You look like nice boys. Well-edjucated. But you're so dirty in your habits. You boys are always kickin' because I don't put you on a car together. . . . If you want me to send you out,you gotta shave and look neat,and *keep away from them dirty Frenchmen.*'
>
> (*ER*, 47; cummings' emphasis)

The *Directeur* dangles the promise of comfortable duty in the hospital before C, for a similar price. He hits 'upon the subject of my appearance; saying that I was come of a good family,that I had enjoyed . . . an education,and that I should keep myself neat and clean and be a shining example to the filthy and ignorant' (*ER*, 92). The irony in the advice of a 'dirty Frenchman' plays softly in the comparison. Neither the *chef* nor the *Directeur* understand the reason for C's dirtiness. When his spirits are lowest, his appearance is most unkempt: 'by being dirtier than usual I was protesting . . . against all that was neat and tidy and bigoted and solemn and founded upon the anguish of my fine friends' (*ER*, 236).

While they can, like uncaring parents, mistreat their prisoners, scolding them for uncleanliness or sending them to bed early, the prison officials are themselves merely toys in the hands of higher authorities. In La Ferté, the *Surveillant*, 'The Wooden Hand' and the *Directeur* must kow-tow to the inspectors and commissioners who visit the camp. In the presence of the commission, even the Wooden Hand (the head guard) reminds C of 'a clothing-dummy,or a life-size doll which might be made to move only by him who knows the proper combination' (*ER*, 218). Behind them all stands the faceless *gouvernement française*, which establishes the concentration camps and runs the war.

Salvation for C springs from an unpromising source, the commission for the *gouvernement française* that reviews individual cases. Fortunately for C, the commission includes one eccentric, 'a Dickens character' who 'ought to spend his time sailing kites of his own construction over other people's houses in gusty weather' (*ER*, 218). This 'little kite-flying gentleman' has some individuality, some ideas and a voice of his own – and thus, in cummings' terms, is something more than an antiquated gentleman. A literary cousin of Dickens' Mr Dick (in *David Copperfield*), he may be able to sympathize with the internees, the dusty kites stored and forgotten in the attic, since he knows the joy of free sailing himself. With his forthright and skilful answers to the commission, C manages to impress this kindred spirit, this child sent to free the children.

However, the paper-sorting will take time, and meanwhile the waiting continues. As the dust and dirt build up in The Enormous Room, C's mind plays games with words, adding the guards to the store of images, 'the maimed and stupid dolls of my imagination': they are 'a collection of vivid and unlovely toys' (*ER*, 225). When B is taken away to a permanent internment-camp, C's enthusiasm for life in La Ferté-Macé wanes. He responds to his remaining, new friends 'in a highly mechanical manner. I felt myself to be,at last,a doll–taken out occasionally and played with and put back in its house and told to go to sleep' (*ER*, 231–2). It seems that the creator's mind threatens to lose control of its creation.

Then snow starts to fall. Snow, with its associations of Christmas and presents, of childhood and innocence, of nature and birth, arrives as if to revivify the artist's imagination. Snowfall also had a more personal meaning to cummings, as explained in a poem about the Parisian prostitute to whom he gave up his virginity in the short period between his release from La Ferté-Macé and his embarkation for New York in mid-December 1917. It begins:

The moon-lit snow is falling like strange candy into the big eyes of the little people with smiling bodies and wooden feet

hard thick feet full of toes

left-handed kiss

I think Berthe is the snow, and comes down into all corners of the city with a smelling sound.   The moon shines all green in the snow.

(Etc, 50).

Except for the unsettling, sinister ('left-handed') kiss, the lines ooze with the sentimentality that weakens other poems in which cummings attaches emotional response to natural phenomena. In *The Enormous*

Room, happily, the image of the snow contains some of the vigorous and evocative conceptualization found in his poem 'SNO', with the opening lines:

> a white idea(Listen
>
> drenches:earth's ugly)mind.
>
> (*TC*, 105)

cummings' image of snow gains symbolic and intellectual importance near the end of *The Enormous Room*, as will be shown presently. He introduces it into the narrative at a time when not only C's optimism but also the reader's perseverance need rejuvenation. It is not so much the writer's linguistic inventiveness that starts to fall off at this point as the reader's stamina in facing the verbal onslaught. In another sense, the author's obsession with word-play weakens his assault on authoritarian systems because the virulence of his attack is undermined by the joke – though the sincerity (a quality much admired in others) of his feelings of outrage are never in doubt.

The narrator's expressions of annoyance towards several inmates in The Enormous Room are usually overlooked in critical studies of the book. Just as negative as his judgements of American ambulancemen or government officials, C's response to certain men sharing his confinement can be unremittingly intolerant. Not everyone in the room, the narrator shows, deserves the attention of the artist. Only one or two of the Belgians are worthy of praise. One nicknamed Brown Bread comes under scrutiny only for his idiosyncrasy. He and his friends are morose and stupid, and therefore worthless subjects for the narrator: 'He was a Belgian,and that's all. By which I mean that I am uncharitable enough not to care what happened to him or for what stupid and morose crime he was doing penance at La Ferté' (*ER*, 106). A few wholly despicable characters are given vivid portrayals: The Fighting Sheeny, especially, and Judas and Rockyfeller less colourfully. Others like Garibaldi (the sweeper), The Trick Raincoat and the unfortunately fat priest's assistant come in for less mitigated criticism. The people of the village sneer at the detainees who 'catch' water outside the camp, but the narrator retaliates with a sharp rebuttal. cummings also makes an assault on conventional American standards in his narrative. Enthusiastic American readers of the book in 1922 turned the pages of the penultimate chapter only to be jabbed by these words: 'The Great American Public [is] the most aesthetically incapable organization ever created for the purpose of perpetuating defunct ideals and ideas' (*ER*, 224). The author performs a sort of narrative blackmail, leaving guilty readers with one option, to disassociate themselves from the organization, from the Great American Public, from the government of the French Republic, to become small individuals set apart from the mob. cummings tells how this can be done. The answer lies in his understanding of the word 'enormous'.

cummings uses the word in a much more complex way than may first appear evident from its descriptive form in his poem beginning 'the bigness of cannon' from 'La Guerre' section of *Tulips & Chimneys*. In the line 'death's clever enormous voice', 'enormous' is attached to something evil, the voice of death – on an immediate level the sound of the thundering cannon. Since that noise is identified as 'clever', also, the calculated, sinister and scientific type of death that the cannonfire brings serves to emphasize the darkly negative impression of the word under scrutiny. Most simply 'enormous' is one of the author's signposts for something 'ungood', something unpleasant, dangerous or wicked. The connection with science yields more fruitful meaning, in which cummings' attitude towards war itself is involved.

For the Cambridge-born poet, war and peace both could be threatening. He once said to his friend and biographer Charles Norman, 'Peace! – it's war' (Norman, 304). In nonlecture four, he quotes from one of his own essays: '"War" and "peace" are not dangerous or alive: far from it. "Peace" is the inefficiency of science. "War" is the science of inefficiency. And science is knowing and knowing is measuring' (i, 68). cummings' ideas about war and peace and their relationship to art can be condensed as follows. Sometimes peace can be just as anathema to the artist as war. Civilization can be deadened by the meaningless luxuries of peace as it can be threatened by the barbarity of war. To create, an artist must 'feel', and the cultivated indolence of quiet times presents as unconducive an atmosphere to the creator as does the unnatural frenzy of war. In peace men die emotionally from over-education, lack of feeling. In war they are mangled physically by inefficient science, the machine inflicting random injury and death. The primitive, feeling man can be buried by culture at rest or torn apart by savagery unrestrained. The artist desires neither the science of education nor the science of warfare, but the art of feeling. Calculated science 'is skilful', but 'Art is a mystery. A mystery is something immeasurable.' Or, he might have said, something 'enormous'.

He identified the mystery of art most closely with nature. His own initiation into the natural world, he explained in his Harvard 'nonlecture' in 1952, came during his childhood when he played in Norton's

Woods. He described the area as ' ... a mythical domain of semiwilderness; separating cerebral Cambridge and orchidaceous Somerville. ... Here, as a very little child, I first encountered the mystery who is Nature; here my enormous smallness entered her illimitable being' (i, 32). Art, he suggests elsewhere in the piece, is an attempt to recapture that child-like understanding. 'Enormous' in this context implies not merely size but the difficult task which the adult artist faces, and the immensity of his or her achievement when an artist is successful.

The incalculability of art echoes nature in cummings' work. As the earth responds to science with the mystery of spring, so the artist opposes science with the mystery of art. Together they surmount death, as another poem in the section of *Tulips & Chimneys* labelled 'La Guerre' emphasizes:

> O sweet spontaneous
> earth how often have
> the
> doting
>
>   fingers of
> prurient philosophers pinched
> and
> poked
>
> thee
> ,has the naughty thumb
> of science prodded
> thy
>
>   beauty   .how
> often have religions taken
> thee upon their scraggy knees
> squeezing and
>
> buffeting thee that thou mightiest conceive
> gods
>   (but
> true
>
> to the incomparable
> couch of death thy
> rhythmic
> lover

thou answerest

them only with

spring)

(CP, 46)

Reminders of cummings' stay in Paris and his sexual initiation through friendship with Parisian demimondaines stand out in the poem – the 'prurient philosophers', the 'naughty thumb' and the 'couch' of death given lewd associations with rational science. Conversely, one's attention is drawn to the understated but omnipotent quality of the earth and spring. The investigations of science, cummings insists, will never yield the answer to the mystery of living things. Nature – as well as art – is immeasurable, ever-changing and vastly complex. This mystery is the 'huger silence' that hushes the 'enormous voice' of battle in 'La Guerre'.

cummings asserts in his Introduction to the 1932 Modern Library edition of *The Enormous Room* that an artist's response to nature must be a personal response, an individual progress towards feeling. His book charts a 'pilgrim's progress' towards understanding and defending the worth of the individual. The philosophic attitude behind that progress is both nativistic and humanistic and, like cummings' behaviour in the Norton-Harjes, anarchic – though his explication of such ideas is usually too confused to be called a genuine philosophy. A human being able to feel, instinctively and emotionally, shares in the eternity of nature. The individual represents the 'enormous' whole, and by doing so transcends mere institutions such as the *gouvernement française* or La Ferté-Macé. cummings explains as much in his 1932 Introduction, using a question-and-answer method:

> Doesn't *The Enormous Room* really concern war?
> It actually uses war:to explore an inconceivable vastness which is so unbelievably far away that it appears microscopic.
> When you wrote this book,you were looking through war at something very big and very far away?
> When this book wrote itself,I was observing a negligible portion of something incredibly more distant than any sun;something more unimaginably huge than the most prodigious of all universes–
> Namely?
> The individual

(Introduction, vii–viii)

So cummings, in *The Enormous Room*, is writing about something larger than war: the individual. Moreover, as an artist he uses war, manipulates the situation into which the First World War threw him, as a person; and from his experience he develops a war narrative that looks through war into ultimate values. These values are personified in the 'Delectable Mountains': the wisdom of The Wanderer, the 'indescribable' communicability of the Zulu, the innocent gaiety and indestructible energy of Jean Le Nègre. Each of these characters grows into a symbolic force, larger than armies or governments. With such inhabitants The Enormous Room takes on 'enormous', immutable and universal significance.

In the text itself, the term 'enormous' is applied in many ways that suggest the catholicity of the author's characters and their predicament. Most simply the adjective is used to describe objects, such as the 'enormous wooden tubs' (*ER*, 158) into which the liquid from the water wagon is emptied. Yet even here the exaggeration of size fits the outline of a landscape where almost everything is presented as larger-than-life. Later on the symbolic value of the water is made clear by connecting the water of the cart with the water of the sea, the link emphasized by the word 'enormous' (*ER*, 189). The word can be manipulated for a clever effect, as in the 'enormous haste' of the Zulu (*ER*, 179). It stands for strength and, conversely, for weakness: Bill the Hollander's 'enormous hairy chest' heaves in waves of anger against The Young Pole, demonstrating the Hollander's forcefulness and indicating the hollowness of his rantings. Most often cummings uses the word for hyperbole, at other times to define innocence, anger or fear. Jean Le Nègre's eyes are 'enormous' after he is set upon by The Sheeny and The Trick Raincoat, reflecting the soul of the innocent abused by injustice.

Though Jean's eyes reveal the helplessness of a child, beneath them are captured the tremendous resources of the individual. Turning again to cummings' Introduction to the Modern Library edition of *The Enormous Room*, one notes the movement from specific to universal, from vast to microscopic, and back and forth again. Here is the humanist, finding in each person's suffering the burden of humanity, in humanity's endurance the indestructibility of the individual. Thus that unfeeling giant *la gouvernement française* seems to cummings 'little, very little'. In a wider view, the vast but petty institution is unimportant, powerless because it is unable to understand or to feel, to know compassion or love.

Because The Enormous Room encompasses the whole world, C's curiosity leads him to good and evil there. His sense of wonder allows him to approach the undefinable mystery of the Delectable Mountains and to see into the heart of La Ferté-Macé. The process reminds one of cummings' encounter with 'that mystery who is Nature', when his 'enormous smallness entered her illimitable being'. A child's 'enormous smallness' gives him a fresh canvas on which to create his original impressions, uninfluenced by genteel tradition and free from social obligation. This way of seeing produced *The Enormous Room*, a work John Dos Passos called 'a distinct conscious creation separate from anything else under heaven' (Dos Passos, 98), thus sanctifying it as a supremely modernist text. cummings' own analysis of his work suggests something more earthy, the creative act associated with procreation, even sexual penetration, however well concealed in metaphor.

cummings' method involves a return to primitive, instinctive understanding. For the educated (and, his work usually implies, masculine) artist it means forgetting his education, living by the Futurist principle that 'to create is first of all to destroy'. The polemic is set forth in the narrative: ' . . . there is and can be no such thing as authentic art until the bon trucs . . . are entirely and thoroughly and perfectly annihilated by that vast and painful process of Unthinking which may result in a minute bit of purely personal Feeling. Which minute bit is Art' (*ER*, 224). True art, for cummings, must come from the sensibilities that the artist shares with the child. Thus he himself wanted to reject his Harvard background, sought purgation in war, and tried to demolish the cultured, museumized past. The word games of his technical experimentation in form and typography are not at odds with his principle of raising feeling above cultivation, for they demonstrate – more than the skill of a refined intellect – a new way of seeing. By observing with unadulterated eye, the child-like artist snatches a minute part of the enormous world of sensations and thereby creates an art-work that adds to the sensibilities of his civilization. cummings' 'minute bit' is *The Enormous Room*.

A few days before leaving 'La Misère', the creator creating his creation turns to the windows of The Enormous Room and sees snow falling: ' . . . I lay down,closing my eyes;feeling the snow's minute and crisp touch falling gently and exquisitely,falling perfectly and suddenly, through the thick soundless autumn of my imagination . . . ' (*ER*, 232). Envisioned through glass and eyelid, the snowflakes mean almost as much to cummings' work as leaves of grass to Whitman's. The tactile image of snow neatly combines the author's ideas of creativity with the ideal of individualism, bound together with the principle of the primitive in his view of art. As the snow descends,

> The Enormous Room is filled with a new and beautiful darkness,the darkness of the snow outside,falling and falling and falling with the

silent and actual gesture which has touched the soundless country of
my mind as a child touches a toy it loves . . .

(ER, 232–3).

Abbreviations

CP Complete Poems
ER The Enormous Room
Etc Etcetera
TC Tulips & Chimneys

Acknowledgements

The excerpts from *The Enormous Room* by e. e. cummings are reprinted
by permission of W. W. Norton and Company. Copyright © 1978 by
the Trustees for the e. e. cummings Trust and George James Firmage.

'a white idea(Listen', 'O sweet spontaneous' and 'The moon-lit snow
is falling like strange candy into the big' are reprinted from *Complete
Poems 1904–1962*, by e. e. cummings, edited by George J. Firmage, by
permission of W. W. Norton and Company. Copyright © 1991 by the
Trustees for the e. e. cummings Trust and George James Firmage.

Notes

1. Though it relates his actual experiences in La Ferté-Macé, the book is difficult
   to label: war memoir, autobiographical narrative, prose-poem, modernist
   novel – these terms all fit but fall short of defining this unique work. The
   composition of *The Enormous Room* as well as cummings' wartime service and
   internment are carefully detailed in Richard S. Kennedy, *Dreams in the Mirror:
   A Biography of e. e. cummings* (New York: Liveright, 1980).
2. See David E. Smith, 'The Enormous Room and The Pilgrim's Progress', *Twentieth Century Literature*, 2 (July 1965): 67–75, in Norman Friedman (ed.),
   e. e. cummings: A Collection of Critical Essays, Twentieth Century Views (Englewood Cliffs, NJ: Prentice-Hall, 1972): 121–32; and for a contradictory view
   cf. Paul Fussell, *The Great War and Modern Memory* (London: Oxford University Press, 1975): 160–1. A more recent study taking a different perspective is
   W. Todd Martin, '*The Enormous Room*: cummings' reinterpretation of John
   Bunyan's *Doubting Castle*', Spring, 5 (Fall 1996): 112–19. On the importance of Cubism to cummings' work, see Rushworth M. Kidder, 'cummings
   and Cubism: the influence of the visual arts on cummings' early poetry',
   Journal of Modern Literature (e. e. cummings Special Number), 7 (April 1979):
   255–91.
3. See John Colley, 'The lure of the primitive: the Village Bohemians and the
   Harlem Renaissance', *Over Here*, 4 (Spring 1984): 10–17; especially 14–15,

which Colley begins, appropriately, by calling cummings 'The enfant terrible of the Lost Generation'.

Works cited

Brown, William Slater. 'Interview with William Blazek'. Rockport, MA, 21 June 1985.

Buitenhuis, Peter. 'The First World War and the Language of Fiction.' Revised transcript of a paper presented at the European Association for American Studies Conference, Rome, 17 April 1984.

cummings, e. e. *Complete Poems 1913–1962*. New York: Harcourt Brace Jovanovich, 1963.

——. *The Enormous Room*, ed. George James Firmage, Cummings Type Script Editions. New York: Liveright, 1922, 1978.

——. Introduction to *The Enormous Room*. New York: Modern Library, 1934.

——. *Etcetera*, eds George James Firmage and Richard S. Kennedy, Cummings Type Script Editions. New York & London: Liveright, 1983.

——. i: *six non-lectures*. Cambridge, MA: Harvard University Press, 1953; New York: Atheneum, 1967.

——. *Tulips & Chimneys*, ed. George James Firmage, Cummings Type Script Editions. New York: Liveright, 1922, 1976.

Dos Passos, John. 'Off the Shoals', *Dial*, 73 (July 1922): 98.

Norman, Charles. *e. e. cummings: The Magic Maker*. Boston and Toronto: Little, Brown, 1958.

Part V
Revising the War Poets

12
Mother's Boy and Stationmaster's Son: the Problem of Class in the Letters and Poems of Wilfred Owen

John Gibson

Two contrary, but related, emotions are endemic in the public and private utterances of Wilfred Owen: they are compassion and contempt. In the letters written before his active service in the trenches, these emotions often appear to be the result of a blurred or double vision in which the same or similar phenomena call forth an opposite reaction. In some of the poems written out of the experience of battle, the emotions are the product of a sharply focused gaze. The blurring is the result of class-related experiences, many of them connected with the traumatic move from Oswestry to Birkenhead and the subsequent ten years' sojourn there, while the focused seeing comes with the sharing of the plight of those Lancashire mill-hands and miners to whom, at best, he had formerly condescended and whom, at worst, he had despised.

An example of the double vision I have in mind is to be found in a letter Wilfred wrote to his mother, Susan Owen, during his time as a teacher of English in Bordeaux. It is dated 14 October 1914.

> ...I can look down on the children coming from a school close by, which never fails to make me tender and poetical. Poor children, these; for the quarter is poor but not low. Indeed, I never see in France any scabby-haired, mud-stockinged arabs, hoarse of voice and hard of eye, such as breed in Liverpool muds, Birmingham cinders, and London fog-smoke.
>
> (*CL*, 288)

English slum children are dismissed, French poor children are romanticized. This markedly different response to poor children may be explained simply as a question of physical propinquity and psychological distance, both related to the Owen family's problematic class status. The young Englishman in a French bourgeois milieu necessarily transcended the world of the *gamins*, unlike the boy Wilfred who had no choice but to be immanent in the streets of Birkenhead, the seaport and shipbuilding town across the Mersey from Liverpool.

It was to working-class Birkenhead that the Owen family moved from the comparative grandeur of Susan's family home, Plas Wilmot, in the Welsh town of Oswestry. Here they lived for the better part of ten years, and here they managed to maintain a middle-class existence, despite the threat to the family's respectability, evident in the daily life of the children as Harold Owen recounts in *Journey from Obscurity*.

> The early refusal to recognize in any way the locality and its inhabitants caused us to be regarded by them as wishing to hold ourselves apart, which we did, and of thinking of ourselves as superior to them, which we did not. The immediate effect was that every emergence by us children from the house held a hunted and nightmarish quality, as of course we were the natural prey of the stevedores' and dock labourers' children, who lay in wait for us and with jeers and screams of laughter set upon us, egged on with the ribald encouragement by the slatternly women who seemed perpetually to fill the dark doorways.
>
> (22/23)

At the end of the first volume of *Journey From Obscurity*, Harold succinctly characterizes the family's marginal social position:

> It was, I feel, an inability to stabilize ourselves socially as a family, or, more correctly, it was that owing to our lack of means, we found difficulty in achieving this social stability. A result was this unpredictability about us and what our real position was, exactly, in the social scale. This led to awkwardness and difficulties in fostering embryonic friendships, and sometimes destroyed them altogether.
>
> (227)

Given the special circumstances of the family – the vanished splendour of Plas Wilmot following the death of Susan's father, the maternal puritan morality, and the role of favoured eldest son ascribed to Wilfred by Susan if not by his father, Tom – such an existence in class-bound Victorian and Edwardian England could hardly fail to imbue Wilfred with the sense of apartness and class-based judgementalism apparent in the Bordeaux letter.

That lower-middle-class judgementalism is reinforced by a romanticized regionalism exemplified in this letter from Ripon in March 1918:

> Have not seen again Warne, but have found under my care other Shropshire lads whose speech betrayed them to me. These and some Welsh chappies we have are indeed, look you, I am prout to say, the muscle as well as the voice, look you, of the company. The Lancashire Mill Hands are weeds, why, Weeds.
>
> (544)

Even in this late letter written after his first battle experiences that culminated in his being sent to Craiglockhart, the voice of class prejudice can still be heard behind the regional romanticism. It stems from the same impulse which caused him to write in a postcard to Susan Owen his reaction to preliminary offers of a commission: 'Both were Lancashire regiments. No thanks!' (21 January 1916).

As the poor health of many of the recruits is well-documented both officially and unofficially, the final sentence of the March 1918 letter – 'The Lancashire Mill Hands are weeds, why, Weeds' – could be read as a comment on the cotton operatives' physical condition, but the word 'weeds' carries the pejorative connotation of the word 'wets' in the mouths of ardent 1900s Thatcherites, that is a lack of moral fibre.

An illuminating contrast to this comment can be seen in the reaction of another grammar-school subaltern, Herbert Read. His troops in a Yorkshire regiment are blast-furnacemen from Teesside:

> Yesterday I had to take the names of men in my platoon who had weak eyes. There were several. It appears that the weakness is caused by staring at molten steel. One man had been blind for a week. Our civilisation again!
>
> (*The Contrary Experience*, 71)

The comment which precedes this is in a much less judgemental vein than Owen's remarks about his Lancashire troops. A judgement of a different kind is being made in Owen's sentences about the Shropshire lads and the Welsh contingent. The allusion to Housman is unmistakable. This is hardly surprising. After the family moved to Shrewsbury, Owen spent time in the surrounding countryside and visited the Roman remains at Uriconium, made famous for his generation by Housman.

Given this, his penchant for Shropshire lads is understandable. As for the Welsh reference, Jon Stallworthy, echoing Harold Owen in his book *Wilfred Owen, A Biography*, tells us that 'Wilfred had inherited from his father the legend that they were descended from Baron Lewis Owen who, during the reign of Henry VIII, was Sheriff of Merioneth-shire' (4). This explains why the parody of Welsh speech is not cruel but loving. In fact, we know that Owen saw a performance of *Henry V* before the war in London, so it is not too fanciful to hear an echo of Fluellen in the stage Welsh of Owen's parody. The lilt of a Welsh intonation and the rustic burr of troops from rural England is more acceptable than the heavily articulated plosives of Lancashire miners and weavers.

I draw attention deliberately to the voices that Owen hears. To this day the most obvious marker of social class in Britain is accent, or more properly dialect, both regional and social. In his Bakhtinian study of the formation of Owen's poetic discourse, Douglas Kerr points to Owen's 'intermediate position' in the poem 'The Dead-Beat': '...intermediacy was a territory entirely familiar to Wilfred Owen, a place in which he was, if never comfortable, at least always at home' (Kerr, 38). This inter-mediacy antedates his army experience and is bound up with the marginal social position of the Owen family that his brother Harold reveals so persistently. Frequently, it expresses itself in a concern with accent. Nowhere is this more obvious than in the account in *Journey From Obscurity* of Harold leaving home as a young apprentice merchant navy officer:

> As I was closing his bedroom door, he called out to remind me how atrocious my English still was, and barked at me that if – when we met again – he found that I had the slightest trace of a Liverpool accent, he would disown relationship for ever.
>
> (vol. 2, 62)

Note the disjunctions that are revealed when we juxtapose this passage with the anecdote related by Peter Parker in *The Old Lie: The Great War and the Public School Ethos*:

> Stephen Spender, taken to meet Sassoon for the first time, was tactless enough to show no interest in his host, asking instead what Owen was like. Infuriated, Sassoon snapped: 'He was embarrassing. He had a Grammar School accent.'
>
> (193)

No wonder Owen showed such deference to the two ex-public school-boys Sassoon and Graves when he met them at Craiglockhart. However, Owen's ambivalence about status and class is complex. His deference to the two poets might well be explained precisely by the fact that they were *poets* whose approval he sought. We find no such deference in a letter from France dated 8 June 1917.

> Dearest Mother,
> Two days ago we started in motors for the Railhead: The Train was there, but there was no accommodation for officers. The O.C. Train, a minute doctor with many papers and much pince-nez, refused to let us board: especially as a Major who was with us expressed himself thus: 'Aw I decline. I ebsolutely decline, to travel in a coach where there are – haw – Men!'
> This major is an unconscionable snob, and consequently suffers something from my humour.
>
> (467)

The charge of snobbery that Owen here levels against the Major might well be brought against that Wilfred who admonished Harold and continued to patronize the Lancashire soldiers in his letters, but the deference and patronizing that derive from his early marginal experiences are absent from his most well-known poems.

Among the voices heard in the poems are those of the other ranks, those of sanctimonious propagandists, and the declaiming, reflecting and ironizing voice of the speaker. These voices enable the poet to realize his professed aims of pleading and warning. They also inscribe social class into the texts in a different way from those comments earlier. In these poems the vision is unblurred, the pity is for the common soldier – even when that soldier is hardly heroic as in 'S.I.W.' and 'The Dead-Beat' – and the contempt is for the unfeeling, those 'dullards whom no cannon stuns', such as the 'Bold uncels, smiling ministerially', the 'brave young wife, getting her fun' and the doctor in the latter poem, and the father (surely an echo of Owen's own father) who exhorts his son with the conventional 'Death before dishonour, that's the style' in 'S.I.W.'.

The term 'common soldier' with its dual significance can be used to highlight further the ambivalences of class in Owen. Consider the language of the following:

> The generality of men are hard-handed, hard-headed miners, dogged, loutish, ugly. (But I would trust them to advance under fire and to

hold their trench;) blond, coarse, ungainly strong, 'unfatigueable',
unlovely, Lancashire soldiers, Saxons to the bone.

(*Collected Letters*, 395)

It could be said that behind this description lurks the pejorative
use of 'common', which he must have heard dozens of times from
his mother. What are 'loutish', 'ugly', 'coarse', if not attributes of
common?

A few weeks later, his assessment of the men is more positive, if still
patronizing:

> I am beginning to pick out the Intelligent and the Smart 'laads' from
> amongst the uncouth and the ungainly...Waiting for the train I had
> more individual dealings, & was wondering whether it would be
> unwise to give my men some cigarettes, but deciding not to, when
> one of the 'Underage' came to me with an offering of apples!! Poor
> penniless scholboy! But you must not think there was anything but
> ingenuousness. These Lancashires are extraordinarily open, honest,
> and incapable of strategy.
>
> (398)

In such a passage, written a month after joining the 5th Battalion, Manchester Regiment and almost six months before going to France, Owen
is beginning to differentiate between his men, and in so doing he is
developing that empathy which will become the hallmark of his changed
sensibility.

Nor is Owen's development an isolated case. In *The Face of Battle*,
John Keegan considers the social composition of the Kitchener and
Territorial battalions such as the 5th Battalion, Manchester Regiment to
which Owen was gazetted on 4 June 1916:

> Officers had to be gentlemen...Britain in 1914 was as sharply Two
> Nations as it had been seventy years before, so that throughout the
> industrial North, the West Midlands, South Wales and Lowland Scot-
> land existed populous and productive communities almost wholly
> without a professional stratum and so without an officer class...Thus
> there came about, during the first two years of the First World War,
> one of the most curious confrontations in British history...It was
> almost always a meeting of strangers...when nicely raised young
> men from West Country vicarages or South Coast watering-places
> came face to face with forty Durham miners, Yorkshire furnacemen,

Clydeside riveters, and the two sides found they could scarcely understand each other's speech.

(224–5)

Training and battle experience, Keegan shows, lead ultimately to a symbiosis that crystallizes in the ritual foot inspection famously commented on by Sassoon. It is this relationship that justifies extending the term 'common soldier' beyond its usual designation of 'other ranks' – privates and non-commissioned officers – to include the subalterns and company commanders engaged in the actual fighting.

This wider definition is strongly suggested in Owen's poems from the front in which the first person plural pronoun dominates. In 'Exposure', for example, everyone unfortunate enough to be in the trenches suffers the insomnia, the bitter cold, 'the poignant misery of dawn', and everyone shares the same dreams of home. Significantly, the only troops to be singled out are the burying party of the last stanza.

Almost as important as the distribution of pity and contempt from the viewpoint of class is the issue of responsibility. And here I turn to a passage in Paul Fussell's book *The Great War and Modern Memory* in which he discusses the reasons for the failure of the Somme offensive of 1916:

> The disaster had many causes. Lack of imagination was one: no one imagined that the Germans could have contrived such deep dugouts to hide in . . . Another cause was traceable to the class system and the assumptions that it sanctioned. The regulars of the British staff entertained an implicit contempt for the rapidly trained men of 'Kitchener's Army,' largely recruited among workingmen from the Midlands. The planners assumed that these troops – burdened for the assault with 66 lbs. of equipment – were too simple and animal to cross the space between the opposing trenches except in full daylight and aligned in rows or 'waves.'
>
> (13)

Not all commentators condemn the General Staff so vigorously. Keegan, for example, suggests that the exigencies of the situation left the army little choice in the matter of training.

In some poets, notably the Sassoon of 'The General', blame for the horrors of the Somme and Flanders is directly placed on the General Staff. This is not quite the case in Owen. Sometimes in his poems the sense of human agency and therefore of human responsibility is lost in abstraction and generalization. We are led to feel that the plight of the soldier is simply part of the human condition. For example, despite the grounding of 'Inspection' in the routine of military life, and despite the sense we get of the common plight of the company commander and the offending soldier, the universalizing of 'The world is washing out its stains' denies any sense of political or military responsibility. The erring private soldier appears to be a representative human being engaged in an act of expiation. In so far as we might take this at its face value, we are, theologically speaking, in the presence of original sin, but the epithet 'Field-Marshal' applied to God insists that we read the whole passage ironically.

A similar problem occurs in 'The Parable of the Old Man and the Young'. Here Abram's actions contradict the divine will. The 'old man/Abram' of 'The Parable', while certainly less vague, is still unsatisfactory. It is a truism that wars are not fought by those who make them, and the poem gives this powerful utterance, but to say this gets us no nearer to the aetiology of this war, nor to the military hierarchy's responsibility for the self-destructive tactics of the British infantry.

In the context of these two poems, one might observe that Owen's tendency to fall back on the supra-human in the face of the appalling facts of his existence in the trenches owes much to the particular religious upbringing to which he was subjected by his mother. His letters reveal that he had not wholly abandoned belief in the existence of God when he rejected the evangelical Christianity of the Revd Wigan of Dunsden. It can be argued that the formation of Owen's consciousness is to some degree a function of marginal lower-middle-class behaviour, where faithful church attendance and religious observance are props to shore up the ever threatened defences of the family against surrounding waves of unrespectability. To acknowledge this is not to deny the reality of Owen's spiritual agonizing, which is reflected in a theme of Owen's letters and poetry: the disparity between the ethics of the Sermon on the Mount and the doctrines of hatred of the Hun propagated by bellicose clergymen. In a letter to his mother in May 1917, he writes:

> Already I have comprehended a light which will never filter into the dogma of any national church: namely that one of Christ's essential commands was: Passivity at any price! Suffer dishonour and disgrace; but never resort to arms. Be bullied, be outraged, be killed; but do not kill. It may be a chimerical and ignominious principle, but there

it is. It can only be ignored: and I think the pulpit professionals are ignoring it very skilfully and successfully indeed.

(461)

The emotion behind such writing fuels the indignation in a poem like 'At A Calvary Near The Ancre' (82).

> One ever hangs where shelled roads part.
>   In this war He too lost a limb,
> But his disciples bear apart;
>   And now the soldiers bear with Him.
>
> Near Golgotha strolls many a priest,
>   And in their faces there is pride
> That they were flesh-marked by the Beast
>   By whom the gentle Christ's denied.
>
> The scribes on all the people shove
>   And brawl allegiance to the state,
> But they who love the greater love
>   Lay down their life; they do not hate.

In this poem, despite the quietism of the last two lines, Owen identifies two targets for his anger: the press and organized religion acting as propagandists for the state. Here are the beginnings of a move towards a critique of English society, although that critique remains at the emotional level of indignation, anger and contempt, as in these two extracts from letters to his mother. The first was written from Scarborough just before he left for France for the last time in August 1918:

> . . . this morning at 8.20 we heard a boat torpedoed in the bay about a mile out . . . I wish the Bosche would have the pluck to come right in and make a clean sweep of the Pleasure Boats, and the promenaders on the Spa, and all the stinking Leeds and Bradford War-profiteers now reading *John Bull* on Scarborough Sands.

(568)

The second extract dated 15 October 1918 was written less than a month after the final draft of the poem 'Smile, Smile, Smile':

> I am not depressed even by Bottomley's 'NO! NO! NO!'.. It has had the effect of turning the whole army against its *John Bull* at last. My

heart has been warmed by the curses I have heard levelled against the *Daily Mail*.

(585)

The second of these comments says much about the responsibility of the editors and press magnates, Bottomley and Harmsworth, for fuelling the war fever to the very end. The first of the comments clearly lumps Bottomley and the war-profiteers together. The relationship between the letters and the poems is again transparent. In this case the poem is 'Smile, Smile, Smile', which opens with a picture of wounded soldiers reading the *Daily Mail*:

> Head to limp head, the sunk-eyed wounded scanned
> Yesterday's Mail; the casualties (typed small)
> And (large) Vast Booty from our Latest Haul.

(*Poems*, 167)

The poem implicitly connects the suffering of the soldiers to human agents. Owen had made this connection before, of course, notably in 'Dulce Et Decorum Est', but nowhere does he so clearly indict the politicians ('We rulers sitting in this ancient spot'), nor so clearly league them with the press magnates. The choice of the word 'rulers' suggests the concept of ruling class, and one is put in mind of the younger Owen in iconoclastic revolt against the opiate of his religious work in Dunsden. His letters from that period detail his contact with rural poverty and degradation, and from time to time express a dissatisfaction with the way things are. In a typical passage, written to his mother on 23 April 1912, he begins with a quotation from an unnamed author:

'The Revolutionary Ideals, crossing the Channel into England, inspired the British school of revolt and reconstruction in Burns, Shelley, Byron, Wordsworth, Coleridge and Tennyson, till its fires have died down today.' Have they! They have in the bosoms of the muses, but not in my breast. I am increasingly liberalising and liberating my thought, in spite of the vicar's strong Conservatism.

(131)

It would seem that in the more than six years that elapsed between that letter and 'Smile, Smile, Smile', Owen has moved from woolly romanticism to a tough opposition to the political establishment. We might say that Owen's propensity to feel pity and contempt has found appropriate subjects in his wartime experiences.

This is surely the case in his poem 'The Calls', which must have been written out of his experience at Scarborough. In the first of two postings at that resort Owen was billeted at the Victoria Hotel from where he wrote on 24 November 1917:

> There was a guest night yesterday, which meant a gorgeous meal, whose menu I am ashamed to give you. It kept my house-lady sweating till after midnight.
>
> (508)

This seems to be the source of the fifth stanza in 'The Calls' (80), in which Owen enumerates the different sounds that call human beings to their tasks:

> A dismal fog-hoarse siren howls at dawn.
> I watch the man it calls for, pushed and drawn
> Backwards and forwards, helpless as a pawn.
>   But I'm lazy and my work's crazy.
>
> Quick treble bells begin at nine o'clock,
> Scuttling the schoolboy pulling up his sock,
> Scaring the late girl in the inky frock.
>   I must be crazy, I learn from the daisy.
>
> Stern bells annoy the rooks and doves at ten.
> I watch the verger close the doors, and when
> I hear the organ moan the first amen,
>   Sing my religion's – same as pigeons'.
>
> A blatant bugle tears my afternoons.
> Out clump the clumsy Tommies by platoons,
> Trying to keep in step with rag-time tunes,
>   But I sit still; I've done my drill.
>
> Gongs hum and buzz like saucepan-lids at dusk,
> I see a food-hog whet his gold-filled tusk
> To eat less bread and more luxurious rusk.
>
> Then sometimes late at night my window bumps
> From gunnery practice, till my small heart thumps

> And listens for the shell shrieks and the crumps,
>   But that's not all.
>
> For leaning out last midnight on my sill
> I heard the sighs of men, that have no skill
> To speak of their distress, no, nor the will!
>   A voice I know. And this time I must go.

From the perspective of my concern – the inscription of class in Owen's poetry – this poem can be taken as representative of the contradictions, deriving from the family's precarious existence on the fringes of the lower middle class and the intensity of Wilfred's relationship with a fanatically pious mother, that joined to form this poet's consciousness. The structure of the poem corresponds to the succession of time throughout the day: dawn – the industrial worker is called to work; nine o'clock – a boy and a girl are called to school; ten o'clock – the congregation is called to church; afternoon – soldiers are called to their drill; dusk – the glutton is called to his dinner; late night – gunnery practice recalls the front and this leads to another memory, that of 'last midnight' when he 'heard the sighs of men, that have no skill'. These sighs are the final call, and they call the speaker back to the fighting. The first and last stanzas are especially significant. In the first stanza, the speaker points to the instrumentality of the industrial worker's life ' . . . pushed and drawn / Backwards and forwards, helpless as a pawn.' The negative characteristics of this call, inherent in the adjectives 'dismal' and 'fog-hoarse' and the verb 'howls', betoken a questioning, at the least, of the industrial system which is condemned in the stanza's final declaration: ' . . . his work's crazy'. Such criticism is not particularly ideological; that is, it does not proceed from a conscious rationale such as socialism, whether of the Marxist or non-Marxist variety. It is not based on an analysis of the class structure. It is the result of a spontaneous upsurge of feeling for the oppressed that one reads from time to time in the letters.

The word 'Quick' (rapid and alive) which ushers in the second stanza lightens the tone perceptibly for the only time in the poem. The words 'Scuttling the schoolboy pulling up his sock' evoke Jacques' speech 'All the world's a stage' ('the schoolboy with shining morning face, / Creeping like snail'), but also remind us of the youthful Owen's disdain of some of his brother Harold's schoolfellows. In the context of his war experience, the otherwise innocent phrase 'I learn from the daisy' might read as a transposition in specifically English terms of Christ's injunction to consider the lilies. Such a reading does have validity in view of the poet's life as a soldier in daily mortal danger, but it is further enhanced by an echo of that bitter poem 'A Terre', in which the blind shell of an officer casualty speaks these words:

> Certainly flowers have the easiest time on earth.
> 'I shall be one with nature, herb and stone',
> Shelley would tell me. Shelley would be stunned:
> The dullest Tommy hugs that fancy now.
> 'Pushing up daisies' is their creed you know.

In contrast to the 'quick treble bells' of the second stanza, the church bells of the third stanza are 'stern', and – a measure of Owen's disenchantment with organized religion – disturb the natural world. The tone becomes downright dismissive in the last line with its colloquial syntax and internal rhyming, accentuated by the punctuating dash of 'religion's' and 'pigeon's'. One might note also the substitution of the commonplace pigeon for the more poetic dove, with its Biblical associations, from both the Old and New Testaments.

The discordancy of the bugle in the fourth stanza introduces another set of ambiguities. The Tommies are 'clumsy' and they 'clump'. The tone reminds us of some of Owen's acerbic observations in the letters. They are also 'trying to keep in step with rag-time tunes'. By this time, Owen has come under the spell of Sassoon, whom he met in the hospital at Craiglockhart. The reference to rag-time tunes is an echo of Sassoon's 'Blighters', published in *The Old Huntsman and Other Poems* in May 1917, whose second stanza begins: 'I'd like to see a Tank come down the stalls, / Lurching to rag-time tunes ...' Once more the final sentence of the stanza, 'I've done my drill' bears two meanings: 'I've done my drill for the day', and 'drill' as a metaphor for combat: 'I know what it's all about, because I've been in the trenches.'

Despite the less than felicitous choice of the word 'rusk' (called for more by the rhyme scheme than by the context), the disgust which the speaker feels for the glutton is powerfully expressed in the animal imagery of the second line combined with the sense of superfluous riches in the 'gold-filled tusk'. Surely he is one of the profiteers noted in the letters. The battlefield looms behind the image of the beating of gongs, since banging on metal was used in the trenches as a signal of a gas attack.

The battlefield is present in the penultimate stanza's call of the gunfire, as the speaker 'listens for the shell-shrieks and the crumps', while the final stanza completes the thrust of the poem with the speaker's pledge to join the men whose fate he consciously shares.

Owen identifies here with the P.B.I., the 'poor bloody infantry', whose ranks were largely drawn from the working class. This identification has not occurred through any political realization about the nature of British society and the causes of the war. Owen's categories are the moral ones dictated by the categories of the Sermon on the Mount of his pious upbringing, not the categories of Karl Marx nor even of his namesake of a hundred years earlier, the utopian socialist Robert Owen. Nevertheless, the problem of class is inscribed in his texts, both in the sense that his own class position helps to account for his ambivalence towards the working-class soldiers under his command, and for his ultimately sympathetic portrayal of those soldiers in poem after poem.

When we compare the writings of Owen after his first tour of duty in the trenches with those of the censorious callow officer in training in England, we can be in no doubt as to the sincerity of the identification that he makes in 'The Calls' and elsewhere.

In conclusion, I would like to link an experience from late adolescence to one of his best-known poems, 'Miners', written after a colliery disaster that killed 155 men and boy miners in January 1918.

In the summer of 1912, during his increasingly uneasy life at Dunsden, Owen went to an Evangelical Summer Convention in Keswick organized by low churchmen and nonconformists. In one of his letters to his mother from the camp outside the town where the Convention was being held, Owen writes:

> There is, in a tent remote from mine, a Northumberland lad who works in the pits, whose soul-life and Christianity is altogether beyond my understanding. . . .
>
> While your sleek Thomas, Hopkins, Dixon, Holden, Scroggie, and the rest of these double-barrelled guns, whose double-barrelled names I refuse to write, while they, I say, preach that preaching is no witness of a Christian Soul, your scar-backed mining-lad acts that acting is efficient. Scar-backed, I say, through running along subterranean 'roads' four feet high and scraping against its jagged roof . . .
>
> Another interesting thing, a good antidote to student-superciliousness, is that this pit-lad is wrestling with a Class-book of Physics – and taking a Correspondence Tuition in the Arts of Mining. He has no holiday and during the week his pay is stopped.
>
> (151)

This Northumberland pit-lad is certainly exceptional, at least as regards his piety. Despite the existence of a chapel-based sub-culture in the mining north-east, the majority of Northumberland pit-lads would have preferred whippets and pitch and toss to Wesley and penitence. Owen's admiration for the young miner begins with his observation of the hardness of the miner's work. It was precisely the vertebral scars of the Lancashire miners that George Orwell seized on as an emblem of the physical tool taken by a miner's work in *The Road to Wigan Pier*. It is those scars and the pit-lad's dedication to learning that call forth Owen's sympathy. It is important to remember this sympathy for the exemplary (in both senses of the word) individual when reading Owen's dismissive comments on working-class soldiers in the mass.

In the poem, 'Miners' (112), sympathy transcends the exemplary individual; it is extended to the collective. The first three stanzas of reverie, occasioned by the speaker's gazing into a coal fire, give place to a different mood and a different seeing:

> But the coals were murmuring of their mine,
>   And moans down there
> Of boys that slept wry sleep,
>   And men writhing for air.
>
> And I saw white bones in the cinder-shard.
>   Bones without number;
> For many hearts with coal are charred
>   And few remember.

Up to this point we can read the poem as being concerned with the literal miners of the title, but the next stanza introduces another kind of miner:

> I thought of some who worked dark pits
>   Of war, and died

The connection between miners and soldiers in the trenches is both meta-phorical and literal; some of Owen's Lancashire soldiers were ex-miners, and both sides used mining and counter-mining in this twentieth-century version of siege warfare. The last three stanzas continue and complete the identification of soldier/miner, and the poem comes to rest on the indifference of the world to the suffering of miners and soldiers:

> The centuries will burn rich loads
>   With which we groaned,

> Whose warmth shall lull their dreaming lids
>   While songs are crooned.
> But they will not dream of us poor lads
>   Lost in the ground.

This is Owen's strongest plea for the common man, and specifically the common man of the working class with whom the declassed officer-poet now identifies. By fusing the miner – the representative type of the industrial worker – with the soldier, the poem affirms the speaker's unequivocal solidarity with the working class and thus pulls down those barriers that had been erected by his family in the streets of Birkenhead.

Works cited

Fussell, Paul. *The Great War and Modern Memory*. London: Oxford University Press, 1975.

Keegan, John. *The Face of Battle*. London: Penguin, 1988.

Kerr, Douglas. *Wilfred Owen's Voices: Language and Community*. Clarendon, Oxford, 1993.

Owen, Harold. *Journey From Obscurity: Memoirs of the Owen Family, Volume 1; Childhood, Volume 2; Youth, Volume 3*. London: Oxford University Press, 1963.

Owen, Wilfred. *Collected Letters*, eds Harold Owen and John Bell. London: Oxford University Press, 1967.

Owen, Wilfred. *The Poems*, ed. Jon Stallworthy. London: Hogarth Press, 1985.

Parker, Peter. *The Old Lie: The Great War and the Public School Ethos*. London: Constable, 1987.

Read, Herbert. *The Contrary Experience*. London: Secker & Warburg, 1973.

Sassoon, Siegfried. *Collected Poems 1908–1956*. London and Boston: Faber & Faber, 1986.

Stallworthy, Jon. *Wilfred Owen: A Biography*. London: Oxford University Press and Chatto & Windus, 1975.

13
The War Poetry of Wilfred Owen: a Dissenting Reappraisal

Malcolm Pittock

I sense that the time is now right for a fundamental reassessment of Owen's war poetry. There have been indications of restiveness with the conventional view for some years now: Joseph Cohen has reductively reinterpreted Owen's response to the war in terms of his alleged homosexuality; Judith Kazantsis (xviii) has criticized Owen's (and Sassoon's) attachment to what she regards as a 'macho ethic', and Merryn Williams suggests that Owen's decision to return to France was 'a cop-out' (176). But Cohen leaves out the context of the war too completely and Kazantsis and Williams bring it in too simply to provide an effective challenge to the prevailing view of Owen, which, with whatever reservations, is still largely an endorsement of the self-image projected by his own draft preface. That Owen was a fine poet and provided a salutary antidote to the viciously sentimental legacy of wartime propaganda is not, of course, in question, but it is necessary now to ask whether his realism and honesty were not, after all, comparative and still confined within a sentimental framework. The implications of Yeats's provocative and much-derided judgement in his *Oxford Book of Modern Verse* in 1935 – the great and early exception to the consensus – which in effect accuses Owen of sentimentality, still have not been properly explored. But Yeats was in an excellent position to cast a cold eye on Owen: he was, after all, an Irishman, to whom the war was 'bloody frivolity' (*Letters*, 600), which, as early as September 1914, he predicted would lead to mutual impoverishment and preparation for a future war (*Letters*, 588). When conscription was extended to Ireland in 1918, he opposed it (Gilbert, 413).

What the significance of Yeats's Irishness can make us aware of is the extent to which a reappraisal of Owen may still be hampered by continuing British (and American?) attitudes to the war embodied in the ceremonies of Remembrance Day, with their partisan pieties, their quasi-liturgical intoning of Binyon's lines, which appear to claim that it is better to die young than to die old (and who can really believe that?), the praise for soldiers who 'gave their lives' or 'made the supreme sacrifice' (but conscripts don't *give* anything and even volunteers, if they couldn't take any more 'giving', were liable to be shot). As for sacrifice, not only must it be uncompelled but it must not involve harming others: 'Christ is not on record as having lobbed many Mills bombs' (Barker, 82).

It may be claimed that Owen's war poetry and those who read it sympathetically are critical of all this. But it is not simply that, as a matter of fact, 'Greater Love' fits in well enough with the ethos of Remembrance Sunday: what more significantly happens is that such sentimentalities can inhibit clear thought even in those who would consider themselves as dissenting from them. As Vernon Scannell puts it, even for him 'whenever the November sky / Quivers with a bugle's hoarse, sweet cry / The reason darkens' ('The Great War', 40). The use of the term 'draft-dodger' even by opponents of the Vietnam War (e.g. Williams, 166) illustrates the continuing influence of that irrationality, for it implies that to fight in an unjust cause is, nonetheless, a duty (one can only dodge an obligation). And it is significant how liberals betray their liberalism – as all of them do – in their tolerance of and even approval for the way in which Graves circumvented Sassoon's famous protest of 1917 so that he ended in Craiglockhart rather than before a court martial. The idea that other people have no right to interfere in your decisions believing that they, not you, know what is best is, one would imagine, a fundamental liberal belief. And yet it does not function here, even though the Sassoon case actually anticipates the way in which psychiatry was misused in the Soviet Union to silence dissidents. In true Soviet style, Rivers regarded Sassoon as having 'a very strong anti-war complex' (Sassoon, *Diaries*, 183, 192) which it was his job to cure.

Strict avoidance of sentimentality does not itself involve the rejection of war as an instrument of policy: it merely means complete clarity as to what is entailed by it. If one accepts that the First World War was a just war and that the Allies were right to fight it to a victorious conclusion, then one must accept that all the suffering was unavoidable and had merely to be endured (though one could legitimately question this or that political or military decision). If one concentrates on the suffering caused by the war as, say, Owen does (even though, as we shall see, he dwells largely on that of this own side), then there must be at least an implicit belief that the suffering is in excess of the ends proposed and that the war should be stopped. Otherwise what one is writing is either reportage or a kind of compassionate grumbling. Such an implication is present in Barbusse through the invocation of Liebknecht's name, for Liebknecht '[urged] soldiers not to fight' (Gilbert, 256).

A soldier, however, who found he opposed the continuation of the war was, of course, in a terrible position: on the one hand he bore moral responsibility for contributing to the suffering which he considered unnecessary and, on the other, his hands were tied. He could not attend political meetings, make public statements opposed to the war or encourage civilians to oppose it, let alone refuse to continue fighting himself, without becoming liable to severe penalties. Moreover, since in any given case, the pressures of one's military situation would cooperate with larger social pressures towards conformity, even private doubters were likely to reveal inconsistency and confusion as well as a tendency to unload responsibility on to others (this point I shall expand on later). Owen's stated hatred of 'washy pacifists' (*Letters*, 498) actually implies opposition to ending the war by negotiation (for that is what pacifism usually meant then), which is inconsistent with what he said elsewhere (*Letters*, 543) and his implicit approval of conscientious objectors (*Letters*, 461).

There was, however, a difference between the situation of commissioned officers and that of other ranks when it came to public dissent. A ranker who refused to continue fighting would have been liable to be shot; nor would he have had any practicable alternative short of direct refusal. But for an officer there could be a hairline crack of opportunity. If temporarily invalided in Britain, he could be in a position to obtain a permanent home posting – particularly if he had influential friends, or he could resign his commission, refuse to go back and face court martial, which he could be pretty sure would lead only to imprisonment. (Plowman was not, in fact, imprisoned at all.) Owen appears for a time to have acquiesced in Scott-Moncrieff's attempts to get him a home posting (Hibberd, *Last Year*, 115); Sassoon, rather than accept such a posting, made his famous statement against the war and refused to consider himself as any longer under military command, and the authorities went out of their way not to court-martial him (Sassoon, *Journey*, 50–4). Max Plowman resigned his commission, was court-martialled and discharged from the Army. Called before a civilian tribunal, he steadily refused to do work of national importance under the Military Service Act: all the tribunal did was to send him back repeatedly to think again – until the armistice intervened (Plowman, *Bridge*, 112, 116, 130).

I think it reasonable to maintain that with First World War writers who are known to have implied or held a position critical of, or opposed to, the war, the way they dealt with that dissent is significant for the manner in which they wrote about the war – and sometimes casts an even longer shadow. Thus in Graves's case the comparative ineffectiveness of his war poetry 'playing at realism' (Parsons, 658), 'he looks but he does not want to see' (Quinn, 22), as well as, at the other extreme, the pose of hard-boiled insouciance in *Goodbye to All That* can be related to his determination to stamp down on his own dissent (he did, after all, agree with Sassoon's statement) and to try to regard himself as contracted to do what he was told, even if it involved him in shooting strikers (Graves, 204–5). That the cost of this suppression was very high is suggested by the way in which when he was a very old man and his defences broke down, he was in anguish over his war guilt, confessing to living in hell (Seymour, 459). Perhaps this suppression explains, too, that determinedly provocative inauthenticity which prevents Graves, despite his enormous talent, from being a major writer.

At the other extreme, Plowman found peace through his steady stand, as his cheerfully serene letters clearly suggest, and though his memoir, *A Subaltern on the Somme* (1927), is the product of only a minor literary talent, it is without bitterness and self-justification and does not even foreshadow the decision he was subsequently to take. In contrast, Sassoon had, I think, a lasting regret that he had not done what he had set out to do but had been deliberately manoeuvred into inauthenticity and ineffectiveness, so that even against Owen's pleas, he decided to return to the front (via Ireland and Egypt as it happened) to escape from a false position. Certainly his long estrangement from Graves, whom he accused of lying to him (Sassoon, *Memoirs*, 513; Seymour Smith, 195–7) and the fact that he could not bring himself to tell the full story even in *Siegfried's Journey* suggests that it was a very sensitive area. It is possible that Sassoon's decline as a poet may be related to it as may also his resort to fictional disguise in his war memoirs with its licence both to omit and touch up. Certainly his account of his military experience subsequent to Craiglockhart in *Sherston's Progress* has a curious defensiveness and evasiveness. Once returned to the Western Front, the gallant Sherston, like the gallant Waverley on the field of Prestonpans, never apparently kills anybody.

In partial contrast, Rosenberg's situation explains some of the features of his war poetry. On the face of it, one might have expected him to have out-Owened Owen. He came from an anti-military background describing his parents as 'Tolstoylians' (Rosenberg, 234) and was ashamed of himself for joining up, which he did for economic reasons (Rosenberg, 214, 219, 227) considering it 'the most criminal thing a man can do' (216). But once a private in the army he was virtually trapped; he could not write home reasonably frankly as Owen could, while he was 'forbidden to send poems home, as the censor won't be bothered with going through such rubbish' (Rosenberg, 242). And so his sole aim was to save his soul alive, determined that 'this war.... [should] not master [his] poeting' (Rosenberg, 248). He therefore preserved his creativity by accepting the war and cultivating a poetic mode of quasi-detachment or symbolic abstraction which would enable him both to understand it and endure it. There was a sense in which he could not afford to protest against the war even to himself. However, unlike Sassoon or Owen he had the integrity never to succumb to a sentimentalist military ideal: he refused to become even a lance-corporal (Rosenberg, 226), while his protective withdrawal into his own creative processes meant that he was frequently punished for absent-mindedness (Cohen, *Life*, 134, 138, 161, 166).

The problem with Owen is that the tenor of his poetry would seem to commit him to some kind of public opposition to the war or to an awareness that it should do so, even if he did not have the requisite strength actually to act. It is to Sassoon's eternal credit that, however much his protest was undermined, he saw this clearly. Yet the most Owen was prepared to do was to seek a home posting, which, anyway, was an act of evasion rather than protest. Since it is extremely difficult to live with an awareness that one ought to do something while doing nothing, the temptation is to avoid awareness by finding a substitute purpose. This is what I think happened to Owen. His poetry itself became the substitute and that it was so was shown by its very limitations: the representation of the war as passive suffering. The re-dating of 'Strange Meeting' is of crucial significance here. Understandably, but erroneously, it was long considered Owen's last poem because, presumably, it appeared to represent a new departure. However, it was actually written between January and March 1918 (*Poems*, 126) before his decision to return to France in May (*Poems*, 139), which was also the date of the preface to the book of war poems which he hoped to publish in 1919. In 'Strange Meeting', Owen had broken through to a position close to Plowman's as expressed in the statement he read out at his court martial in 1918: 'I believe that God is incarnate in every human being.... [and] that killing men is killing God' (Plowman, *Bridge*, 772). Significantly, Owen could not sustain such a level of guilt and insight and the poems after 'Strange Meeting', including the ones he wrote or revised following his return to France, 'Spring Offensive' and 'Smile, Smile, Smile' (*Poems*, 167, 170) represent a reversion to the limitations of his earlier war poetry.

When war broke out, Owen's long-standing ambition to be a recognized poet in the prophetic-romantic tradition, together with the accident of his residence in France, meant that, though broadly speaking he had taken a conventional view of the conflict, he was not only exempt from the insistent pressure to join up which he would have experienced back home, but 'felt no personal call to do anything about it at all. . . . his only strong feeling was to preserve for himself the opportunity to continue with his poetry at all costs' (H. Owen, 118). So when he finally volunteered in 1915 he could hardly be said to be enthusiastically committed. But once in the army, he felt strong pressures to conform. Indeed, being from a lower-middle-class family, painfully conscious of its status, he had been attracted by the chance to become an officer and a gentleman. The snobbery that surfaces in his letters (*Letters*, 539, 563) shows how important that was to him.

Experience of fighting activated the ethical sense he had already manifested at Dunsden. The force with which in one letter to his mother he expresses the view that Christianity is a pacifist faith and his description of himself as 'a conscientious objector with a very seared conscience' may indeed show the influence of Tolstoy, who was, after his conversion, an uncompromising Christian pacifist (*Letters*, 461). As Rosenberg's reference to 'Tolstoylians' suggests, Tolstoy's views were widely known, and Owen even possessed a volume containing some of his post-conversion tales with a forty-page introduction.

But the fact that experience of fighting also led to a nervous breakdown and he had been 'officially recorded as having suffered a loss of morale under shell fire' (Hibberd, *Owen the Poet*, 76) subjected Owen to different pressures. He had not behaved as an officer and a gentleman was supposed to and that left him with a sense of a debt unpaid to that ideal. He was to feel that he needed to 'get some reputation of gallantry' (*Letters*, 498). The experience of Craiglockhart and acquaintance with Sassoon, however, reawakened his cherished desire to become a significant poet. Sassoon's example gave him an appropriate subject and role: he was to be the poet who was to express the pity of war. After flirting with the possibility of a home posting, which, in view of what was regarded as his loss of morale, he had little chance of obtaining anyway (Hibberd, *Last Year*, 148) and which clearly would have entailed a feeling of guilt at training soldiers for the front (*Letters*, 562), his final solution was to embrace what in ordinary terms could not be avoided. By redeeming himself as an officer and a gentleman, he would also fulfil his poetic destiny. That redemption would authenticate his war poetry, freeing it from the taint of Craiglockhart. By adopting the role of pleader for his suffering men, which would also involve the distinct possibility that he would be killed, he would fulfil what in terms of the sentiment of the time would give him a kind of Christian role, silencing any remaining scruples.[1]

There is no doubt that Owen's return to France, the award of the Military Cross and his death in battle did promote his war poetry. He became an acceptable icon: the compassionate but gallant officer who in his poetry had shown that war was hell but had, nonetheless, done his duty (Cohen, 'Agonistes', 253). The anti-war attitudes in the 1930s to which his poetry contributed were, however, superficial (Orwell, 567) for, whatever good reasons there were to fight the Second World War, it was undoubtedly marked by public approval for the mass slaughter of civilians. The way Owen explains his acceptance of a return to France serves as a useful introduction as to what is wrong with much of his war poetry:

> I came out in order to help these boys – directly by leading them as well as an officer can; indirectly, by watching their sufferings, that I may speak of them as a pleader can.
>
> (*Letters*, 580)

This is simply incompatible with the reality of warfare. Owen, like other junior officers, was subordinate to the commands of his superiors which he could not question, while, like all soldiers, he was not merely watching suffering but contributing to it. The latter part of the statement appears to pass muster only because it is ultimately compatible with the sentimental picture of British soldiers as so many Christs laying down their lives for their friends. One of the most telling, because unwitting and implicit, criticisms of Owen's position came from his own family. If Dominic Hibberd is right (Hibberd, *Last Year*, 174) they appear to have doctored the official citation for the Military Cross so that it contains no reference to the fact that he 'personally manipulated a captured enemy M.G. from an isolated position and inflicted considerable losses on the enemy'. Reality had to bow to the icon.

It is not altogether surprising, therefore, that Owen falsely represents his subjects as victims (passive sufferers) with no hint that they combine the roles of victim and executioner. How far this could actually involve Owen in drawing on current stereotypes is at its most obvious in 'Greater Love'. In the second line of the opening verse, if the reader substitutes 'German' for 'English' the poem no longer works because it depends on stock responses still not available for the other side.

Red lips are not so red
  As the stained stones kissed by the German dead
Kindness of wooed and wooer
  Seems shame to their love pure.

'Greater Love', unusually for Owen, is openly partisan. Such poems as 'Hospital Barge', 'At a Calvary near the Ancre', 'Miners', 'The Letters', 'Conscious', 'Dulce et Decorum Est', 'the Dead-Beat', 'Asleep', 'Futility', 'S.I.W.', 'The Chances', 'The Send-off', 'Disabled', 'A Terre' are covertly so, for all, however varied in their approach, deal with the British victims of the actions of their opponents – even if they can sometimes also be regarded as indirect victims of the complacency of civilians back home. However, when a poem does not deal with an actual victim as, say, 'Insensibility', the reference can be ambiguous. Although it may appear to have a universal significance, a line like 'sore on the alleys cobbled with their brothers' (l. 5) actually also invites a restricted and partisan application without readers being consciously aware that this is so. This is significantly true too of Owen's famous statement in his draft preface. 'My subject is War, and the pity of War' (*Poems*, 192) sounds universal enough; however, not only would the contents of the projected volume have dealt prodominantly with British sufferings but the statement itself is restricted by its context: 'This book is not about heroes. English poetry is not yet fit to speak of them' on the one hand, an obligatory swipe at 'Prussia' on the other.

'Anthem for Doomed Youth' is a very telling example of Owen's sleight of hand. The title has a universal application, and it is actually quite possible to read most of the octave as applying to both sides represented, not as the victims of each other, but of their weapons, which, rather extraordinarily, appear to go off without the intervention of human agency. But even by the end of the octave the reference is being restricted: 'And bugles calling for them from sad shires' (l. 8). 'Sad shires'? how very British, not to say English: there is even a touch of Housman. And, though one might struggle to make the sestet refer to grieving Frauen and Fräulein, it would be an uphill task. As Stallworthy points out: 'And each slow dusk a drawing-down of blinds' (l. 14) can be associated with Binyon's famous lines (*Poems*, 77).

Of course, Owen cannot altogether avoid the fact that soldiers on his own side fought and killed too. Graves was haunted by the fact that he had killed – murdered was his preferred word – over a hundred Germans (Seymour-Smith, 567; Seymour, 459–60). But, apart from 'Strange Meeting', the poems which seem to take account of this are characterized by generalizing evasiveness as to what happens in combat: not for Owen the unblinking realism of Keith Douglas in 'How to Kill'. This evasiveness is closely associated with the question of his moral responsibility as a participant. In 'Spring Offensive', Owen actually manages to keep himself out of the poem altogether (that it was written or at least revised after his return to France is significant). The third person is used throughout, while the description of combat is betrayingly vague:

> And there out-fiending all its fiends and flames
> With superhuman inhumanities,
> Long-famous glories, immemorial shames –

> (41–3)

But it is not merely vague, it is morally ambiguous. Not only does 'long-famous glories' not fit into the sequence (unless one invokes that universal solvent of all difficulties – irony) but the sequence as a whole is boastful, as if out-fiending the fiends was something to be perversely proud of. That the evasiveness and the moral bluffing is Owen's own, distanced by attributing it to an impersonal 'they', is shown by a parallel passage in his letters: 'The fighting passed the limits of my abhorrence. I lost all my earthly faculties, and fought like an angel' (*Letters*, 580). But in the very same letter he shows himself shy of detail and in the action which was to win him the MC he claimed to have shot only one man. 'The rest I took with a smile.' This, of course, is not consistent with the official citation.

'Apologia pro Poemate Meo' does use the first person. But the only reference to actual fighting is: 'For power was on us as we slashed bones bare / Not to feel sickness of remorse or murder' (ll. 7–8). 'Slashed bones bare' is the only realistic combat detail in any of Owen's poems bar 'Strange Meeting'. But, again, even though he confesses to murder, he appears to be actually celebrating the callousness which makes it morally possible. Most of the poem is indeed a perversely sentimental attempt to claim that for the British troops, despite everything, life in the trenches involved spiritual transformation. Owen is very much the officer shuttling between participant and observer:

> Faces that used to curse me, scowl for scowl,
> Shine and lift up with passion of oblation,
> Seraphic for an hour; though they were foul.

> (ll. 14–16)

We are back to the old cliché of sacrifice, but here seen through mud-covered spectacles.

'Insensibility' is less crude than 'Apologia'. There is no attempt to present the callusing of the sensibility as somehow heroic, and any possibility of heroism is further undermined by sardonic irony. The callousness manifested by the troops is, moreover, surpassed by the callousness with which they are regarded:

> Men, gaps for filling;
> Losses, who might have fought
> Longer; but no one bothers.

> (ll. 9–11)

But there is even less reference to actual fighting than in *Apologia* and though combat is implied (at least for most of the time) 'besmirch / Blood over all our soul' (ll. 41–2) seems to be the only passage where we can be reasonably certain that the blood referred to is non-British. Revealing, too, is the fact that it takes Owen 37 lines to stop talking about the troops as if he himself were elsewhere and to use the first person plural. And, at this point, another element of falsity enters. For the 'we' is not, after all, an inclusive we, but an elite we, 'We wise', who, naturally sensitive, have to desensitize themselves using those who are basically insensitive as a model:

> How should we see our task
> But through his blunt and lashless eyes?
> Alive, he is not vital overmuch;
> Dying, not mortal overmuch.

> (ll. 42–6)

Behind this social snobbery and the sentimentalization (see 'Inspection' as an example) is the role of the junior officer (who was after all armed with a revolver to shoot recalcitrant rankers).

The unsatisfactoriness of 'Apologia' and 'Insensibility' is compounded by an accusatory rhetoric which, in 'Insensibility', is particularly strident and is followed by a decline into verbiage: 'Whatever shares / The eternal reciprocity of tears' (ll. 58–9). It is other people who are to blame: 'cursed are dullards whom no cannon stuns. . . . by choice they made themselves immune / To pity' (ll. 50, 54–5). But Owen had already claimed to be a member of a moral elite who surely must have *chosen* to desensitize themselves ('How should we see our task...?'). More-over, though he may use the first person plural pronoun, 'We wise', he is really talking about himself. Blaming other people, however reason-able it may be in relation to a collective, is a form of bad faith when an individual resorts to it to exonerate himself from responsibility however badly placed he may be. That a soldier has not an absolute duty of obedience was even recognized at the Nuremberg trials.

In some of Owen's minor poems, in his determination to exteriorize responsibility, he is prepared to make common cause with the other side. In 'The Parable of the Old Man and the Young', for example, it is youth in general ('half the seed of Europe') who are collectively seen as the victims of the older generation. In 'Soldier's Dream', the blame is put on God, conceived as Blake's Old Nobodaddy. But again Owen is evading the issue. The majority of British soldiers, for instance, did not look on the war as pointless slaughter – a view which the poems just mentioned clearly imply – and were broadly in agreement, whatever their grumbles, with official policy (Stephen, 77–9).

Yeats's criticism of Owen for representing the war as passive suffering is true not only in the sense that he concentrated on British soldiers in their role of victims, but also in a moral sense: as if nothing else but passive endurance could be envisaged. And yet the mutinies of the French and Russian troops, as well as the Kiel naval mutiny, show that when soldiers lost their belief in the war they could no longer be trusted to remain passive. As far as Owen himself is concerned, Yeats's invoca-tion of Arnold's decision to exclude 'Empedocles on Etna' from his 1853 collection is suggestive: Arnold thought that the representation of suffering which finds 'no vent in action' was depressing and monoton-ous (Arnold, 592).

There is, however, one poem that can be closely associated with poems like 'Spring Offensive', 'Apologia' and 'Insensibility' which, morally and imaginatively, is much more adequate. Significantly, it shows some of the same structural features as 'Strange Meeting': a dream or fantasy of escape from the scene of battle, which, turning out not to be an escape at all, leads back to renewed suffering and fresh insight. 'The Show' takes the evasiveness of 'Spring Offensive' to such an unacceptable extreme that Owen is, I think, through that exaggeration showing a critical awareness of it. This time the poet represents himself as a non-combatant observing a struggle between what appear to be two sets of caterpillars impelled by instinctive drives and therefore one to which normal moral judgements do not apply. He is, however, only *au-dessus de la mêlée* because he is in a humanly impossible position: dead, but

with a continuing consciousness: an uninvolved observer, one might
say, at last. Naturally, the unreal vision collapses:

> Whereat, in terror what that sight might mean,
> I reeled and shivered earthward like a feather.
> And Death fell with me, like a deepening moan.
> And He, picking a manner of worm, which half had hid
> Its bruises in the earth but crawled no further,
> Showed me its feet, the feet of many men,
> And the fresh-severed head of it, my head.

> (ll. 33–9)

What this strange and potent image appears to signify is the poet's
awareness not only of his own likely death but of his dehumanization and
moral responsibility. His head is that of a caterpillar-worm with the
platoon as its body. So in human terms the members of the platoon are
reduced to instruments of his own instinctive will. But his head is not that
of caterpillar, the members of the platoon are not parts of his body but
independent beings. His head is a human head capable of reason, responsibility and choice. A false way of seeing and feeling has been diagnosed.

'Strange Meeting' is, however, the only poem in which Owen fully
faces up to the reality of his own experience. The most obvious sign of
its uniqueness is a frankness about the details of combat:

> 'I am the enemy you killed my friend
> I knew you in this dark: for so you frowned
> Yesterday through me as you jabbed and killed.
> I parried; but my hands were loath and cold.'

> (ll. 40–3)

Not only is such explicitness really new, but an actual German enters
Owen's poetry for the first time and one whom not any Briton but the
poet himself has killed. Moreover, these lines impact with a calculated
force because up to that point the Other could have been on the same
side – a Sassoon, for example. (Indeed, in an earlier related fragment, the
Other is clearly a friend who is being invited to 'stay behind' with the
poet.) The sudden change from a visionary to a realistic mode strength-
ens the effect still further.

The poem is not only about the inescapability of personal guilt (no
blaming of other people here) but it implicitly undermines the purpose

expressed in Owen's preface: 'Yet these elegies are to this generation in no sense consolatory. They may be to the next. All a poet can do today is warm' (*Poems*, 192). For what the body of the poem envisages is that the world will be made worse by the war and will not be in a position to heed any kind of warning. There is, indeed, some connection with the Yeats of 'The Second Coming'. The idea of a poet fighting and warning at the same time is recognized as unsustainable. Not only would that involve staying alive – and the poet envisages his own death – but more importantly, as the use of a doppelganger motif shows, it may involve killing someone with a vision and purpose similar to one's own, an Ernst Toller for example ('I know at last that all the dead, French and German alike, are brothers and I am their brother too' (Toller, 71)). But, of course, by fighting, he is destroying the life and creativity of others and the world cannot but be the worse for such destruction. Moreover, by making his victim his doppelganger, Owen is alluding to a central feature of that myth: that in killing one's double one is killing oneself. The grave friendly courtesy of the enemy is an embodiment of the civilized intercourse that both have violated. The contrast between such intercourse and that which war imposes on them is contained in the near oxymoron 'I am the enemy you killed, my friend'.

Insight at this level with its acknowledgement of guilt and punishment: 'I knew we stood in Hell' (here Owen joins hands with the dying Graves), was simply unsustainable in the light of the choices Owen actually made. But the fact that he was capable of it illuminates the distortions and limitations of his other war poetry.

Note

1. I have felt it necessary to omit consideration of the vexed question of Owen's homosexuality as this would involve a detailed rehearsal of the evidence, though clearly it could have been a relevant factor. Three positions have been maintained: (a) that Owen was not homosexual; (b) that he was so in temperament only; (c) that he was an active homosexual. Without prejudicing the issue, I should say that (b) is the most likely.

Works cited

Arnold, Matthew. *Poems*, ed. K. Allott. London: Longman, 1965.
Barker, Pat. *Regeneration*. London: Penguin Books, 1992.
Cohen, Joseph. *Journey to the Trenches: The Life of Isaac Rosenberg, 1890–1918*. London: Robson Books, 1973.
——. 'Owen Agonistes', *English Literature in Transition*, 8 (1965): 253–68.
Gilbert, Martin. *First World War*. London: HarperCollins, 1995.

Graves, Robert. *Goodbye to All That*, revised edition. Harmondsworth: Penguin Books, 1960.

Hibberd, Dominic. *Owen the Poet*. London: Macmillan – now Palgrave, 1986.

———. *Wilfred Owen: The Last Year, 1917–1918*. London: Constable, 1992.

Kazantzis, Judith. *Scars upon My Heart: Women's Poetry and Verse of the First World War*, ed. Catherine W. Reilly. London: Virago, 1981.

Orwell, George. 'Inside the Whale', in *Collected Essays, Journalism and Letters*, eds Sonia Orwell and Ian Angus, 4 vols. Harmondsworth: Penguin, 1970, vol. 1, 540–80.

Owen, Harold. *War*. London: Oxford University Press, 1965 (Vol. 3 of *Journey from Obscurity: Wilfred Owen 1893–1918*, 3 vols, 1963–65).

Owen, Wilfred. *Collected Letters*, eds Harold Owen and John Bell. London: Oxford University Press, 1967.

———. *The Manuscripts of the Poems and the Fragments*. London: Chatto & Windus, 1983 (Vol. 2 of *The Complete Poems and Fragments*, ed. Jon Stallworthy, 1983).

———. *The Poems*, ed. Jon Stallworthy. London: Chatto & Windus, 1985.

Parsons, Ian. 'The Poems of Wilfred Owen', *Criterion*, 10 (1931): 658–69.

Plowman, Max. *Bridge into the Future: Letters*, ed. Dorothy L. Plowman. London: Andrew Dakers, 1944.

Quinn, Patrick. *The Great War and the Missing Muse*. Selingsgrove, PA: Susquehanna University Press, 1994.

Rosenberg, Isaac. *The Collected Works*, ed. Ian Parsons. London: Chatto & Windus, 1979.

Sassoon, Siegfried. *The Complete Memoirs of George Sherston*. London: Faber, 1972.

———. *Diaries, 1915–1918*, ed. Rupert Hart-Davis, London: Faber, 1983.

———. *Siegfried's Journey 1916–1920*. London: Faber, 1945.

Scannell, Vernon. *Selected Poems*. London: Alison & Busby, 1971.

Seymour, Miranda. *Robert Graves: Life on the Edge*. London: Doubleday, 1995.

Seymour-Smith, Martin. *Robert Graves: His Life and Work*. London: Hutchinson, 1982.

Stephen, Martin. *The Price of Pity: Poetry History and Myth in The Great War*, London: Leo Cooper, 1996.

Toller, Ernst. *Prosa, Briefe, Dramen, Gedichte*, ed. Kurt Hiller. Reinbek bei Hamburg: Rowohlt, 1961.

Tolstoy, Leo. *Short Stories*. London: Walter Scott, n.d.

Williams, Merryn. *Wilfred Owen*. Bridgend: Seren Books, 1993.

Yeats, W. B. *The Letters*, ed. Allan Wade. London: Rupert Hart-Davis, 1954.

———. (ed.) *The Oxford Book of Modern Verse*. Oxford: Oxford University Press, 1935.

14

'Thoughts That You've Gagged All Day': Siegfried Sassoon, W. H. R. Rivers and '[The] Repression of War Experience'

Patrick Campbell

On 4 December 1917, the distinguished psychoanalyst W. H. R. Rivers gave a talk to the Royal Society of Medicine. Entitled *The Repression of War Experience*, it was subsequently reprinted in a collection of essays called *Instinct and the Unconscious* (1920). To any student of the First World War it is a significant document. For the paper offered the view that current therapeutic practice, which urged the 'shell-shocked' victims of the war 'to banish all thoughts of war from their minds', was misguided. Instead, what Rivers advocated, citing a number of clinical case studies from Craiglockhart as evidence, was the need to face up to rather than repress these distressing thoughts so that they 'no longer raced through [the] mind at night and disturbed . . . sleep by terrifying dreams of warfare' (190). For Rivers believed that 'repression', as opposed to 'suppression' ('the state of inaccessibility') was a conscious procedure, 'the active or voluntary process by which it is attempted to remove some part of the mental content making it inaccessible to memory and producing the state of suppression' (190).

Before illustrating some of the 'effects which may be produced by repression', Rivers outlined his theory:

I hope to show that many of the most trying and distressing symptoms from which the subjects of war-neurosis suffer are not the necessary results of the strain and shocks to which they have been exposed in warfare, but are due to the attempt to banish from the mind distressing memories of warfare or painful affective states which have come into being as the result of their war experience.

219

Everyone who has had to treat cases of war-neurosis, and especially that form of neurosis dependent on anxiety, must have been faced by the problem what advice to give concerning the attitude the patient should adopt towards his war experience. It is natural to thrust aside painful memories just as it is natural to avoid dangerous or horrible scenes in actuality. The natural tendency to banish the distressing or the horrible is especially pronounced in those whose powers of resistance have been lowered by the long-continued strains of trench life, the shock of shell explosion, or other catastrophe of warfare. Even if patients were left to themselves, most would naturally strive to forget distressing memories and thoughts. They are, however, very far from being left to themselves, the natural tendency to repress being in my experience almost universally fostered by their relatives and friends, as well as their medical advisors. Even when patients have themselves realised the impossibility of forgetting their war experiences and have recognised the hopeless and enervating character of treatment by repression, they are often induced to attempt the task in obedience to medical orders. The advice which has usually been given to my patients in other hospitals is that they should endeavour to banish all thoughts of war from their minds. In some cases all conversation between patients, or with visitors, about the war is strictly forbidden, and the patients are instructed to lead their thoughts to other topics, to beautiful scenery and other pleasant aspects of experience.

(187)

Rivers' themes, adumbrated and then illustrated in his talk, are important in other, more specific ways. Six months earlier, Siegfried Sassoon had written a poem also entitled 'Repression of War Experience'.[1] It is a watershed poem, as significant, in terms of its exploitation of a key moment in his psychic development, as anything Sassoon wrote during the war. That he realized that the poem was both an example of 'repression' and an attempt to come to terms with its operations is clear from a title which not only employs a term drawn from Freudian psychoanalysis but also pays homage to Rivers' professional interest in 'anxiety-neurosis' and subsequently the subject of his December lecture.

It is unlikely that Sassoon waited six months before giving the poem a title. Soon, very soon after composing it, Sassoon would be at Craiglockhart War Hospital, in daily contact with Rivers and undergoing treatment to relieve his 'anti-war complex'[2] and other distressing symptoms apparently brought on by 'repression' of his trench experiences. In a letter dated 26 July 1917, the first reference to his new mentor, Sassoon refers to 'Rivers, the chap who looks after me . . . I am very glad to have the chance of talking to such a fine man' (Sassoon, *Diaries*, 177). Less than a year later, Rivers, no longer vainly trying to persuade Sassoon from his pacifist views, had assumed in the poet's eyes a God-like eminence. 'I must never forget Rivers. He is the only man who can save me if I break down again. If I am able to keep going it will be through him' (Sassoon, *Diaries*, 246). All this was in the future. For the moment, and the pastoral setting of the poem makes this clear, Sassoon was resting at his mother's home at Weirleigh, There he was recuperating both from the effects of a physical wound resulting from 'a sniper's bullet through the shoulder' (Sassoon, *Diaries*, 155) and from psychical trauma in the form of an 'anxiety neurosis' not only occasioned by memories of front-line atrocities but also by his decision, taken as recently as 15 June, to confront the establishment by publicly denouncing its war policies. It is worth reminding ourselves of its opening salvo:

> I am making this statement as an act of wilful defiance of military authority, because I believe that the war is being deliberately prolonged by those who have the power to end it. I am a soldier, concerned that I am acting on behalf of soldiers. I believe that this War, upon which I entered as a war of defence and liberation, has now become a war of aggression and conquest.
>
> (Sassoon, *Diaries*, 173–4)

Now at the moment of composing the poem, he was awaiting official reactions, in the certain knowledge that they would be powerfully antipathetic and that his artistic reputation, his military career, even his life, could be in jeopardy. In a follow-up letter to his commanding officer, Sassoon gloomily confessed, 'I am fully aware of what I am letting myself in for' (Sassoon, *Diaries*, 177). Robbie Ross, writing to Gosse on 19 July (the day before Sassoon went to Craiglockhart), had already remarked his 'very abnormal state' (Sassoon, *Diaries*, 182). Wounded, 'shell-shocked', Sassoon had now taken on the authorities in a head-on gesture whose wisdom even his friends Graves and Ross seriously doubted. It can be safely concluded that his state of mind at the time of writing 'Repression of War Experience' was turbulent, troubled, shot through with conflicting emotions. As Rivers would later remind him, it was a condition probably exacerbated by his officer 'training in repression' and his consequent inability to 'dwell upon . . . painful experience . . . in such a way as to relieve its horrible and terrifying character' (Rivers, *Instinct*, 191). The poem, in form an irregular and unrhymed ode, is not significant just because it charts, both consciously and unconsciously, a key episode in Sassoon's war. It deals with the whole notion of 'repression' – albeit before he had discussed the process with Rivers – in a richly ambivalent way. Though it is the only poem, apart from 'To Any Dead Officer', written during the heart-searching period that culminated in his statement of 'wilful defiance', it contains no overt reference to the protest; if it was one of those thoughts which, in the words of the poem, he had 'gagged all day' and which now threatened to 'come back to scare him', it was single-mindedly eliminated from the conscious observations and images that constitute the poem. To sublimate these emotions, to give poetic embodiment to them (though 'to Any Dead Officer' had tried) was simply too painful an experience to contemplate during the lengthy and necessarily intense process of creation.

Not that Sassoon seems to have been entirely unaware of the Freudian theory of 'repression' and its attendant dangers. He might not have read Freud in depth but the fact that he uses the term suggests that he could hardly have been ignorant of the basic principles of 'repression' which Freud had expounded in his *Introductory Lectures on Psycho-Analysis*. Here, in his 19th Lecture, Freud had developed his celebrated metaphor of a 'door-keeper' standing 'on the threshold' between the 'ante-room' of the unconscious and the 'reception room' of the conscious. This 'personage' examines the various mental excitations, censors them and denies them admittance to the 'reception-room when he disapproves of them'. At this juncture, Freud explains, these thoughts, are 'incapable of becoming conscious'; we call them, *repressed* (Freud, 337).

Not everything in Sassoon's poem is 'repressed'. After all Sassoon does allow, across the threshold into consciousness and into the public domain of the poem, some ghoulish memories that he has 'gagged all day'; he is attempting to confront that problem that beset all convalescing soldiers: how to cope with these memories that you would rather repress out of consciousness at the consequent risk of their terrible resurfacing in dream and nightmare. And not only in dream. The state of evening reverie was equally vulnerable. As Rivers explained: 'If unpleasant thoughts are voluntarily repressed during the day, it is natural that they should rise into activity when the control of the waking state is removed by sleep or is weakened in the state which *precedes and follows sleep and occupies it at intervals* [emphasis added]' (*Instinct*, 199). That his 'treatment' by Rivers, aimed at the 'removal of repression' (*Instinct*, 194) would in the future help him cope much better with an 'anxiety neurosis' to which he was consistently prone, is evidenced by the Craiglockhart poems themselves. Many of these would reveal a Sassoon able again to relive his 'war experience' through their cathartic expression in verse. For the present – and the 'evidence' is in the poem – facing up directly to the worst circumstances was more difficult. Only at the conclusion of this poem, with his deflecting strategies undermined by the insistent noise of gunfire, is Sassoon able to repudiate the distancing devices of poetic language and, in a rough-hewn and demotic unleashing of pent-up emotion, openly declare: 'I'm going stark, staring mad because of the guns.'

Read in this way, 'Repression of War Experience' is a dialogue between the 'I' and 'you' of the divided self in which the 'I' of the present, apparently relaxed moment is constantly pressured by another self that is traumatized by invasive memories of an ineradicable past. Such 'disassociation' or 'splitting of consciousness' was, in Rivers' estimation, often exacerbated by 'some shock or illness' (*Instinct*, 195). In such a state, being alone with one's thoughts, albeit at home, was not necessarily a tranquillizing experience. For the therapies which the poem describes – talking to himself, performing mechanical little rituals such as lighting candles or his reassuring pipe, contemplating the weather or watching a fluttering moth – are less than convincing strategies for suppressing the looming spectres of war. What the poet must do, for his apparent peace of mind, is to control the way in which these memories encroach on his consciousness and enter the world of the poem. They may be glimpsed through the 'door-keeper's' portals but they are blurred and indistinct, premonitions rather than hard-edged images. The 'ugly thoughts' of the poem remain thoughts – disembodied and abstract; significantly only when they are metamorphosed into images of 'old men with ugly souls' does Sassoon allow reality – and it is a reality unconnected with the trenches – to intrude. Even the dead, at least the rotting corpses of men killed in battle, are manifestly erased from the poem's memory; instead they are replaced by old men, ghostly presences of 'horrible shapes in shrouds'. Only at the end can anger, an emotion repressed for 28 of the poem's 38 lines, be no longer thrust aside. Finally, maddeningly, the actual sounds of war invade his consciousness, thereby provoking an uncensored irruption of feeling.

Such an understated, indeed largely unstated, view of war's horror might be seen as a vitiation of the poem's effectiveness as well as – according to the Rivers' theory of 'repression' – damaging to the psyche of the anxiety-ridden soldier/poet. But poetry traditionally employs the oblique mechanisms of figurative language and much of the uneasy ambivalence of 'Repression of War Experience' derives not only from Sassoon's refusal to confront the 'experience' unequivocally but also from his richly connotative use of metaphorical tropes.

It is worth considering how this links with psychoanalytical theory. For Freud, repressed thoughts issued in dreams, via the processes of condensation and displacement, as images of a visual and usually symbolic cast. Rivers, summarizing Freud, expresses it thus: '... the manifest content becomes the expression of the wish through a process of distortion, whereby the real meaning of the dream is disguised for the dreamer' (Rivers, *Conflict*, 4). Admittedly 'Repression of War Experiences' is a poem and not a dream. Nonetheless it is a highly associative poem, in which the use of ellipsis suggests a creative reverie in which the processes of symbolization and metaphoric displacement can flourish. Such metaphoric displacement is evident in the resonating images of the poem – candles, pipe, books, rain, roses and, above all, the solitary moth. All are familiar presences, variously associated with domesticity, leisure, an English summer evening. They are there, physical, observed objects incorporated in the poem, to assist the process of personal recuperation, reassuring things that help the soldier/poet forget the horror of the trenches. But it is late evening, a vulnerable time of day, and all these images generate associations that the poet would like to repress; it is only because these latent and metaphoric meanings are *initially* unacknowledged by the poet that they survive in the text. Each time the poet introduces an image, it is to find that it brings with it unwanted overtones that he has sought to smother, that he has 'gagged all day'. The prosaic lighting of candles acquires associations of votive offerings to the dead, then in the moth's likely incineration, the scorching, maiming effects of war that confront the would-be hero ('And scorched their wings with glory, liquid flame'). The comforting pipe is, after all, not so comforting. Lighting it reminds him uneasily of its function in the trenches. Here, as there, he tries to calm himself by the reassuring observation, 'Look! What a steady hand'. But the fact that he has to count to 15 before he is 'as right as rain' is sure proof that he is anything but calm; whether pipe or gun, the trembling way it is grasped betrays his fragile state of mind.

The cliché 'right as rain' fails to reassure; instead the process of free association leads the daydreamer to wish for a real downpour and 'bucketfuls of water'; he is desperate for a purifying agent to 'sluice the dark' and wash away the recurrent sense of horror. Even the roses are charged with symbolic force as the pathetic fallacy, an echo perhaps of Keats's 'droop-headed flowers all' and the consequent invitation to 'glut thy sorrow on a morning rose',[3] invests them with the poet's own guilt-laden and mournful emotions. More disturbingly, the symbolism of 'hang' and 'dripping heads' is redolent of the carnage of the battlefield; these images remorselessly return him to areas of experience he is trying to forget. He searches desperately for yet another source of solace. Books...a constant source of consolation in the trenches and here reassuringly lining the walls, books are, he reflects, 'a jolly company'. But the innocuous personification refuses to suggest a comforting jollity. Instead the word 'company' reminds him of a military unit; the orderly ranks of tomes 'standing so quiet and patient', of soldiers awaiting orders. The desperate injunction, 'O do read something', is yet another strategy for repressing these resurgent memories – after all books encapsulate the 'wisdom of the world'. But again unsought associations proliferate: of soldiers dressed to die in '*dim* brown' (emphasis added), and finally turned 'black and white and green', to 'every kind of colour' in death and putrefaction.[4] The poet averts his imaginative gaze by staring prisoner-like at the blank ceiling, only for the moth to reappear. Initially, we recall, the poet attempted to reject its symbolic implications with 'No, no, not that, Its bad to think of war.' Now its presence, 'one big dizzy moth that bumps and flutters' painfully reminds him of his own confused state of mind. Like the moth he is liable to self-destruct, fatally attracted to the very things that may destroy him.

Even the garden beyond, a sanctuary for moths and men alike, provides no consolation. The very air is 'breathless', at once holding itself in dreadful anticipation of some catastrophe, and devoid of life; the spectral trees conjure up images not of the heroic dead of earlier poems such as 'The Last Meeting', but of ghoulish apparitions, ghosts of old men who, far from dying courageously in battle, have 'worn their bodies out with nasty sins'. That this particular 'nasty thought' was very much on Sassoon's mind at the time is indicated by a diary entry written four days after his 'statement' in which he had asked: 'Is there anything inwardly noble in savage sex instincts?' before embarking on a denunciation of 'the elderly male population ... old men like ghouls, insatiable in their desire for slaughter, impenetrable in their ignorance' (Sassoon, *Diaries*, 175). Like the diary entry, the imagery in the poem conflates twin aversions: one, a hatred of old men; two, a disgust at the gross physicality of heterosexual intercourse. That these men are presumably copulating with young women while young men die vainly for a lost cause is doubly abhorrent.

At this juncture, the poem appears to provide evidence of another level of 'repression' of which the poet's 'door-keeper' was probably unaware, that of sexual repression. Freud is instructive here, since he uncompromisingly links repression to sexual drives, maintaining that 'the symptoms serve the purpose of erotic gratification for the subject; they are a substitute for satisfactions which he does not obtain in reality' (Freud, 340). Sassoon, we are reminded, was not yet a patient of Dr Rivers, and though he would talk with him about his dreams, it is unlikely that he discussed his sexuality with an analyst more concerned with repression engendered by 'war experience' than by sexual proclivities.[5] But the fact remains that Sassoon was a homosexual, though on the evidence of the diaries as we have them, he would only discuss it openly with his friends after the war. One aspect of his war experience, an intensely fructifying one, was his daily contact and kinship with other young men. Of course one didn't have to be 'just so'[6] in order to develop loving relationships: the pressure-cooker atmosphere of the front line ensured that. Moreover, most officers would already not only have encountered a whole tradition of homoerotic literature, but would have experienced non-physical 'crushes' at public school: J. R. Ackerley observed that while he 'never met a recognizable or self-confessed adult homosexual' during the war, 'the army with its male relationships was simply an extension of my public school' (Fussell, 273). Homoerotic feeling *was* acceptable in the trenches; homosexuality was not. As a consequence, Sassoon was obliged to sublimate his homosexuality: in platonic friendships, in sentimentalized hero-worship, by writing pastoral elegies to dead comrades or, as in this poem, by adopting a puritanical, even misogynistic stance. Not that these responses in any way invalidate the truth and intensity of his own emotions. Indeed these erotic feelings were, I believe, as much a source of tension to him as the now publicly documented conflict between Sassoon the pacifist and Sassoon the warrior.

Such emotions reside in the subtext of 'Repression of War Experience'. They are 'gagged' out of existence more successfully than the memories of war, but they occasionally slip into sight, shadowy evidences from the palimpsest of the poem. Such parapraxes were, as Rivers knew from his reading of Freud, often revelatory of the psyche's inner workings. 'Slips of the tongue', he explained, 'are the expression of tendencies lying below the ordinary level of waking consciousness ... the expression of some unconscious or subconscious train of thought [which] intrudes into a sentence with which it has no obvious connection' (Rivers, *Instinct*, 232). So while these 'ugly thoughts' refuse precise, conscious identification, they do slip in – in potentially subversive ways. Thus his pipe, which is subsequently 'let out', has, on this reading, potentially erotic associations; the procedure of 'count fifteen / And you're as right as rain' is a relief mechanism not entirely devoid of sexual connotations. The poet dares not 'lose control' of these feelings; if he does, they will 'drive [him] out to jabber among the trees'; he will be regarded as 'mad', perhaps recognized as sexually deviant and ostracized in consequence. The garden, the poet observes in a phrase that says more than it intends, 'waits for something that delays'. But however 'dizzy' and dislocated the thinker's present state of mind, now is not the time for revelations about his sexuality. Indeed, by a process of transference, his own sense of self-disgust issues in the denunciation of the 'nasty sins' of old men, 'wearing out their bodies' in heterosexual congress, an activity which is nonetheless part of a 'natural' sequence of erotic events that may be denied the speaker.

So what conclusions should we stress in relation to 'Repression of War Experience'? Writing poetry is, in psychoanalytic terms, a sublimatory activity, a rechannelling of basic drives so as to make them socially acceptable and potentially useful. I have argued that in the poem Sassoon is sublimating, however obliquely and erratically, his repressed sexual instincts. Rivers is again instructive here. Talking about neurosis, he offered the opinion that new symptoms often arise in hospital or the home which are not the immediate and necessary consequence of war experience, but are due to repression of painful memories and thoughts . . . arising out of reflection concerning this experience' (Rivers, *Instinct*, 186). In other words, war anxiety might trigger the release of other deep-seated and quite unrelated repressions. That such suppressed feelings do surface in this poem is almost certainly the case.

But Sassoon's primary repressions centred on memories of the trenches; they were the direct consequence of a war recently experienced, nightmarishly recalled, and now, in his statement, finally rejected. In *Instinct and the Unconscious*, Rivers would identify three kinds of 'war-neurosis'. The first, he suggested, produced anaesthetizing physical manifestations such as blindness, paralysis or mutism; a second form led to extreme lassitude, enervation and disorders of sleep; a third form resulted in 'mental instability and restlessness with alternations of depression and excitement . . . similar to those of . . . insanity' (232). It does not take much to realize that Sassoon, though displaying some symptoms of the second kind of neurosis (from 2 June to mid-July he seems to have written only two poems) was mainly a victim of the third variety. That much at least is clear from a remarkable poem that both reveals the processes of 'repression' and, at the same time, attempts to come to terms with them by exorcizing these horrors through the act of giving them poetic embodiment.

If Sassoon does not altogether succeed in exorcizing these battlefield ghosts, he also fails to repress them effectively, since they crop up in the unlikely guise of homely symbols and metaphors. What Rivers *would* succeed in doing was to help Sassoon to give expression to his deepest memories and fears. One unlikely by-product of this release is the Craiglockhart poems 'Glory of Women' and 'Their Frailty', pieces which give vent to the poet's inherent distaste for women and especially their role as rival lovers for men. Much more important, his stay at 'Dottyville' under Rivers allowed Sassoon to release his pent-up feelings in powerful poems – 'Prelude: The Troops' and 'Counter-Attack' for example – in which he dares to relive, in graphic detail, his ghastliest moments of the war. We must be grateful that the Riversian exorcism probably helped Sassoon to come to terms with his homosexuality and its attendant complex of attitudes. Much more significantly, it helped him to understand the mental mechanisms of 'repression' and to deal with a now declared pacifism that must have intensified his desire to escape from all those memories of a trenchscape 'where all is ruin, and nothing blossoms but the sky' (Sassoon, *War Poems*, 104).

Sassoon's stay at Craiglockhart was not, as might be expected, entirely happy, but that it did help him deal with these 'war experiences' is evidenced by a body of work which not only faces up to the terrible effects of 'shell-shock', or recalls, in such expressions as 'butchered frantic gestures of the dead' (Sassoon, *War Poems*, 105) the remorseless scenes of carnage at the front, but returns to an imagined event more often repressed than any other by all combatants, the actual 'experience' of dying, of 'choking', of 'drowning', of 'bleeding to death' (Sassoon, *War Poems*, 106). Though Sassoon was not able, any more than his surviving comrades in arms were, to ameliorate his abiding sense of horror and outrage, he would, thanks to the renewed therapy of poetry and the good offices of 'my reasoning Rivers' (Sassoon, *War Poems*, 131), continue to exorcize some of these ghosts in the *Counter-Attack* of 1918.

Notes

1. It is difficult to date the poem with precision. Sir Rupert Hart-Davis suggests 'July 1917' in his edition of *The War Poems*. Sassoon's statement was composed on 15 June and sent to his CO on 6 July. An editorial note in the *Diaries: 1915–1918* (173) states that 'S. S. left Chapelwood Manor on 4 June and spent his time until 12 July in his London club and at Weirleigh'. On 13 July he was in Liverpool for the Medical Board prior to going to Craiglockhart.

So the poem was composed between 15 June and 12 July. On the evidence of material in the diary and reworked in the poem, late June is the likeliest date.

2. River's term for Sassoon's condition. See Sassoon's letter to Robert Graves, 19 October 1917 (*Diaries*, 192).

3. John Keats, 'Ode on Melancholy'. Sassoon had been reading the poet since the arrival, on 9 April, of a 'little India-paper edition of Keats bound in green vellum' (*Diaries*, 192).

4. Compare Graves's description of the dead in *Good-bye To All That*: 'The colour of the dead faces changed from white to yellow-grey, to red, to purple, to green to black, to slimy' (137).

5. There is a reference to Sassoon as Patient B in *Conflict and Dream*, 'in hospital on account of his adoption of a pacifist attitude while on leave from active service' (166).

6. A covert term used by Graves in a letter to Sassoon (early May 1916) implying homosexual tendencies.

Works cited

Freud, Sigmund. *Introductory Lectures on Psychoanalysis*, trans. James Strachey. London: Penguin Books, 1973.

Fussell, Paul. *The Great War and Modern Memory*. Oxford: Oxford University Press, 1975.

Graves, Robert. *Good-bye To All That*. Harmondsworth: Penguin, 1960.

Rivers, W. H. R. *Conflict and Dream*. Cambridge: Cambridge University Press, 1923.

——. *Instinct and the Unconscious*. Cambridge: Cambridge University Press, 1922.

Sassoon, Siegfried. *Diaries 1915–1918*, ed. Rupert Hart-Davis. London: Faber, 1983.

——. *The War Poems*, ed. Rupert Hart-Davis. London: Faber, 1983.

15
Siegfried Sassoon: the Legacy of the Great War

Patrick J. Quinn

At the conclusion of the Great War, there was little doubt as to whom the mantle of the greatest living soldier-poet should fall: Captain Siegfried Sassoon of the Royal Welch Fusiliers had spoken more effectively than any of his contemporaries about the horrors facing the ordinary soldier in this war, which had exploded any conceptions of chivalry and left over 18 million bodies in the trenches of the Somme, the mountain passes of Italy, the steppes of Russia and the poppy fields of Belgium. Wounded painfully in the shoulder while fruitlessly leading his company of infantry into the centre of German machine gun emplacements in April of 1917, Sassoon was moved to a London hospital at Denmark Hill where he scribbled in his diary the following lines, entitled 'To The War Mongers':

> I am back again from hell,
> With loathsome thoughts to sell;
> Secrets of death to tell;
> And horrors from the abyss.
> Young faces bleared with blood,
> Sucked down in the mud,
> You shall hear things like this,
> Till the tormented slain
> Crawl round and once again,
> With limbs that twist awry
> Moan out their brutish pain,
> As the fighters pass them by.
> For you our battles shine
> With triumph half-divine;
> And the glory of the dead

> Kindles in each proud eye.
> But a curse is on my head,
> That shall not be unsaid,
> And the wounds in my heart are red,
> For I have watched them die.

(Diary, I, 158–9)

This hastily scribbled verse may not be successful poetry, but the sentiments articulate the frame of mind of the young officer who, on one hand, had received the Military Cross for his bravery at the Somme, but on the other, later entered into an anti-war protest on behalf of his men, who, he felt, were being sacrificed needlessly in France for the sake of the pocketbooks of munitions manufacturers. From 1917 on, Sassoon's war poetry became a bitter attack against those 'who are excluded from the martyrdom (of experiencing battle) and who can be held in some way responsible for its continuance. The counter attack is directed chiefly against the Nation at Home – the Church, the State, the civilians (whether ignorant or indifferent) – and the "brass hats" of the General Staff' (Thorpe, 19).

Sassoon wrote a number of vituperative attacks on the General Staff while he was recovering from wounds. 'Base Details' is a classic example of his invective against complacent staff officers, and the double entendre of 'base' in the title is not accidental. However, the most effective of Sassoon's poetic counter-attacks is the simple seven-line poem 'The General'. Using his familiar method 'of composing two or three harsh, peremptory, and colloquial stanzas with a knock-out blow in the last line' (*Journey*, 29), Sassoon exposes the incompetence of the General Staff as they direct their naively willing subordinates into battle:

> 'Good-Morning; good morning!' the General said
> When we met him last week on our way to the line.
> Now the soldiers he smiled at are most of 'em dead,
> And we're cursing his staff for incompetent swine.
> 'He's a cheery old card,' grunted Harry to Jack
> As they slogged up to Arras with rifle and pack.
> But he did for them both by his plan of attack.

The light, cheery greeting in the first couplet is darkened by the second. This juxtaposition between the chummy greeting and the evidence of the general's incompetence is exposed ironically in the first two lines of the triplet as we listen to the kindly words of the innocent slogging off to the slaughter. The message is driven home in the last line, when the reader realizes that the two glum heroes, Harry and Jack, will be deprived by yet another bungled attack of ever seeing the future.

Sassoon's anti-war poetry was written primarily to shock the complacent British public into an awareness of the dehumanizing conditions that were prevalent across the Channel. He soon came to realize, however, how little his poetic effort had really touched the propagandized population of Great Britain. And only when the poet himself contrasted the horrors on the Somme with his convalescent life, lounging amid the yew hedges and rose gardens of England, could he admit finally that his satiric poetic voice would not be effective enough to affect in any way a desensitized British public.

By mid-June of 1917, within a month of being invalided home a second time, Sassoon, with the aid of the pacifist circle supported by the Member of Parliament Philip Morrell, wrote his famous statement of protest to be read in the House of Commons, its main tenet being Sassoon's protestation that the war 'upon which [he] entered as a war of defence and liberation has now become a war of aggression and conquest' (*Diary*, I, 173). The statement announced Sassoon's refusal to serve. The stirring language of the final lines of his protest clarify his reasoning:

> I have seen and endured suffering of the troops, and I can no longer be a party to prolonging those sufferings for ends which I believe to be evil and unjust. On behalf of those who are suffering now, I make this protest against the deception which is being practised on them. Also I believe that it may help to destroy the callous complacence with which those at home regard the continuance of agonies which they do not share and which they do not have sufficient imagination to realise.
>
> (*Diary*, I, 174)

The authorities defused Sassoon's protest by placing him in a hospital for the shell-shocked where he was given psychiatric care. But the 'catch-22' of the situation was clear: Sassoon could be released only if he admitted that his protest was ill-advised; yet once he did that, he would be sent back to the front. For five months, he received therapy in the same hospital as fellow soldier-poet Wilfred Owen. Once Owen was discharged and sent back to France, Sassoon could only follow the example of his friend, however reluctantly, and return to war. This decision to re-enter battle was undoubtedly influenced by the loyalty and compassion that he felt for those under his command; Sassoon could no longer stay in the safety of England while the men of his regiment continued to fight. Thus, at the end of 1917, he returned to battle only to be shot in the head seven months later and sent home a third time to convalesce. Before he had fully recovered, however, the war had ended. Sassoon summed up his feelings on the night of the Armistice: 'It is a loathsome ending to the loathsome tragedy of the last four years' (*Diary*, I, 282).

Sassoon spent the ensuing decade trying unsuccessfully to expiate the memories of the war from his consciousness and reminding the British government of its promise that the returning soldiers should have an improved lifestyle with a fair share of the cultural and economic benefits of a victorious England. He became, for a short period, literary editor of the Socialist newspaper *The Daily Herald*, but was temperamentally unsuited for the pressures of the position. Continuing to search for meaning in a world that seemed to him more self-centred and materialistic than before the war, yet disillusioned by what he saw, Sassoon returned to writing poetry through which he hoped to expose the superficiality of his life; by extension this implicated many of the returning officers who had fought in the war. 'Picture Show' gives his readers a glimpse of Sassoon's disengagement from postwar life:

> And still they come and go; and this is all I know –
> That from the gloom I watch an endless picture show,
> Where wild or listless faces flicker on their way,
> With glad or grievous hearts I'll never understand
> Because Time spins so fast, and they've no time to stay
> Beyond the moment's gesture of a lifted hand.
> And still, between the shadow and the blinding flame,
> The brave despair of men flings onward, ever the same
> As in those doom-lit years that wait them, and have been
> And life is just the picture dancing on a screen.

The second line of the poem suggests that the speaker is dispirited, aware of the superficiality of his peacetime existence; his participation in the war has set him outside the deceptive flicker of everyday life which drifts past him and fails to engage him with its petty concerns. He can only observe 'reality' much in the way that a viewer relates to life portrayed on a movie screen: the viewer is sympathetic, even empathetic to what is being observed, but at the same time always aware that he is outside the action. He cannot engage the shadows as they pass by him as they are oblivious to his presence, and being unable to participate in the community of existence prevents him from grasping life's essentials. In this condition, the excluded can only observe an endless stream of images dancing across the retina of his eyes.

By the mid-1920s, tired of satirizing the materialism, the superficiality and the growing philistinism of his age, Sassoon began an introspective journey of self-investigation which was to lead eventually to his 1928 volume of poetry entitled *The Heart's Journey*. The voyage towards spiritual self-discovery was a result of Sassoon's inward-looking personality, but the intensely personal struggle was closely aligned with mankind's struggle to make some sense out of a postwar world, where traditional values and certainties had been obliterated. From this point on, Sassoon was to turn inward for inspiration, to sift repeatedly through his memories, constantly refining them in order to produce the six semi-autobiographical works which he was to produce over the next 18 years. The first three of these novels, which combined to form the trilogy entitled *The Memoirs of George Sherston*, took him back to his youth and the experience of war.

It was while writing the second part of the trilogy, *Memoirs of an Infantry Officer*, in 1930, that Sassoon began to face up to the ominous political developments taking place in Europe. Emerging from his reveries of self-discovery and reliving halcyon days of the Edwardian twilight, he wrote a short poem which was to become the prefatory verse to his volume of prophetic poetry published in 1933 (a full six years before Hitler invaded Poland) called *The Road to Ruin*. In these brief 12 lines, Sassoon spoke to the generation which was to lead the way into the 1930s:

> My hopes, my messengers I sent
> Across the ten year continent
> Of time. In dream I saw them go,
> And thought, 'When they come back I'll know
> To what far place I lead my friends
> Where this disastrous decade ends'.
>
> Like one in purgatory, I learned
> The loss of hope. For none returned,
> And long in darkening dream I lay.
> Then came a ghost whose warning breath
> Gasped from an agony of death,
> 'No, not that way; no, not that way'.

> (*Collected Poems*, 199)

The poet's voice here offers a premonition of inevitable disaster. For ten years, he has tried to forewarn his readers (his friends) that the corruption and craving for power by those in control might lead to another war, but no one listens. When a ghost from the distant past (perhaps from the battlefields where Sassoon fought) cries out in agony that this is not the route to peace, we, the readers, sense that his dire warnings will be ignored in much the same way as the poet's. It would appear that as early as 1930 Sassoon realized that Allied policies were leading to resentment of the victors by the defeated fuelling nationalistic designs. The path was leading to the 'road to ruin' despite assurance ten years earlier that the Great War had been the war to end all wars and that the world would be made safe for emerging democracies.

In the first poem in his *The Road to Ruin* volume, 'At the Cenotaph', the evils of war are personified in the convenient guise of the Prince of Darkness, 'standing bare-headed by the Cenotaph / Unostentatious and respectful.' The Prince offers up the following prayer:

> Make them forget, O Lord, what this Memorial
> Means; their discredited ideas revive;
> Breed new belief that War is purgatorial
> Proof of the pride and power of being alive;
> Men's biologic urge to readjust
> The map of Europe, Lord of Hosts, increase;
> Lift up their hearts in large destructive lust;
> And crown their heads with a blind vindictive Peace.

Sassoon's Prince pinpoints one of the main causes of Germany's grievances against the victorious Allies: in the Allies' attempts to punish Germany after the Armistice, they had imposed severe economic sanctions on the fledgling Weimar Republic. The more colourful of these results can be seen in history texts, whose photographs invariably show shabbily dressed fathers trundling wheelbarrows full of Deutsch marks through German cities in order to buy bread for their poverty-stricken families. Most historians agree that part of the success of the National Socialist Party in Germany and its achievement in the 1933 election was tied in with its promise to redress the embarrassment suffered at the hands of the English and French after the Great War. Sassoon cuts to the essence of the problem: his Prince of Darkness prays for the continuance of this 'destructive lust' of the victors. The poet, in essence, sees more clearly that the politician where retributive policies will lead.

In 'News From the War-After-Next', published two months after Hitler had ascended to power in Germany in January 1933, Sassoon moved from criticism in the abstract to criticism of the particular. He spells out quite clearly the type of man Germany had selected as its Chancellor:

> The self-appointed Representative
> Of Anti-Christ in Europe having been chosen
> As War Dictator, we are pledged to live
> With Violence, Greed, and Ignorance as those in
> Controllership of Life. . . . The microphone
> Transmits the creed of Anti-Christ alone.
>
> The last Idealist was lynched this morning
> By the Beelzebub's Cathedral congregation –
> A most impressive and appropriate warning
> To all who would debrutalize the Nation.

Despite the unfortunately awkward use of Old Testament vocabulary in this poem (but then again, perhaps Sassoon was stylizing himself purposely as a Hebrew prophet), his depiction of the emerging German state is aptly sketched. Hitler's plan over the five years following his rise to Chancellor was to build a German war machine that would terrorize and destroy a large sector of Europe. Threats of violence and acting in ignorance – how often have those excuses been given through this century to deflect criticism from less-than-honourable actions by man towards our fellow man – would become the status quo in Hitler's Germany. And Sassoon's symbol of the microphone as the transmitter of the new Aryan creed is a brilliant touch; for is there any film footage of the twentieth century more poignant than that of Hitler ranting behind a microphone in front of masses of hypnotized Germans, arms lifted in the salute of promises to come? Sassoon paints images of the Fascist state before its realization in Germany is complete: what he calls in the final stanza 'the inauguration of a super-savage Mammonistic State'.

In what may be the most powerful and prophetic of the poems in *The Road to Ruin*, 'An Unveiling' looks ahead to the end of the Second World War and parodies a future President's propaganda eulogy in honour of 'London's war-gassed victims'. The string of clichés and weasel words demonstrates both the futility of war and the ceremonious cant that follows holocaust. And since the end of the Vietnam and Gulf Wars, the litany of this poem has become all too familiar:

The President's oration ended thus:
'Not vainly London's War-gassed victims perished.
We are a part of them, and they of us:
As such they will be perpetually cherished.
Not many of them did much, but all did what
They could, who stood like warriors at their post
(Even when too young to walk). This hallowed spot
Commemorates a proud, though poisoned host.
We honour here' (he paused) 'our Million Dead;
Who, as a living poet has nobly said,
'Are now forever London'. Our bequest
Is to rebuild, for What-they-died-for's sake,
A bomb-proof roofed Metropolis, and to make
Gas-drill compulsory. Dulce et decorum est . . . '

The meaningful pause before his reference to the million fallen in battle gives the politician ample time to milk the enormity of the losses. In its barren futility, this memorial echoes images of the Menin Gate and prepares the reader for a 'gas choked future' (Thorpe, 62). The world depicted here is a world of war-mongering, but a world still giving lip service to the old lie exposed by Wilfred Owen in his ironic 'Dulce et Decorum Est'. The old values of honour and valour are trotted out for yet another round of convincing the masses that this war was worth dying for.

Less than a year before the invasion of Poland, most of Sassoon's worst fears had been realized, and all of Allied Europe was preparing for the imminent Nazi invasion. Sassoon, like most people in England, was holding his breath waiting for the bomb to drop. In this anticipatory and melancholy mood, he wrote down his final thoughts on the coming darkness. 'Thoughts in 1938' is a poem of three stanzas that opens with the poet riding on horseback across Salisbury Plain on a mild afternoon in November. The mood is solitary and quiescent, and, as he gazes across the plain, he reflects on man's place in this 'liberal landscape'.

There on that ancient drove-road, leading to nowhere now,
    my horse
Grazing and then gazed, as I did, over the quietly
    coloured miles.
Though sign-posts pointed toward the dread of war,
    ourselves, of course,
Were only humdrum joggers on through time.
    Remembering it one smiles.

For the prophet of war, there can be little respite from despair. But we must focus on that smile, that Giaconda smile, which is both enigmatic and telling: enigmatic, for Sassoon may have been smiling in 1938 at his own anti-war poetry of twenty years previously and at the futility of his attempts to halt the inevitable effects of national aggression; or telling perhaps, because he knows this coming war will create new poems of futile protest for a new age. Most importantly, though, Sassoon's smile is one of knowing. He knows from grim experience that war may be an affront to natural laws, but ultimately man's place is subordinate to the elemental power that forms the beauty of a mild winter's sunset and the vital mystical forces which permeate Salisbury Plain, whereupon sits the unfathomable enigma of Stonehenge itself.

Works cited

Hart-Davis, Rupert (ed.) *Siegfried Sassoon Diaries 1915–1918*, Vol. I. London: Faber, 1983.

Sassoon, Siegfried. *Collected Poems*. London: Faber, 1947.

——. *The Road to Ruin*. London: Faber, 1933.

——. *Siegfried's Journey*. London: Faber, 1945.

Thorpe, Michael. *Siegfried Sassoon: A Critical Study*. London: Oxford University Press, 1966.

Index

Letters', 212; 'Miners', 202,
203, 211; 'The Parable of the
Old Man and the Young', 196,
215; 'The Send Off', 212; 'The
Show', 215–16; 'S. I. W.', 193,
212; 'Smile, Smile, Smile',
197–8, 209; 'Soldier's Dream',
215; 'Spring Offensive', 209,
213, 215; 'Strange Meeting',
72, 209, 212–13, 215, 216–17;
'A Terre', 201, 212

Pankhurst, Sylvia, 42, 52n, 69, 82
Parfitt, George, 12, 13
Parker, Peter, 192
  The Old Lie, 192
Parsons, I. M., 68
Penguin Books, 15, 16, 107n
Périn, Cécile, 95, 96, 97,
  99–101, 106
  The Captured Women, 99; *The
  Mothers*, 99–100
Phelps, William Lyon, 149
Phillips, Ray, 114, 116, 138n
  The White Feather, 116, 138n
Picasso, Pablo, 164, 165
Plowman, Max, 207, 208, 209
  A Subaltern on the Somme,
  208
Poetry (Chicago) 73, 78–9, 83, 87n
Pope, Jessie, 68
Post-colonial Theory, 2
Pound Ezra, 69, 79, 87n, 159,
  160–1, 162, 165,
  'Sestina: Altafore', 159
Price, Annie, 72, 74
Prothero, Sir George, 12
  *Analytical List of Books Concerning
  the Great War*, 12
Psycho-analytic Theory, 224, 227
Punch (London), 27, 30, 31

Racine, Nicole, 93
Rado, Lisa, 78, 80, 87n
Ransom, John Crowe, 79
Raphael, Lev, 151
Read, Herbert, 191
Reilly, Catherine, 68, 93
  Scars Upon My Heart, 68

Remarque, Erich Maria, 1,
  23, 25, 34
  All Quiet on the Western Front, 1, 23
Richards, Frank, 13
  Old Soldiers Never Die, 13
Riding, Laura, 68
Riegel, Léon, 93
Rivers, W. H. R., 4, 206, 219–24, 226–8
  Conflict and Dream, 229n; 'Instinct
  and the Unconscious', 219–20,
  227; 'The Repression of War
  Experience', 4, 219–20
Rixon, Annie, 114, 115, 116
  The Scarlet Cape, 114; *Yesterday and
  Today*, 114
Roberts, Heather, 121
Rosenberg, Isaac, 68, 208–9, 210
Ross, Robert, 221
Rossetti, Christina, 69
Ruddick, Sara, 93–4, 96, 104
Russo-Japanese War, 27, 29

Samuel, Raphael, 40
Sassoon, Siegfried, 3, 4, 13, 68, 192–3,
  195, 201, 205, 206, 208, 209, 210,
  216, 220–8, 230–8
  'At the Cenotaph', 235; 'Base
  Details', 231; 'Blighters',
  201; 'Counter-Attack', 228;
  Counter-Attack, 228; 'The
  General', 195, 231; 'Glory of
  Women', 228; *The Heart's
  Journey*, 234; 'The Last Meeting',
  225; *Memoirs of an Infantry
  Officer*, 234; *Memoirs of George
  Sherston*, 234; 'News from the
  War-After-Next', 236; *The Old
  Huntsman and Other Poems*,
  201; 'Prelude the Troops', 228;
  'Picture Show', 233; 'Repression
  of War Experience', 4, 220,
  221–2, 223–8; *The Road to Ruin*,
  234–7; *Sherston's Progress*, 208;
  'Thoughts in 1938', 237–8;
  'Their Frailty', 228; 'To Any
  Dead Officer', 222; 'To the
  War Mongers', 230–1; 'An
  Unveiling', 236–7; *The War
  Poems*, 228n